Kenneth Grange

Designing the Modern World

Kenneth Grange

Designing the Modern World

Lucy Johnston
Foreword by Sir Jonathan Ive

With over 500 illustrations

Contents

Foreword

Sir Jonathan Ive

Sir Kenneth Grange is profoundly modest. His extraordinary body of work speaks unfailingly to his selfless ambition to make wonderful products for others. He came of professional age in the golden era of public service, devoting his life to service through design. When I think of his work, I do not immediately think of the designer, but of the millions of users that have been beneficiaries of his care and thought.

For so many of us growing up in the United Kingdom, his work formed a substantial part of our shared visual culture. It represented a selfless optimism and trust, both in one another and in our collective future. He created products that assumed such a rare cultural significance that they ultimately became icons. In honesty and deference to the user, his iconic products were a brilliant example to a generation of designers trying to navigate the excesses of consumerism. I think of his marvellous parking meter, its purity so perfectly describing its context and place among the noisy clamour of so many other objects vying for our attention.

Grange uses materials sparingly and with thoughtfulness and respect. His profound understanding of their nature and value is rooted in his love of making. For me, it is this fundamental knowledge of materials and process that ultimately describes a sense of rightness – an inevitability – in his designs. While there is a joyfulness and truth that characterizes his work, it is accompanied by a fierce resolve to protect fragile ideas, and to see drawings and models evolve to become prototypes and products.

My favourite is without doubt the InterCity 125. I remember taking a day return from London to Bath solely to ride on his train. I love its complete rejection of arbitrary form, or space-age design aspirations without function. It is not a rocket – it is a beautiful, simple train. True simplicity is not achieved through the absence of complexity or artifice, but in the expression of essential purpose and utility.

For his service and humility, for his love of making and his enormous impact on our visual culture, Sir Kenneth Grange is a hero of mine and of British design.

Below. Grange at the meeting table in the Pentagram studios in Needham Road, Notting Hill, late 1980s. On the wall behind him is Pentagram partner Theo Crosby's large collection of ethnographic masks.

Preface

Lucy Johnston

While I am writing this, an art transport team is busy in my studio downstairs packing fifty large boxes with sketchbooks, diaries, technical drawings, portfolios, letters, press cuttings, magazines and thousands of photographs and transparencies, all to be transported to London and officially accepted into their new home in the permanent collection of the Victoria and Albert Museum. This moment marks the final miles in the journey of a remarkable archive, the flatwork half of which I have been custodian for the past two years. The whole archive, a rare and sizeable volume of material, has been compiled across eight decades and also includes a large collection of original products and models already safely in V&A storage. But this moment marks as well, for me, the culmination of an extraordinary four years of collaboration and close conversation with the owner of the archive, now well into his ninth decade, to document a lifetime of memory and bring together this book as a comprehensive record of an unparalleled life in design.

I have known Kenneth, or of Kenneth, for most of my life, through the work of my grandfather Dan Johnston, who was Head of Industrial Design at the Council of Industrial Design (CoID, later the Design Council), during Kenneth's fledgling years as an independent designer in the early 1960s. Dan was one of a small, dedicated team who joined the CoID in the early 1950s, in the halo of the Festival of Britain years, who were passionate in their belief in the necessity and value of design for industry, manufacture and commerce. Involved in promoting access to good design for everyone, through exhibitions and awards programmes at the bright and optimistic Design Centre in London, Dan delighted in seeing Kenneth quickly gaining wide recognition with a number of early client commissions through the CoID's Designer Selection Service. He witnessed Kenneth's exceptional career trajectory from within a context of huge positivity and energy at the heart of the British design and manufacturing industries,

a time he found endlessly exciting and rewarding, and which I never cease to find fascinating.

I first met Kenneth in person three decades ago when – at the same age Kenneth himself had been when he enrolled in the art school at Willesden Technical College – I was fortunate enough to be accepted for a work experience placement with him and his team in the Pentagram studio. That first-hand glimpse into Kenneth's world, and into the context of the profession of which my grandfather had been such a dedicated champion, made a particular, indelible impression on me. And this, combined with an inherited appreciation for the social history of the incomparable British design and manufacturing industries, would prove to be the tiny seed for the making of this book.

However, it has only been through two decades of wider industry work and research, during which I would cross paths with Kenneth every so often, and then through these last years of close collaboration with him, that I have finally felt able to do any justice to articulating his story and just how far his positive impact on modern industrial design has stretched. And, importantly, that has also meant bringing together many of the threads in the evolution of Britain's wider industry scene, the history of which has so often intertwined with Kenneth's own. These threads of biography capture a remarkable time in the evolution of British design and of the dynamic fabric of the modern manufacturing industry as it evolved and reacted. This was an era when modern consumer culture boomed, when choice and competition spurred brands to 'invest in design', and when a relative few working in the young profession of design first closely integrated with the large and centuries-old manufacturing industries, resulting in a powerful blend of creative instinct and industrial expertise never before seen. Through Kenneth's journey, we see how British industrial design expertise was first exported to the world – the distinctive British movement in modern industrial design, of which Kenneth was the figurehead for so many years, contrasting in its sensibility with the leaner European style and the big personality of the US approach.

No other creative individual has consulted across such wide-ranging industry sectors – translating beneficial ideas and innovative techniques in material, structural and production efficiencies from one field to another – across such a formative period. From numerous Kenwood appliances that forever transformed the kitchen experience, best-selling razors for Wilkinson Sword produced in their millions, and a Kodak camera so popular it became a cultural icon, to revolutionary sewing machines for the Japanese manufacturer Maruzen, a radical pen for Parker that transformed the international fortunes of the company, and that other cultural icon, the visionary streamlined form of the InterCity train, Kenneth has been a fearless, dynamic figure at the forefront of the rise of industrial design, notably working in close collaboration with industry, not apart from it, to steer consumer culture into the modern age.

The range and versatility of his skill and application can be clearly seen through the forty-five product stories in this book, many of which also act as concise documentary of the evolution of their respective industries. His thoughtful, tactile approach and dedication to considering the user at all times shines through each and every project – from introducing the smallest incremental improvements to complete reimaginings of what was expected. Even if his type of understated celebrity means the user might not necessarily be aware that certain designs are by his hand, the pleasure and satisfaction in the using make them undeniably and wonderfully his creations.

Kenneth's singular career span has borne witness to the growth of a profession from humble beginnings before the concept of 'design' had crystallized, let alone become a subject that could be studied in higher education, to a world in which it is a powerhouse industry. His journey reveals a consistent strand of curiosity, imagination and bravery, sharing with many a determination to leave things better than they were found and a passion to tackle challenges and find solutions to improve life and bring pleasure in the day-to-day for millions of people. And what a journey it has been.

Kenneth Grange
A Life in Design

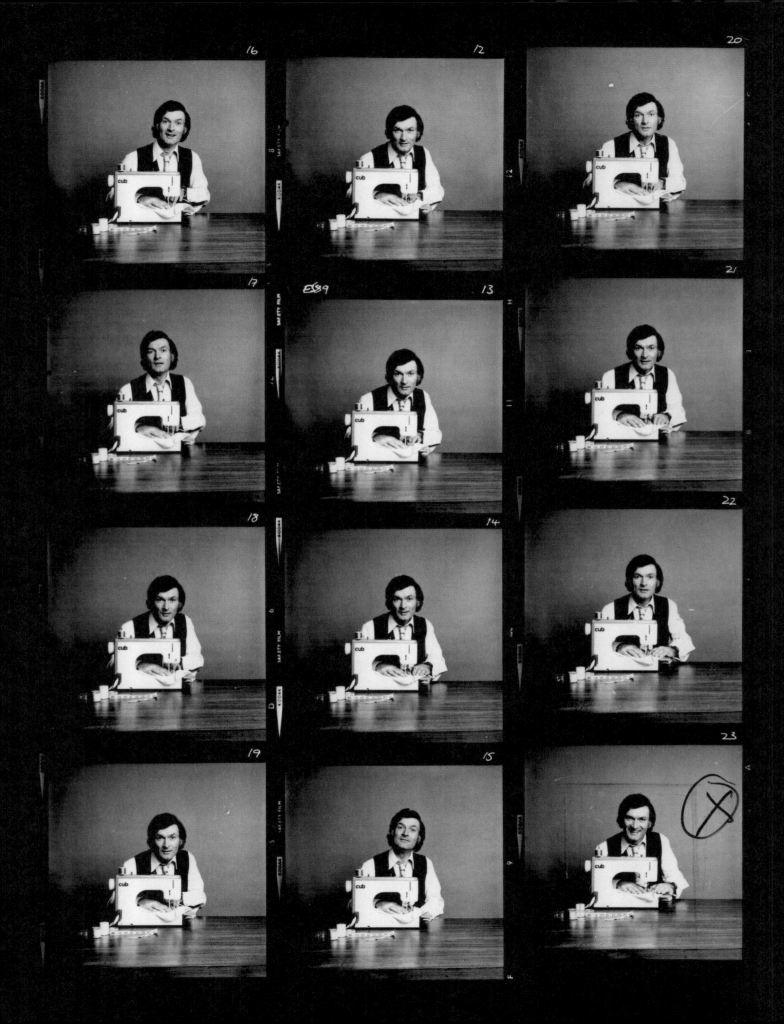

1
Childhood and Formative Years
1929–1949

Kenneth Henry Grange was born on Wednesday, 17 July 1929 at the Royal London Hospital, Whitechapel, east London, to Harry Alfred Grange and Hilda Gladys Grange (née Long). Home for his early years was a terraced house on a quiet cobbled street in Stepney, east London, within his father's assigned beat as a constable in the Metropolitan Police. Grange recalled fleeting early memories of horse-drawn milk carts and of being 'the only English family in the street' – most of the residents were Jewish immigrants who worked in trades connected with the nearby Thames docks – and, aged three, of being bundled off into the care of a kindly woman next door while his mother was in hospital for the birth of his sister, Shirley.

Harry and Hilda were a lively, striking couple, he with a creative streak in contrast with his profession in the police force, and she more practical, making a comfortable home and working for most of her life as an expert machine operator, first in the British Thomson-Houston armaments factory in Willesden, North London, during and after the First World War, and later long-term making metal springs in the International Springs & Washers factory in Harlesden in north-west London. Hilda took great pleasure and satisfaction in her work and although she attempted to retire several times in later age – memorably asking for 'a very large spring from an army tank' as a retirement present, of which Grange recalled she was extremely proud and which she displayed on the sitting room floor 'in the place where other people might have a floor-standing lamp' – she was loath to actually leave, loving the social life of the factory and continuing to work until she was ninety.

The pair enjoyed evenings of live music and demonstrated proficient skills on the dance floor, together perfecting the Charleston, the foxtrot and the waltz. They married in 1927 after meeting at the dance hall in Willesden where Harry, who was also a talented musician, played the banjo in a dance band to supplement his young policeman's salary.

He also performed for a few years as part of the Police Minstrels, a popular theatrical troupe of the era. This shared love of popular music and dancing – encouraged at family parties particularly during the Second World War years – was a mainstay of family life, with Hilda whistling songs from her favourite musicals around the house and the radio often being on. Hilda even insisted on addressing Grange as 'Bill' rather than Kenneth for the rest of her life, after one of her favourite songs, 'My Boy Bill', which was written in 1945 by Rodgers and Hammerstein for the musical *Carousel*. This joy in music would rub off on Grange, who as a teenager joined the local boys' band of the Salvation Army, where he learned to play the trombone. And he later enjoyed nights of dancing at the London dance halls in his teens and twenties

1

Previous. A contact sheet from a PR photo shoot for Japanese sewing machine manufacturer Maruzen with Grange the celebrity European innovator, to launch the Cub sewing machine (see also pp. 44 and 153).

1. A young Grange, dressed in his Sunday best, *c.* 1933.

2. Entering school poster competitions to support the war effort was a popular activity for Grange. During the war years he would often sit at the dining table with his father in the evenings, drawing, painting and making models.

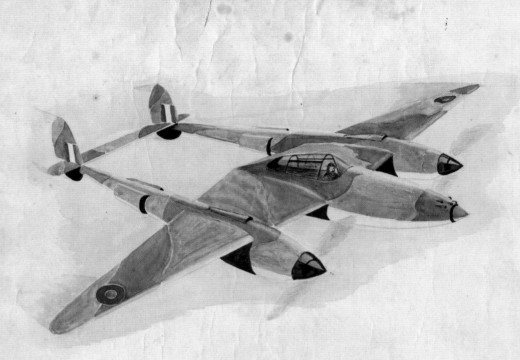

WEMBLEY WANTS WARPLANES

3

where, with a natural sense of rhythm, he became proficient in the tango and the swing. He explained recently that while dancing was the 'thing to do back then' it was also 'a great learning source' for balance and coordination, which much benefited him in his later-found love of sports, including tennis and skiing.

In terms of his wider family, throughout his childhood Grange only briefly knew his paternal grandparents, who lived in Willesden; glimpses in his memory are of his grandfather's uniform as a former officer in the Royal Navy. But his maternal grandparents, Jack and Clara Long, feature centrally and warmly in his recollections. For many years, at weekends and during school holidays, he, his sister and his mother would head down on the train from London to stay with Jack and Clara in Strood, on the north Kent coast, where his mother had herself grown up before heading to London to find work. Setting out each day from his grandparents' cosy terraced house, Grange would spend blissful times playing on the foreshore of the muddy Medway Estuary, watching the testing of newly built flying boats at the Short Brothers factory across the water at Rochester. He would weekly carry his grandparents' heavy glass accumulator battery to the local radio shop to swap it for a charged one – one of his first tastes of British product engineering. Jack, who had fought in the First World War though never spoke of it, was a quiet, gentle man who encouraged Grange's explorations and would recount to him the industrial stories of the area. Clara was a warm, welcoming and self-reliant presence frequently to be found up a ladder decorating the house or cooking for the wider family of aunts, uncles and cousins, who all lived and worked nearby and frequently came round.

In 1933 Grange's father was promoted to sergeant and, as was usual in the police force,

was relocated to a new division. So the family were moved to Tufnell Park, north London, where home became a maisonette in a pretty street of three-storey Victorian terraced houses, with a fig tree in the small front garden. Here Grange attended Burghley Road School, where he stood out as a bright and thoughtful child and was bullied by the tougher boys in the neighbourhood on his walks home. But he took great pride in his pair of hobnail boots, a desirable statement for boys of the era and a source of 'satisfactory click-clacking sounds' along the pavement; his pair was regularly mended by his father, to last until he outgrew them. And it was also during these years that Grange first encountered the building play set Meccano, and gained his first taste of 'the satisfaction found in making stuff', when a friend of his father generously gifted a large tea-chest full of the pieces that had belonged to his late son.

Grange recalled how his father, a 'somewhat disciplinarian but warm character', would study night after night at the dining table, to pass the examinations required to rise through the ranks of the police force. He would later fade through a struggle with drink – as Grange explained, police stations at that time often had a private bar for the staff after work – but his early example of graft and 'the drive to better oneself' lodged permanently with Grange, who back then would never slack on his homework, also sitting for hours at the table and taking pleasure in putting the time in after school and at weekends.

In 1936 the family moved again, this time to Commercial Street, Aldgate, when his father was promoted to the role of inspector. The spacious flat was in a police section house and held the status, notably to Grange, of being their first home with an inside toilet and bathroom. And it also featured, rather than old carpet, fashionably modern lino

3. Grange, back row third from right, as goalkeeper for 'cup winners' Tokyngton Youth Club football team in Wembley, 1943.

4. Grange on graduating from the art school at Willesden College of Technology in 1946 before setting out on his new path as an assistant in the offices of architectural firm Arcon.

5. Self-portrait, 1949. Grange kept up his attendance at local art classes during his time on National Service, and has honed his life drawing skills throughout his life.

4

5

floors, which required regular polishing; thus one of Grange's treats after homework was done was sliding up and down the hallway with dusters tied to his feet, an ingenious solution in place of a standard floor-polishing machine. Here, in the heart of the City of London, the seven-year-old Grange would attend Sir John Cass's Foundation School for boys, a smart fee-paying school, which through the Cass charitable foundation offered free places to the children of officers of the armed forces: it was a 'wonderful opportunity' he has looked back on with lasting gratitude. He vividly described witnessing, while walking to school one morning in 1938, the scene of a group of men in red overalls handing out the newly launched *Picture Post* at Aldgate East Underground station – his first, memorable taste of consumer marketing. His father would subscribe to the popular weekly photojournalism magazine for years afterwards, and they enjoyed reading it together; Grange devoured the style of the striking visuals, and their impact would last a lifetime.

Grange was ten years old when war was declared in 1939. He had been prepared for evacuation the year before when the threat of war first arose – together with hundreds of other inner-London children – and was ready with a smart coat and a gas mask in a cardboard box to hang around his neck. But by the time war finally broke out his parents were set to move the family once again, this time to Wembley, his father having been seconded to work in the Bomb Disposal Division of the force. Their new home in

Wembley – this time a semi-detached house with a garden and shed – was, unlike Aldgate, considered far enough outside the centre of London to be safe from the threat of bombing, so Grange remained living at home. He had had to leave Sir John Cass's Foundation School, where he had excelled, and his parents' assumption was that he would gain a place at the local grammar school in Wembley; but to his great disappointment the syllabus differed and he did not qualify to sit the entrance exam. Although this rejection stayed with him, true to character Grange bounced back and went on to be 'happy enough and prosper' at Wembley Elementary School. And it was around this time he was given his first bicycle, a trusty model that had belonged to his uncle, through tinkering with which he continued to 'learn how things work'.

The war years would prove to be extraordinary in Grange's memory. For his father, serving in the Bomb Disposal Division in central London caused a great deal of strain, but he 'took it in his stride', never letting his children sense his concern. For a teenage Grange, his father's role was a constant source of pride and provided him with plenty of 'bomb fuses and bits of shrapnel' to take to school in his pockets and show off in the playground. And wartime London also imprinted in him many long-lasting visual memories, from the huge mesmerizing beams of the aircraft searchlights at night to the futuristic barrage balloons floating on long wires. Towards the very end of the war, when the technological innovations

6   7

of conflict were reaching a peak, while on his regular journey home from school and crossing the pedestrian bridge over the train tracks at Wembley, he spotted a German V2 rocket far off in the sky, cruising down silently to target the railway junction and factories at Willesden. He graphically described the turmoil of the explosion as if in slow motion, the 'freight train axles spiralling up into the air' followed a short time later by the sensation and sound of the blast. In the early postwar years, Grange also recalled, he experienced his 'first understanding of modern architecture', when he gazed upon the beautifully sculptural concrete cooling towers of the power stations he glimpsed from the train windows on journeys to his National Service postings. Each of these visual moments he stored away in his creative mind's eye, later drawing on them for inspiration for many forms in his product designs.

The family moved home once more during the early war years, to another rented house in Wembley, where – being years before television was a commonplace source of home entertainment – the young teenage Grange's evenings were spent on creative endeavours. His father was a capable watercolour painter and draughtsman and would encourage Grange and his sister to draw, mainly learning by copying early Disney characters from comic books and the revolutionary animated film *Snow White and the Seven Dwarfs* and later *Fantasia*, which the pair saw many times at the cinema. It was during the war years too that Grange discovered his love of model making, a skill he would hone and that would see him well through his entire career. Studying photographs in his father's newspapers and magazines, Grange started making his own intricate models of fighter planes and ships in balsa wood,

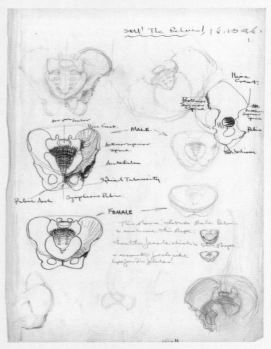

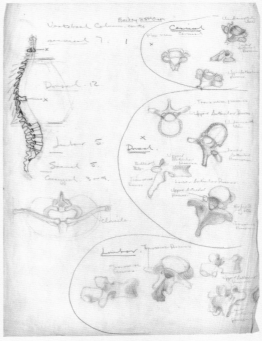

8   9

6 / 7. Catalogue for the first open art exhibition for which Grange's work was accepted for show, 1950. One of the pieces he entered, the wooden sculpture *Reclining Nude*, he later gifted to his mentor and employer Jack Howe.

8 / 9. Sketches from the life drawing classes that Grange attended during his time at art school at the Willesden College of Technology.

10. Sketch of Grange's own right leg, from his portfolio of personal drawings compiled during his two years of National Service (1947–49).

11. Sketch of a resting policeman at Marylebone Police Station, where Grange's father moved to work as an inspector after the Second World War.

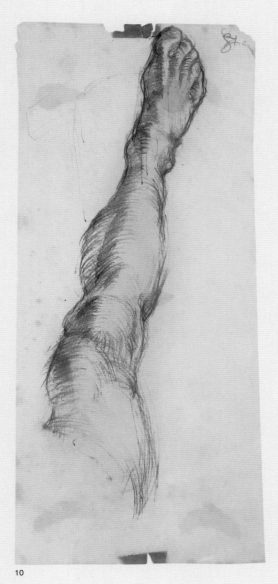

10

11

painting them in patriotic colours. There were also frequent competitions at school to design and paint wartime posters, a challenge Grange took up with great enthusiasm.

Then, in 1943, when Grange was nearly fourteen, the door to his future career path unexpectedly presented itself, at the end of school assembly one morning. The headmaster announced there were bursaries available for places in the art school at Willesden College of Technology for the following academic year, and asked for students to put themselves forward. Grange immediately put his hand up to apply, an action that surprised him as he had never before been a 'confident, audacious kid'. He was sent for an interview, taking a small portfolio of examples of his drawings, posters and models, and was subsequently offered a place; much to the 'bafflement and concern' of his parents, belonging as they did to an era when secure careers did not lie in the creative industries. Indeed, until she died,

and long into Grange's successful career years, his mother would always end their conversations by asking, 'Have you got enough work, Bill?'

Grange went on to spend four happy years at the art school, the first two in the study of general academic subjects alongside the artistic basics, before choosing commercial art as his focus for the remaining two, forever conscious of the necessity to turn passion and graft into the ability to earn a living. Of the study schedule he would much later recall: 'The art school had little formal education. Never a lecture. But somewhere along the way I picked things up.' This included a lasting love of life drawing, a skill he would continue to explore over the following decades, as can be seen in his personal sketchbooks; later, he even encouraged after-work life drawing classes for his team at Pentagram, always believing in the importance to a designer of exploratory freehand drawing. Describing the newly constructed school building itself, Grange explained that 'the ground floor was for engineering, with full machinery workshops, the first floor was for the building students, and the top first was the art school, of which commercial art took up half. And never would any of the floors mix ...' – a great missed opportunity, in retrospect, but a standard convention of the time.

When the war finally ended, in September 1945 – Grange still clearly recalls the dancing in the streets – he was into his final year at art school. The younger teaching staff would not return from active service for a while yet, so during this time he continued to study under an older generation, including Tom Gentleman – father of the celebrated illustrator David Gentleman – whom Grange recalled as 'an excellent draughtsman in comfy, characterful clothes', who taught them poster design and 'how to solve problems and make things'; and Charles Mansell, a 'superb lettering artist' who made his living from book jacket designs and took sufficient interest in his students to allow them to 'watch over his shoulder as he worked on his personal commissions'.

At the end of his final year, aged seventeen, in the summer of 1946, an official from the BBC came to the school to recruit two new scenery painters for the recently installed television studios in the historic Alexandra Palace. Grange was offered one of the positions, so, alongside a part-time job in the spring factory in Harlesden where his mother worked, he embarked on this new experience. He was tasked with creating 'primitive' scenic backdrops, which involved painting with long brushes on huge canvases laid flat on the floor. Unfortunately, just a couple of months into his employment, the head of the studios was informed by the unions that

permanent jobs should be prioritized for the previous workforce returning from the war, so Grange was unceremoniously dismissed and sent on his way. He immediately returned to the head of the art school, the kind and generous Mr Lockie, to ask for guidance; Lockie in turn asked for advice from a friend who worked in the Institute of Town Planning. It was through this connection that Grange was given his first 'extraordinarily lucky break' in the industry: the friend took a look at his portfolio and recommended him for an apprenticeship with the leading architectural firm of the era, Arcon, which had recently won a government contract to develop prefabricated housing solutions to tackle the postwar housing crisis.

Based in a smart office on Piccadilly – with sleek furniture and lighting, piles of architecture magazines shipped to the studio from Europe, a tendency to hold 'terrific parties', and senior partners showing off their latest design-conscious purchases such as the radical new Biro ballpoint pen that had just been introduced to Britain – this environment was a wide-eyed Grange's first taste of how the modern world could look. Describing the office as 'a natural gatherer of the talent of the age', Grange absorbed all he could for the following nine months, making himself useful by applying his newly learned skills in graphic design to put together brochures for Arcon's housing proposals, while also finding an appreciative audience for his model-making skills. Notably, this talent would later be specifically remarked upon in a treasured reference letter written for him when he left Arcon in September 1947 to serve his two years of National Service. However,

12

12. A page from one of Grange's early personal sketchbooks, capturing a sleeping passenger, while he was on the train travelling back to his National Service posting after a long weekend home in London, 1947.

13. Artwork for a book jacket designed by Grange as part of the Commercial Art programme at Willesden College of Technology, where he studied under lettering artist Charles Mansell and draughtsman Tom Gentleman.

14. Abstract in pastels from Grange's portfolio from the art school at Willesden College of Technology.

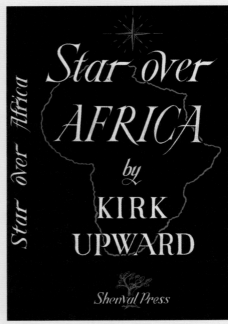

13

14

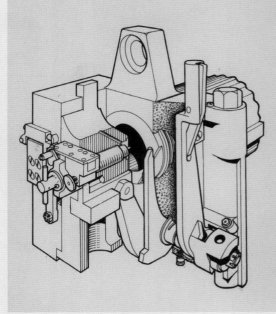

15

16

15. A brochure cover design by Grange for a postwar housing scheme by leading architectural firm Arcon, where he worked for nine months as an assistant.

16. During his National Service, Grange was sent to the printing unit of the Royal Armoured Corps in Dorset, where he was tasked with dismantling artillery pieces and making technical drawings of them for training manuals.

undoubtedly in Grange's mind the most important and fortunate aspect of his time at Arcon was the connection he forged with a certain Jack Howe, associate partner of the firm, under whose watch Grange spent part of his apprenticeship. Grange endeavoured to keep in touch with Howe throughout his period of National Service, and over the following decade this connection would develop into further employment, mentoring and a strong working friendship that proved to be the most consequential of Grange's career.

Grange's two years of National Service were spent on obligatory general training with the Duke of Cornwall's Light Infantry in Bodmin, Cornwall, before an interview to find him his next position. In another 'lucky break', the interviewing officer took a look at his portfolio of work for Arcon and from art school, and rather than recommending him for officer training, as Grange had anticipated, advised a position as an architectural draughtsman. In this capacity he was first sent to the Royal Engineers in Malvern, Worcestershire – this time undertaking 'gruelling but interesting' training in physical aspects of building and construction, including how to install a Bailey bridge, a 'Meccano-like truss structure on rollers' the ingenuity of which Grange still raves about to this day. After three months he was moved to work in the Royal Engineers' printing unit, attached to the Royal Armoured Corps in Bovingdon, Dorset, where he made technical drawings for manuals and learned about the printing process. Finally, he spent a stint in another printing unit with the Royal Armoured Corps in Lulworth, Dorset, dismantling and making drawings of artillery.

So in these years too Grange continued to gain industry experience while also learning many valuable life skills, including how to cope with a gruelling physical schedule as well as how to 'get on with all sorts of people, from different walks of life'. He would later regularly point to those rigorous two years as providing him with the experience and stamina he would need 'to cope with the late nights, deadlines and intensity' of the career journey that lay ahead. And while his mother worried about him eating properly – though in fact he 'grew very well' on the large army rations – and would send him regular parcels of peanut butter and jam along with clean underwear, he greatly enjoyed the living and the social scene. The time passed fast and before he knew it his service was complete and he was on the train back home to London and ready for the next chapter of his life.

2
Professional Beginnings
1949–1958

By 1949 Grange's father had returned to peacetime work in the police force, in another position as an inspector, and his parents had moved once again to police family quarters in a mansion block in Marylebone, in the West End of London. So it was this home to which Grange returned on completing his National Service. While taking a part-time job again at the spring factory where his mother worked, he set about seeking more creative career employment. Wielding a combination of boundless enthusiasm, honed draughting skills and the treasured reference letter from his apprenticeship at Arcon, he naturally gravitated back to the city's architectural practices. He met again with Jack Howe, who by now had established his own small practice, but the

business was not yet financially able to employ an additional design assistant, so instead Howe recommended Grange for an assistant role at the nearby architectural practice of Bronek Katz and Reginald Vaughan.

The architecture industry in London was growing fast as the mammoth vision for the Festival of Britain of 1951 gradually came into focus on the horizon. As an assistant to Katz, Grange worked on draughting, detailing and graphic design for the studio's commercial projects across retail and exhibitions, including early drawings for the studio's design of the Homes and Gardens Pavilion for the festival; the pages of his diaries from this time give a feel of the thrill and sense of mission flowing through the

1. The outdoor kiosks of the Sports Pavilion at the Festival of Britain, 1951, by architects Gordon and Ursula Bowyer, for whom Grange worked as a design assistant. He would regularly visit the exhibition after hours to tidy up and make alterations and repairs.

2. The treasured reference letter given to Grange on leaving his apprenticeship at Arcon to sign on for his National Service, 1947. His mentor, and later employer, Jack Howe, is noted on the letterhead as an associate.

1

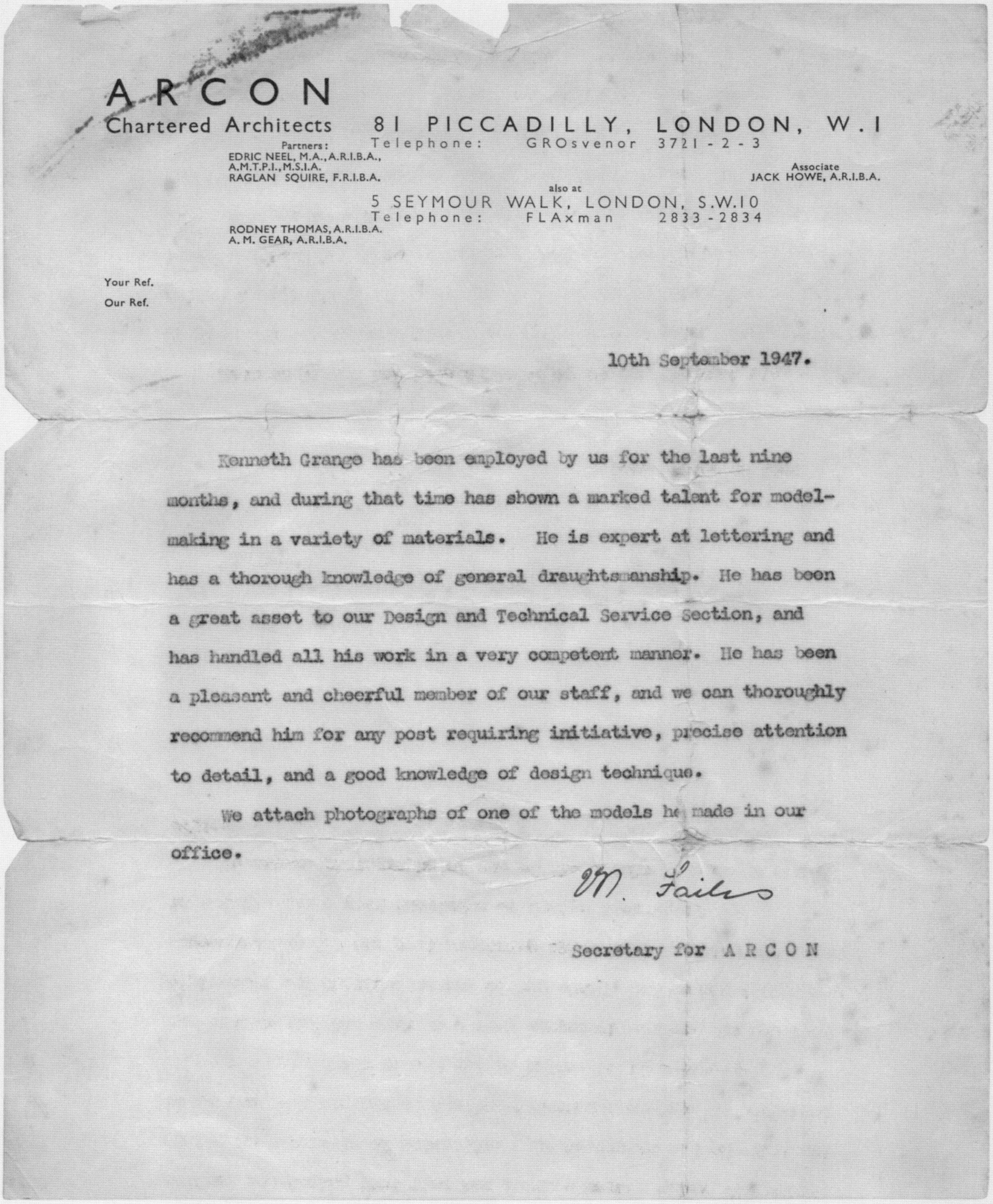

ARCON

Chartered Architects   **81 PICCADILLY, LONDON, W.1**

Partners:
EDRIC NEEL, M.A., A.R.I.B.A.,
A.M.T.P.I., M.S.I.A.
RAGLAN SQUIRE, F.R.I.B.A.

Telephone: GROsvenor 3721 - 2 - 3

Associate
JACK HOWE, A.R.I.B.A.

also at

5 SEYMOUR WALK, LONDON, S.W.10
Telephone: FLAxman   2833 - 2834

RODNEY THOMAS, A.R.I.B.A.
A. M. GEAR, A.R.I.B.A.

Your Ref.

Our Ref.

10th September 1947.

Kenneth Grange has been employed by us for the last nine months, and during that time has shown a marked talent for model-making in a variety of materials.   He is expert at lettering and has a thorough knowledge of general draughtsmanship.   He has been a great asset to our Design and Technical Service Section, and has handled all his work in a very competent manner.   He has been a pleasant and cheerful member of our staff, and we can thoroughly recommend him for any post requiring initiative, precise attention to detail, and a good knowledge of design technique.

We attach photographs of one of the models he made in our office.

M. Failes

Secretary for A R C O N

2

industry. Grange found a friendly employer in Katz, an émigré Polish architect, who on one occasion after an evening working late in the studio gave Grange a lift home in his car – a Hillman, and a luxury for the young Grange, who, until that point, had not personally known anyone with a private car. On the way back Katz took a short detour to his own home, in order to show Grange some new interior furnishings but predominantly to proudly show off his newborn baby daughter, Carol. More than two decades later, in the early life of the Pentagram studio, Grange would offer one of Theo Crosby's new architectural assistants a lift home in his car after an equally long evening working in the studio, only to discover delightedly during their conversation that she was this same Carol, Katz's daughter.

As the Festival of Britain drew nearer, more architectural practices picked up work across the vast project and, in September 1950, Grange transferred to work for the notable young architects Gordon and Ursula Bowyer, who had been engaged to realize the festival's Sports Pavilion. Grange was initially appointed to design the graphics and details of the displays for the pavilion. And then – as the empty pages of his diary for May and June 1951 demonstrate – he was for a while consumed by long days on-site at the South Bank setting up the various exhibits. Once the pavilion had launched, he returned to assisting with other exhibition stand designs, including his first for the General Post Office (GPO),

but his regular daily task was still to visit the Sports Pavilion most nights after hours to clean up and make wear-and-tear repairs and amendments to the exhibits. Of the months of the Festival of Britain, when millions of people flocked to visit from across the UK, Grange later related, 'it is impossible to describe what it was like, for someone now to imagine themselves in the shoes of someone back then – who was witnessing that level of colour and vibrancy and innovation for the first time. Where quite literally nothing like it had ever existed before as a vision of the future.'

Proving himself to be skilled and industrious, Grange was accepted during this period as a member of the Society of Industrial Artists (SIA; later the Society of Industrial Artists and Designers, SIAD), having been recommended for membership by Gordon Bowyer. This was a big moment for Grange, which he recorded with great excitement in his diary, not least because it was presented to him by the then president of the SIA, the eminent designer Mischa Black. And it was also during this period that Grange started to develop a real awareness of the bright potential of modern living, finding great inspiration in the sleek European architecture magazines subscribed to by the studios where he worked and also in the homes of his employers. He would regularly babysit for the Bowyers' children and later recalled: 'It was very good because it was an opportunity to spend time in a home that was totally

3

3. A 1949 Christmas card design by Grange for the studio of Katz & Vaughan, for which he worked as a design assistant.

4. Working sketches by Grange for his own sideboard design, inspired by the work of Ernest Race, whose furniture design prototypes he had seen presented at Arcon in the postwar years.

5. During his employment with Jack Howe, Grange recorded in his diary spending endless hours meticulously building this model of Howe's design for the Highbury Quadrant Primary School, which was presented to the client at London County Council (LCC) in the autumn of 1952.

4

'I joined Jack's practice in 1952 as an interior designer but the work involved a variety of commissions for door handles, cabinets, street lighting and pieces of hardware alongside the architectural practice. It was therefore via architectural design that I first became involved in designing products.'

Kenneth Grange

unlike mine. Where it was all modern furniture, and lots of books and beautiful bits of art. Gordon had a real eye for quality.'

Following the highs of the summer and autumn of 1951, work on the festival finally came to a close and there followed a marked lull in the pace of new commissions being received by the network of architectural practices that had thrived within its halo. By the end of the year the Bowyers could no longer keep him on full time, and Grange recorded in his diary that he needed to seek new employment and 'a new experience'. Gordon Bowyer, who valued his skills, asked Grange to stay on for one day a week for the following year. Longer term the two would remain in touch, meeting for lunch regularly. They ended up collaborating a number of times over the following years and once Grange had set up his own practice, working together on projects including the design of

a UK visitors centre for Kodak in 1961 and the design of displays for the British Pavilion for Expo '70 in Osaka, Japan.

And so it was that, in early 1952, as Grange was departing employment with the Bowyers, his next 'lucky break' happened: Jack Howe approached him with the offer of a position, now having work steadily coming through the door of his practice, Jack Howe & Partners. Grange once again gratefully found himself employed as a design assistant, this time working for his mentor. By now he had gained enough experience to take on more responsibility for making presentation drawings and models, including for Howe's highest-profile architectural commission, Highbury Quadrant Primary School. Grange's diaries record that his meticulous scale model of the school took two months to build, demonstrating skills that had initially been praised in his referral letter from

5

6

7

Arcon a few years previously. Other projects on which Grange worked at that time included the redesign of the interiors of Charing Cross Underground station and exhibition stand designs for key early industrial design clients of Howe's such as Gent's clocks and Chubb.

By the mid-1950s interest in the potential of a vibrant modern consumer world was surging and manufacturers across the spectrum were starting to invest in design to bring their visions of modern living to market. This led to rapid expansion in the requirement for commercial exhibition stands, an area of design that formed a large and lucrative part of the portfolios of many architectural practices over the coming decades. Vast trade exhibitions, which had been dormant during the war years, were back and bigger than ever; shows including the Ideal Home and Building Trades exhibitions at Olympia, London, and the British Industries Fair in Birmingham offered sizeable opportunities for architects to demonstrate innovation and build their professional reputations, with Grange recalling that 'it is not possible to overstate the importance of those fairs for introducing new ideas in design to industry and the public'. For Grange too, exhibition stand design for UK fairs and certain world's fairs would prove to be an important source of early work when he later set up his own independent practice. He would later reflect: 'These were years of enormous energy and unprecedented material abundance. The level of extravagance was remarkable to someone like myself, who had grown up in a modest family where wit in the interests of economy was the norm. Working on interiors and exhibitions made this visible to me for the first time.'

Crucially, however, his employment with Howe was also the chapter when Grange first properly gained insight into the concept of industrial design,

as it emerged as a profession from within the architectural trade. Through the 1950s Howe was developing a strong reputation as one of the first recognized industrial designers in Britain, working on commissions ranging from street furniture and architectural hardware to early electrical products and later even to trains. So Grange's time in Howe's design office also notably involved assisting on draughting for early industrial design jobs, including bus shelters for the British Transport Commission, as well as visiting manufacturing facilities to view the production of designs such as Howe's street lamps for Spun Concrete. Thus these years proved a pivotal and hugely influential part of Grange's career development, as he continued to expand not just his commercial design skills but also his understanding of the use of innovative materials and fabrication techniques. Later in his career, looking back on this era, Grange would explain that 'the originators of the profession, with a few exceptions, were almost all architects ... at the time there were probably only around twenty of us in the whole country. So you could grow very well.'

Alongside documenting his working life, Grange's diaries from the early 1950s are filled with enthusiastic descriptions of his home life and social scene: tennis and swimming, shopping trips and dinner parties, regular evenings at the cinema or dancing the night away with friends at Wembley Town Hall, and even his own home furniture-making projects. His father had by now retired from the Metropolitan Police and become the landlord of a pub at Elephant and Castle, south London, so Grange had recently moved to live with his parents in the flat there. However he was by now also spending a lot of time at the home of the family of his fiancée, Assunta Santella, a fashion model, up in Harrow. At the weekends he would regularly help his future

6 / 7. Perspective sketches made by Grange for alternative bus shelter designs by Jack Howe for the British Transport Commission. The left image shows Grange's distinctive early style of sketched figures.

8. An evening freelance job, for which Grange designed a small Atoms for Peace outdoor exhibition stand for the UK Atomic Energy Authority (UKAEA), led to much bigger things and the launch of his own design studio.

father-in-law Felix, an émigré Italian butcher, with the rounds to his London restaurant clients; they often returned home together quite merry after sampling the hospitality while collecting payments, with bags of gifted food alongside the cash. And Grange also put his architectural experience to good use in helping Felix manage the conversion of a substantial period property in Crouch End into flats for the family and two tenants. One of the flats subsequently became his and Assunta's home together, and later also housed Grange's first studio, following their marriage in August 1952. Another flat became home to Grange's close friend and best man, Alf Meyer, a child survivor of Auschwitz who had come to London in the late 1940s; he had subsequently

worked as an assistant in architectural offices, through which he had met Grange, while studying at night school to qualify with the Royal Institute of British Artists (RIBA). Grange's diaries from this time are highly visual, describing colour and texture from the world around him, including commenting on the 'grass turning black' during the winters of London smog and the 'tricks of perspective' caused by the fog.

Back in the office, ever the mentor figure, into the mid-1950s Howe encouraged Grange and the other assistants to take freelance work on the side, to broaden their skills and industry experience. It was through one such freelance job, a small Atoms for Peace outdoor exhibition stand for the fledgling UK Atomic Energy Authority (UKAEA)

8

> 'For sheer rigour of ethics or honesty, Jack had no equal. I never did really come up to his standards, but I'm privileged to have been befriended by a rare human being.'

Kenneth Grange

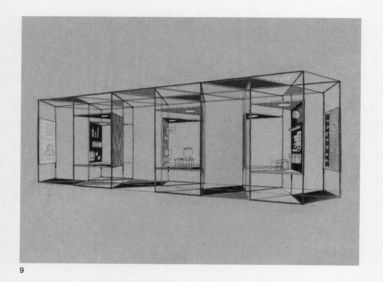

9

9. Perspective drawing of an exhibition stand design for the brand Bakelite, 1957. The majority of early commissioned work for Grange when he first set up his own studio was designs for commercial exhibition stands at UK industry trade shows.

10. The iconic Venner parking meter design, which Grange developed after winning a pitch for the project through the CoID's influential Design Selection Service. This was his first independent industrial design commission, and from here his career rapidly took off.

in 1955 (see pp. 66–69), that Grange would be unexpectedly presented with the doorway to the independent career that lay ahead. Having recently been given another early boost by being elected to the Chartered Society of Designers, in 1956 he enthusiastically accepted the commission for a substantially larger exhibition stand, this time for the UKAEA's presence at the second UN Conference on the Peaceful Uses of Atomic Energy, to be held in Geneva in 1958. After bringing this sizeable project commission back to Howe, who declined to take it on and encouraged Grange to 'go it alone', his next move was set. Standing at the 'biggest turning point in his life', Grange had no alternative but to take the opportunity that had been presented, leaving Howe's full-time employment and setting up his own practice. The departure was amicable, as would prove to be Grange's trademark character in working relationships throughout his career. He continued to work part-time for Howe for the next couple of years as a consultant designer, and Howe would also proceed to recommend a notable number of opportunities to Grange at his new practice.

And so it was that during 1956 the fledgling Kenneth Grange Design Office was founded in the spare room of his marital home, where he was initially joined in the evenings and at weekends by a typographer friend from the tennis club, Peter Jackson, who worked on the display graphics for the UKAEA exhibition while Grange worked on the structural designs. Alongside the work for UKAEA, other commissions started to roll in via referrals from all three of his previous employers, Katz, Bowyer and Howe. Among these early jobs were small exhibition stands and graphic work for the GPO and Bakelite, as well as Grange's first high-profile industrial design job: the redesign of the Venner parking meter for Westminster Council (see pp. 70–71). He won the pitch for the project in late 1956 after being shortlisted by the Council of Industrial Design (CoID), a flourishing postwar government body set up to promote the value of good design in industry (later to become the Design Council), and its Design Selection Service, an influential advisory service matching manufacturers with recommended design talent listed on its books. When he landed the project, Grange had only recently been placed on this professional listing at the nomination of Howe, who himself had been one of the first of a new era of industrial designers to be recognized by the CoID.

This recommendation was one of a number of generously supportive gestures of Howe's that, as

10

11

11. Perspective drawing by Jack Howe of his design for the Kodak Pavilion at the 1958 Brussels World's Fair. Howe employed Grange, now set up with his own design office, to design the interior exhibition displays.

Grange later gratefully recognized many times, 'set him up for life' – particularly the connection to the CoID. But there was one project in particular, which Howe directly commissioned him to work on, that Grange often later acknowledged as having truly sparked his 'big breakthrough'. The job was a large-scale exhibition design for Kodak, to fill the interior of the Kodak Pavilion designed by Howe for the 1958 Brussels World's Fair. It was while on-site in Brussels that a chance conversation took place, long since settled into legend and much recalled, that led to Grange's 'luckiest break'. A casual comment by Grange regarding the 'ugliness' of the American-style cameras was overheard by a gentleman who later turned out to be a sales director at Kodak. Their apparently inconsequential exchange led, on his return to London, to a phone call during which Grange was commissioned to design a camera for Kodak for the European market (see p. 79). 'What a day!' Grange would later recall. The episode would change the course of his career.

Thus it was that after a decade of gradually learning his trade – combined with a talent that had now been firmly acknowledged, the generosity of his previous employers and a chance conversation about cameras – Grange would be rapidly propelled to a stellar career in industrial design that would endure for more than six decades and involve many long-lasting client relationships. By the time of the Brussels World's Fair and the UN Atoms for Peace conference, both in 1958, and his first overseas work trips, Grange was employing three permanent staff and a pool of freelancers as the studio's workload escalated. The rise of Kenneth Grange Design was well under way.

Jack Howe

Jack Howe RDI FRIBA FSIAD (1911–2003) was a key figure in British architecture and design during the mid-twentieth century. Working initially on a number of breakthrough modernist architectural projects for some of the biggest names in the industry, he went on to found his own highly respected practice with a wide range of notable commissions across both architecture and industrial design.

Howe studied architecture at London's Regent Street Polytechnic from 1928, where he excelled with the 'practical solutions' approach to the teaching programme. After graduating with a first-class degree in 1931, he continued the latter part of his studies in the evenings, funding his training with a full-time assistant job in the office of the acclaimed early modernist architect Joseph Emberton. There he was soon given his first contract to run: Emberton's design for the Royal Corinthian Yacht Club at Burnham-on-Crouch, Essex, which was to be Britain's submission for the International Exhibition of Modern Architecture in New York in 1932. Other notable contracts with Emberton followed, including the HMV building on London's Oxford Street and Simpsons of

1

Piccadilly; Howe worked on the interior of the latter with the Bauhaus professor László Moholy-Nagy.

In 1934 Howe was further inspired by the Bauhaus vision when he attended a lecture at the RIBA given by the celebrated founder of the movement, the architect Walter Gropius, who was soon to flee Germany for London, where he would briefly work in partnership with the British architect Maxwell Fry. Fired up with enthusiasm, Howe quickly secured a job in Fry's office. And when Gropius was approached by Henry Morris, the renowned Chief Education Officer for Cambridgeshire, with the now famous commission for Impington Village College, it was Howe who became his chief assistant on the project – the only assistant to Gropius in Britain. When before long Gropius departed for the USA, Howe delivered successfully on the request from Gropius to refine the design and 'get the building built', on a tight budget and before the Second World War broke out.

From 1940, for the majority of the war, Howe worked as drawing office manager for the large building firm Holland, Hannen & Cubitts Ltd,

'I owe Jack my beginnings. He was a mentor and friend, and a rigorous and unswerving employer. Never, ever – sometimes to his personal disadvantage – did he settle for a convenient solution. If he decided that a design, or a tactic, or a smart answer would ease a path that he thought unworthy, then the response would be simply: start again …'

Kenneth Grange

2

3

4 Leopold Avenue Wimbledon SW19 7ET Telephone 020 · 8 946 7116

5 August 2002

Dear Kenneth

Fond though I am of you please forgive me if I
say that you are being a little tiresome. You
ought to know me better than to think that I
can be persuaded by pressure, flattery or other
inducements, to change my mind. I have given you
my decision which will remain unless I have good
reason to think otherwise.

In regard to Richard Carr I do remember that he
was assistant to John Blake editor of 'Design'
but I have not read his book on Ettore Sottsass.
I am no lover of Sottsass and if Carr admires his
work he is not likely to think much of mine, so
please do not get me involved with him.

I have not seen the British Library building
but plan to do so in my own time. Thanks very
much for the invitation.

yours
Jack

Mr Kenneth Grange
Tibridge Farm
Coryton
Lewdown
DEVON EX20 4PP

4

1. Jack Howe, holding the desk clock he designed as his award for winning the Duke of Edinburgh's Prize for Elegant Design in 1969 for his design of the Chubb automated cash dispenser.

2. Howe's design for a Gent & Co. wall clock for schools was a well-recognized visual symbol for millions of children sitting in classrooms.

3. Howe's refined design of streetlight columns for the UK firm Spun Concrete. Grange assisted on the project and recalled this being one of his first opportunities to visit a factory and 'see how things were made'.

4. A characteristically forthright letter from Howe after an enthusiastic Grange attempted multiple times to persuade him to make a National Life Stories recording with the British Library. Grange recorded his own in 2003 but Howe, ever a private and unassuming character, never did participate in the project.

on the Royal Ordnance Factories in Wrexham and Ranskill, before returning to practise in London as associate partner of Arcon in 1944. One of the most notable architectural practices in the country at that time, the firm was hard at work conceiving a programme of prefabricated housing, for which Howe developed experimental building methods in light alloys, steelwork and plastics. This led to the design for the Mark 4 pre-fab house, 41,000 of which were subsequently produced. It was here at Arcon, in 1946, that Howe first met the young Grange, just out of art school, when he came to the studio on a nine-month apprenticeship.

In 1949 Howe started his own practice, where he would a few years later directly employ Grange as his design assistant. His prominent architectural projects then included the refurbishment of Charing Cross station and another commission from Morris, this time for the award-winning Highbury Quadrant Primary School, on which substantial project Grange would work for him. Alongside this Howe also worked on lighting and street decoration for the 1951 Festival of Britain, and was later commissioned to design the Kodak Pavilion for the Brussels World's Fair in 1958 – on which Grange again collaborated, by then in an independent capacity – and the pavilion for the British Trade Fair in Moscow in 1961. Howe also quickly developed a strong reputation as an early modern pioneer in industrial design; Grange later argued that his iconic series of Gent & Co. wall clocks for schools

was 'likely the first point of contact with modern design for a generation of school children'. Howe's other notable industrial design projects included bus shelters for the British Transport Commission, the Blue Pullman diesel train for British Rail and the first Chubb automated cash dispenser, which won him the 1969 Duke of Edinburgh's Prize for Elegant Design, which Grange had also been awarded a few years previously.

Working at the heart of the fast-growing British design industry of the postwar decades, Howe became the recipient of many further awards, honours and nominations to industry bodies, including the Council of Industrial Design (CoID) and the illustrious Royal Designers for Industry (RDI) faculty of the Royal Society of Arts (RSA). Throughout his career he would stay true to his concept of 'user design', now an industry standard, which he envisioned as the practice of focusing on how a product would be used and how it would relate to the user, rather than any 'superficial surface dressing'; in his words 'the design quality must be in it, not on it' – an ethos that greatly inspired and influenced Grange in his own lifelong practice.

3
Flying Solo: Kenneth Grange Design 1958–1972

Soon after his initial meeting with Dr Pitt at Kodak in mid-1958, Grange set about considering the design of his first camera; the Brownie 44A. This was the brand's first product aimed specifically at the European market, and Grange's first experience of working on a consumer product for mass production. While he continued to find an outlet for his more 'extrovert tendencies' in his work on exhibition stand designs, he explained he was 'happy also to have to curb these tendencies and to consider the more rigorous implications of work on a mass-produced product', these constraints compelling him 'to pull in my belt and think somewhat differently about the factors determining design'.

Grange's first few months of work with Kodak met with approval, and papers in the Kodak archives from 1959 record that 'Mr Kenneth Grange is appointed consultant for appearance design', a role he would hold for twenty years (see pp. 78–89). Grange said of that time: 'They were very happy years with Kodak and I learned much of what I know from those men,

highly ethical, enjoying a supremacy in their industry, and generous with it.' This was an ethos he admired and would apply in his own professional conduct throughout his career. The Brownie 44A launched later in 1959 and soon afterwards won Grange his first award from the Council of Industrial Design (CoID) – the first of ten CoID awards he collected across his career – as well as seeing him receive his first coverage as a name in industrial design since setting up his solo practice.

Meanwhile, as he was cementing this relationship with Kodak, another new client came calling: one that was to become the most prolific and enduring of his career (see pp. 94–107). In 1958 a salesman by the name of Ken Wood was looking to employ a consultant designer to reinvent the look of his early kitchen appliances, namely his food preparation machine, the Chef. Recommended to Wood by the CoID on a shortlist of three designers, over just a few days Grange constructed a now famous presentation model of his proposed design: a mirrored half-model

1

1. The office move notification card for Grange and his team's transfer to the first full office premises of Kenneth Grange Design at 7a Hampstead High Street. Pictured marching in line are Grange (right) followed by Bernard Sams, Ian Langlands and Klaus Lehmann. The picture was taken at Whitestone Pond in Hampstead.

2. Bespoke Christmas card designs sent by the studio each year were a favourite endeavour of Grange and the team, and were a popular and competitive creative outlet across the industry; the design pictured here featured a photograph of a winking, face-painted Grange.

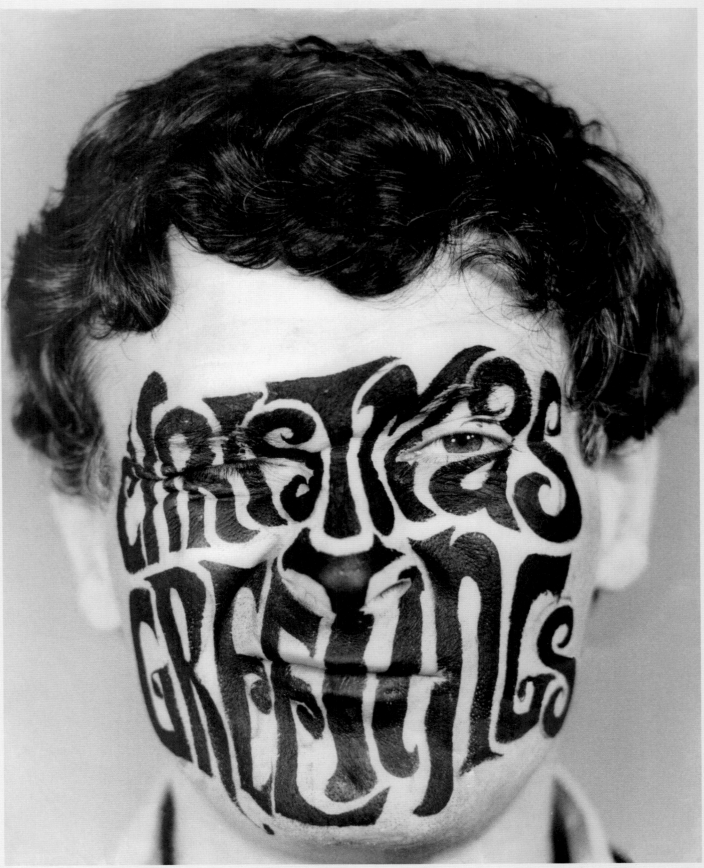

2

'By the end of the 1950s I was employed by three very different types of company, in Venner, Kodak and Kenwood. The richness of this experience furnished me with a training in industrial design which cannot be gained in any other way.'

Kenneth Grange

that he ingeniously spray-painted using his mother-in-law's vacuum cleaner; running out of time, he cut the model in half and took a mirror with him. He presented the model to Wood, who admired this creative trick and his flair for selling an idea, and employed Grange on the spot. So, with Kodak increasingly gaining him attention too, Grange's reputation for designing elements key to modern life was forged. His revised Chef launched in 1960, and over the following decades millions of units of his Kenwood designs were sold. His retained relationship with the company lasted until his retirement from Pentagram in 1997. Recognizing these early years to have been a rare and extraordinary learning experience, Grange described how Wood 'ran the company in an autocratic manner and I was thrown in at the deep end, negotiating with the draughtsmen and presenting work directly to him'. Looking back

on this time, Grange reflected: 'By the end of the 1950s I was employed by three very different types of company, in Venner, Kodak and Kenwood. The richness of this experience furnished me with a training in industrial design which cannot be gained in any other way.'

By the dawn of the 1960s Grange's profile as one of a new era of modern industrial designers was firmly established; his recognition by the CoID, and the organization's promotional activities, brought growing attention as more manufacturers became aware of the potential benefits to their businesses of investment in design. One such client, and a fond favourite in Grange's memory, was Henry Hope & Sons Ltd, a long-established British manufacturer of metal window frames (see pp. 90–93). The owner, Michael Hope, who sat on the board of the CoID, was impressed by Grange's approach and retained him on

3. The Kodak Brownie 44B viewfinder camera followed the successful 44A (see p. 78), for which Grange won his first Design Centre Award from the CoID in 1960. Among other small differences, the 44B had a focusing rather than fixed lens, and a leather rather than plastic case.

3

4

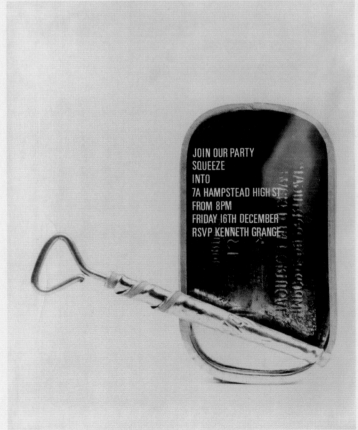

JOIN OUR PARTY
SQUEEZE
INTO
7A HAMPSTEAD HIGH ST
FROM 8PM
FRIDAY 16TH DECEMBER
RSVP KENNETH GRANGE

5

projects for a number of years, becoming something of a mentor to Grange in the industrial sector, while Grange brought a fresh perspective to Hope's traditional business. This work took Grange to visit the firm's factory in Birmingham for 'a very enjoyable few days each month'; the opportunity to experience the machinery of heavy manufacturing and to 'learn how things were made at scale' was a part of the job that captivated him, a fascination stemming from his time with Jack Howe. Recalling his visits to the Hope factory, and to those of other clients including Needle Industries and Imperial Typewriters, he described how he 'never forgot the first sight of industry, the awesome foundries, the sheer size of the machines'. And he would draw on his insight into the economics of materials and of production techniques gained in these environments to benefit clients across the board, knowledge that proved hugely valuable as the era of mass production gathered pace.

Meanwhile alongside enjoying visits to the offices and manufacturing sites of his clients around the UK, Grange also enthusiastically embraced these trips as opportunities to appreciate new places; a passion for travel has always stayed with him. Ever full of energy to explore, he made the most of his free time to sample social and cultural life, his love of music and live shows often drawing him to music halls and theatres in the evenings. In one much-enjoyed anecdote, on an occasion in early 1963 while staying in Birmingham for his work with Hope's, he told of stumbling upon a pleasant evening of variety entertainment at the Hippodrome; the programme ended with 'a set by a little-known young quartet called The Beatles'.

Throughout this time of his practice's initial growth, Grange and his founding team continued to work from his marital flat in Crouch End. But having initially set up in the spare room in 1956, by late 1960 Grange found the piles of work and his employees rapidly overflowing the space and even taking over his father-in-law's garage, where they had set up a

6

6. An outtake from the team photo shoot at 7a Hampstead High Street, *c.* 1970 (see image on previous page). Grange (far left) is turned away from the camera, with (left to right) Ian Buchanan, David Balding, Bruce Watters, Chris Sidgreaves, Tony Lowe, Ellen Montgomery, Jill Westwood, Alan Wall, Roger Jones, and Tamar Eburn ('Mrs E').

7. Grange pictured in his office at the 7a Hampstead High Street studio, *c.* 1966, with some early product designs on display around him, including his first Ranger barometer set for Short & Mason and his Chef and Mini mixers for Kenwood.

model-making workshop. It was clearly time to find a new home for the Kenneth Grange Design Office, particularly as Grange was keen to further expand the workshop facilities. So January 1961 saw the team moving into new premises at 7a Hampstead High Street, a much-beloved address in the memory of Grange and all those who worked with him during that time. Grange signed a lease on the whole building, taking the first, second and third floors for the studios, while leasing the ground floor unit to an existing tenant, a paraffin shop – the smell from which he can still recall – and later to a publisher and bookseller. Grange set up his office on the first floor, and his design assistants and secretary spread out across a warren of smaller rooms on the second floor.

The third floor was given over to the workshop with its ever-growing assortment of tools and machinery, the weighty equipment painstakingly dismantled and carried up the stairs by the enthusiastic and dedicated bunch.

The workshop quickly became, and would remain, the heart and soul of his studio practice for decades and a nexus of activity that captivated clients and collaborators alike; and, as can be seen on a number of occasions through his career journey, it was always a priority consideration for Grange when employing talent and expanding resources. Most famously for Kenwood, but also for Kodak and many other clients, model making was always the focus of both Grange's design development process and his

7

8 9

8. A 'very nervous' Grange (right) standing with Prince Philip, Duke of Edinburgh, at the Design Centre, after winning the Duke of Edinburgh's Prize for Elegant Design from the CoID in 1963.

9. The Dave Clark Five in the band's trademark white Jaguar E-Type convertible for a photo shoot. Grange owned an identical vehicle, which he lent to the band during the filming of their movie *Catch Us If You Can* in 1965.

presentations, being, he asserted, 'the only medium in which I had confidence to sell my ideas'. As he later noted in his writings at Pentagram, 'models prove valuable as three-dimensional reference points to the designer, are more meaningful to the engineer, and certainly more understandable for the client'. He also explained how models meant the designs 'could be handled, and therefore provide a truthful basis for a tactile assessment', as well as communicate a statement of function and style. Impressively, Grange's models were also recognized by a number of clients across the years – from Kenwood to Maruzen – as being so meticulously made that they could later be used instead of drawings by the engineers to make the final tooling for manufacture.

As the pace of the consumer industries rapidly accelerated into the 1960s, so did the number of commissions landing in the studio, often arriving with inquisitive clients in tow. Now with more space for hosting, Grange found that clients were more than happy to leave their own desks and visit for meetings, fascinated to see at first-hand the creative environment and particularly the workshop activities. Grange later said of this time: 'By the early 1960s all the formative factors for a fully consolidated industrial profession were presented in Britain and we were ready to show the rest of the world what we could do. I was very lucky to play a part in the design aspect of what would prove to be one of the most exciting decades that Britain has experienced.'

In 1963 Grange was acknowledged with his first high-profile award, the newly established Duke of Edinburgh's Prize for Elegant Design (later the Prince Philip Prize), for his design of the Milward Courier cordless electric shaver. From here he and Prince Philip would maintain correspondence and cross paths many times through the various institutions and industry events that the Duke so fervently supported

across a few crucial, influential decades in British design and industry. Grange's royal connections would soon also extend further through a CoID-related acquaintance with Antony Armstrong-Jones, Lord Snowdon, husband of Princess Margaret, who alongside welcoming him into the social whirl of Kensington Palace recommended his talent to a number of companies, including the premium loudspeaker manufacturers Bowers & Wilkins, with which Grange would later forge a highly successful working relationship (see pp. 202–215).

Another notable encounter the following year would greatly impact the path of Grange's career in a different way, this one coming about as a result of his position as design consultant to Kodak, for which he would attend creative pitches from other studios. One such impressive pitch by the renowned graphic studio of Alan Fletcher, Colin Forbes and Bob Gill sparked a friendship and led to a number of collaborations between the trio and Grange during the following few years, later with Theo Crosby replacing Gill to form the studio Crosby/Fletcher/Forbes. But little did any of them anticipate at that time where this meeting of minds would ultimately lead by the turn of the decade.

That same year Grange and his wife divorced and he moved to a flat in Shepherds Hill, within easy driving distance of the Hampstead studio. Alongside a busy social scene, Grange's schedule across these mid-decade years became ever more packed with work activity, including numerous industry functions, as his studio continued to grow in prestige and Grange threw himself into making the most of every opportunity. Also during this period, feeling driven to find ways to 'give back to the industry which had formed him', Grange started accepting invitations to speak to students and visit diploma shows at the booming art schools across the country that

10

were now training the next generation of industrial designers. He joined the governing body of Hornsey College of Art, and also became closely involved with the CoID and its judging for the Design Index and its activities to recognize new designers.

Alongside collecting further honours, his career successes of the mid-decade were also bringing substantial income and Grange, though never one to flash his growing wealth, was finding pleasure in being able to set himself up with the kind of lifestyle he had so much admired in his early employers. Among his more 'extrovert' purchases were cars; though, as he explained later, it was less about choosing status symbols and 'really always for fun, whether cheap or expensive'. Over the years he owned a great variety of cars: from a Fiat 500 to a Ferrari Dino and a Jaguar Mk2 to a Citroën Dyane – this last much to the 'horror' of his style-conscious partners at Pentagram, when he rolled into the partners' car park at the studio. But the design of one car more than any other left a lasting impression on him. Reading the papers one Sunday morning soon after the studio move to Hampstead, Grange turned a page to be faced with 'the most extraordinary vision of the future I had ever seen'. This vision was a full-page advertisement for the newly unveiled Jaguar E-Type, which had recently stolen the show at its launch in Geneva. On closer calculation of the finances required to purchase one of his own, Grange conceded he would need to begin by buying a second-hand one; this he did, after a patient wait, and later replaced it in 1965 with a brand new one. This car later found its fifteen minutes of fame when one day there was a knock on the door of the Hampstead studio from a film producer asking to borrow it – Grange had as usual left it parked at the kerb outside. It proceeded to feature in a film project for the rock-and-roll band the Dave Clark Five, who were to be seen cruising around London in a number

of the cars, all white, in their film *Catch Us If You Can*. Meanwhile, so self-conscious was Grange of how his taste in expensive cars might be received by clients that for years he also kept his previous runaround, a beloved Ford Prefect van, bought with the proceeds of his early jobs for UKAEA in the 1950s, into which he had manually cut rear windows and installed a back seat. He would often arrive at client meetings in this rather than the Jaguar, leading on one occasion to Dr Pitt of Kodak spotting the well-worn van in the car park and ticking him off, telling Grange that 'he really should charge more'.

By now the studio's burgeoning portfolio of clients was frequently taking Grange to meetings not only across the UK but also in Europe, particularly Germany, in his work with Kodak, Kenwood and soon Wilkinson Sword as well. And before long the USA also beckoned, first through Kodak and then when his client Imperial Typewriters was bought by a US firm. Through these trips Grange recalled being presented with his 'first taste of US modernism' and his awe at the scale and dynamism of the country's embrace of modern living. He vividly described, having been invited to the spectacular home of the renowned US architect Philip Johnson, his amazement that the home had four Eames chairs, which were actually 'being sat on'; he had only ever previously gazed at these precious symbols of 'the height of modern design' in magazines. He would go on to hugely enjoy his trips to the USA over the following decades, from exploring the jazz clubs of New York to settling into animated dinner table conversation when, as a sign of his personable character, he was often invited to stay with his clients in their family homes rather than be put up in hotels.

In 1967, his journey as a truly internationally recognized designer was further advanced when a call came requesting him to consult for Maruzen in Japan. His initial visit to Japan was also his first

10. Grange and a happy design team from Japanese sewing machine manufacturer Maruzen, on a weekend hiking trip during one of Grange's many visits to the country in his two decades of working there from the late 1960s.

11. A faxed letter from Osamu Nakamachi, the sales director of Maruzen, to his European agent, Derek Quitmann of Frister & Rossmann, who had recommended Grange to the Japanese firm. Nakamachi gives glowing feedback on his early meetings with Grange and outlines an expansion in the scope of design work being commissioned.

MARUZEN SEWING MACHINE CO., LTD.

OSAMU NAKAMACHI
DIRECTOR
EXPORT DEPARTMENT

June 19, 1968

Mr. D.L.H. Quitmann
FRISTER & ROSSMANN
350/356 Old Street
London E.C.1.
England

Dear Mr. Quitmann :

I thank you very much for your letter of June 13th forwarding to me
a copy of June issue of "Which ?" and calling my attention to their
latest report on the portable typewriters. I have also appreciated
your prompt cable advice on the matter of the solid state control
proposed by the Kenwood.

Mr. Grange has left here this morning to home via United States.
I think it is a must for me to brief you of the outcomes of his
recent visit. First of all, he has greatly impressed all of us with
his proposed design on our new family machines. It is a consensus
of mine and Mr. Mikuni's impression that his professional talent
would help us in many ways on our forward project planning and we
have decided to subscribe to his service on our full lines of products.
He has built our confidence in his professional capability and personality during the course of his recent work at our plant.

Mr. Nishigami, our project engineer in charge, has covered in details
the engineering problems involved in his original design proposal.
I understand from them that they have resolved those problems sufficient
enough to build a prototype machine in the proposed model. It is
scheduled now to be completed some time in the first part of August.

In the course of discussion, we have explored a possibility of single
tooling utilizing his design proposal for both version of flatbed and
freearm excutions. It is proposed by us since his new concept in
the machine construction indicated a possibility of identical structure
for both version of models. In another words, the underbase mechanism
has to be modified toward those required for the free arm construction.
However, at a close of discussion, we have concluded that we should use
separate tooling for freearm machine based on the cost indication that
we would be adding extra cost for the flatbed machines, as well as for
the aesthetic consideration that we might kill the clean and smooth
finish of the flatbed machines with the additional parting lines.

- Cont'd -

HEAD OFFICE & EXPORT DEPT.   34 SATA-HIGASHI-MACHI 3 CHOME MORIGUCHI CITY
CABLE "MARUMACHIN" MORIGUCHI   OSAKA, JAPAN TEL OSAKA 991 5154(5) 6231

11

12

12. In the late 1960s Grange bought a small villa in Malta, where he spent many holidays over the years.

13. Grange receiving a CoID award from Prince Philip, Duke of Edinburgh, for his work on the Star radiotelephones range for STC in 1970.

long-haul journey beyond the USA, and being 'quite oblivious of geography' led to him leaping to his feet in panic as the BOAC plane touched down to refuel in Alaska, thinking he had boarded the wrong flight. But the trip immediately sparked a three-decade-long love affair with Japanese culture; he was instantly charmed by the 'care that characterized every social and creative activity', bringing back many influences to his own domestic environments in the UK, while the Japanese industry would embrace 'the European innovator' in its PR and make him a star. His new-found knowledge of working in Japan would separately prove beneficial when a little later, in 1969, his early employer Gordon Bowyer asked Grange to collaborate on the interior design of the UK pavilion for the 1970 World Expo in Osaka, on the theme of 'Progress, Promise and Variety', led by Sir Hugh Casson and architectural practice Powell & Moya.

As the 1960s wore on, a relentless schedule of work commitments led his secretary, Elizabeth Burney-Jones, to urge a somewhat worn-out Grange to take more holidays. This idea he immediately put into action, picking the first beach destination he spotted in the window of a travel agent on Hampstead High Street, and finding himself in Malta. Quickly smitten with the island, and in characteristically enthusiastic fashion, by the time he returned he had purchased a property there; a small and simple villa that would prove a restorative bolthole for him over a number of years and which encouraged his later love of international travel for

pleasure, during which he always kept sketchbooks of the details he noticed around him. It was also around this time that Grange took up skiing, which became a long-time obsession and a source of great enjoyment for a few weeks every springtime with friends. And he also embarked on a course of flying lessons at the Elstree Aerodrome in Hertfordshire. The industry's work-hard, play-hard lifestyle also naturally led to plenty of parties, particularly around Christmas, when the hot tickets would include invites to the furniture company Hille's famously luxurious affairs. Not to mention the time when Grange gatecrashed a *Magical Mystery Tour* fancy dress party hosted by The Beatles in December 1967, for which he dressed as a witch doctor; his helmet with horns was meticulously constructed by his head of workshop, Bruce Watters. Unsurprisingly this alarming costume saw his entry to the party unchallenged, and he found himself seated next to George Harrison at dinner.

By the last years of the 1960s, with the continued patronage of a number of key manufacturers and his design of the Kodak Instamatic camera rocketing on launch to become a cultural icon, Grange was acknowledged as Britain's most successful modern industrial designer of the time. In 1969 he was honoured as a Royal Designer for Industry (RDI), the most prestigious recognition of a designer's

13

> **'In Jack's and then my own generation it was far more possible for a designer to span between industry sectors, from architecture to trains, unlike today with such high levels of specialization. If a client trusted in the designer's ability, that was what mattered.'**
>
> **Kenneth Grange**

14. Full-scale model of an early self-service fuel pump design developed for BP, built in the workshop at Hampstead by Grange and his head of model making, Bruce Watters.

achievements as nominated by the industry itself, once again joining his former employer and mentor Jack Howe in the honour. However, looking at his portfolio timeline, many of his biggest impacts on the landscape of industrial design were still very much yet to come: the client who would bring him his most high-profile and enduring single project (see pp. 132–147) had arrived in a low-key manner in 1968, in the form of British Rail, with a commission for a railway timetable design; his design of a highly futuristic concept in video conferencing called Confravision for the General Post Office was on the cusp of being trialled (see pp. 72–77); and his star was still on the rise in Japan as he spent more and more weeks each year working there.

One of the last new clients to land during the Hampstead studio years was British Petroleum (BP), notable not so much for the output of the project as for where this collaboration with Crosby/Fletcher/Forbes would lead. The project itself entailed a substantial body of research and conceptual work looking at the future of the self-service filling station, though little record remains today, and it was presented to the client in late 1970 (see pp. 168–173). Following its completion, the office diaries through 1971 fascinatingly document an increasing flurry of meetings between Grange and the trio, and with another eminent graphic designer of the time, Mervyn Kurlansky. Then, the last days of December 1971 in Grange's studio diary are blocked out for what is recorded in large penned writing as 'the Move', to 61 New Wharf Road in 'gritty, unfashionable Paddington' – the first home of Pentagram.

An early Pentagram promotional book explains how the BP project was recognized as 'outstanding among those in which Crosby/Fletcher/Forbes and Kenneth Grange discovered their mutual dependence', directly leading to the formation of the world-renowned studio. Grange has explained the arrangement in characteristically casual terms, noting that they 'slipped into partnership' through all

needing to move to larger studio space, though he conceded it was also due to their collaborations all 'being very agreeable'. And he would later muse that 'the best things seem to happen to me by accident. I have never had success if ever I thought of an initiative and tried to make it happen. Other forces guide you in.'

And so, in the first days of January 1972, Grange's merry band of now ten employees found themselves setting up a new studio – and most importantly a sizeable new workshop, to which Grange particularly aspired – and a new era began.

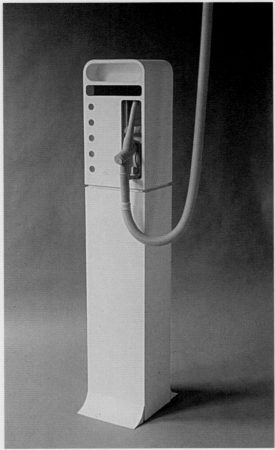

14

4
The Pentagram Years
1972–1998

The announcement of this high-profile new partnership, and the explanation of a proposed new working model for a design office, was met with curiosity and fascination by the industry – as was the chosen name, Pentagram, which, so the legend tells, was suggested by Alan Fletcher, who had been reading a book on witchcraft. This suggestion was thrown into the ring in jest after many hours of discussion and after Theo Crosby's popular idea of Grand Union – suggested for the canal alongside the building and as a wordplay on this being 'quite a coming-together of talent' – had been thrown out after someone pointed out it translated into French as 'trade union'. As they would all later recall, the name Pentagram 'just somehow stuck'.

At that point in the evolution of the design industry there were no other large, multidisciplinary design offices in the UK, and Grange described how they felt to be 'stepping into a brave new world'. The anticipation and excitement for the potential ahead

of them is palpable in the glamorous confidence of the five in their original press photograph. A launch feature in *Design* magazine explained that the desire to grow a bigger organization had originated with Fletcher and Colin Forbes as far back as 1962 when, on looking ahead twenty years, they 'dimly perceived that big clients would be more interested in dealing with other organisations than with freelancers': a prescient vision. Pentagram Design Partnership was officially incorporated in June 1972, and launched with a big party at the studio to which 'every journalist and newspaper turned up, and all the great and the good'. Grange would later recall: 'We just called up all the folks we knew. It was a great beginning and we never looked back from that, really.'

The building the partners leased, a converted warehouse adjacent to the Grand Union Canal and to Paddington Station, gave the five ample space to set up their individual sections; not least Grange, whose desire to increase the size of his workshop

1. Grange at the launch party for Pentagram, attended by 'all the great and the good', at the agency's first studios at North Wharf Road, Paddington, 1972.

2. Grange was a great admirer of the work of British cartoonist Mel Calman, much appreciating his style of wit. The Pentagram partners commissioned a series of cartoons from Calman to use in their presentations, bringing his 'little man' character (made famous in cartoons for the *Times* newspaper) to comment on the world of design.

1

2

3. The five founding
Pentagram partners in their
photo shoot for the launch of
the agency. Industrial designer
Grange (second from left)
with (from left) architect Theo
Crosby and graphic designers
Colin Forbes, Mervyn Kurlansky
and Alan Fletcher.

3

4

4. A contact sheet of out-takes from a PR photo shoot, featuring Grange, for Japanese sewing machine manufacturer Maruzen, taken to launch the Cub sewing machine (see also pp. 13 and 153).

and model-making facilities had been the 'deciding factor' for him in joining the partnership, having worried more than the others about the potential loss of individual identity. His substantial team, the biggest of any partner, situated itself at one end of the open-plan space behind a glass wall to shield the rest of the company from the noise of the workshop machinery; the glimpses of activity this offered would prove endlessly fascinating to the marketing executives and other clients visiting the more serene graphic design partner sections across the studio.

Grange's department brought with it the strong camaraderie developed in Hampstead, with practical jokes a constant source of amusement shared between them – a form of wit Grange greatly enjoyed and appreciated, having inherited this good-natured sense of humour from his mother. The exceptional model-making skills honed by his team often proved central to the success of these jokes: on one occasion, the head of the workshop, Bruce Watters, fashioned a highly realistic lookalike of his own finger, finished with a bloodied end, which he popped into a matchbox and presented to Grange's unsuspecting secretary, Elizabeth Burney-Jones, asking her innocently 'what he should do with it'. Burney-Jones promptly fainted, but came to in good spirits. Grange remembers that attempts to engage the wider

company in some of these escapades, including trying to convince Fletcher through a forged letter that he was expected to wear a kilt to an upcoming partners' away-weekend, 'went down like a lead balloon', so the team learned to keep its comic efforts to itself.

The partnership approach of the new organization was open and democratic, considered an association of equals with each partner continuing to retain his own clients and run his own projects. The new factors were that administrative costs were pooled, each partner would receive the same income, and profits were shared, regardless of the value of projects that each partner brought in. By way of comparison, for similar income Grange's projects had substantially longer timescales and were heavier on resources than other partners' graphic design projects with shorter turnaround times. Regular partner meetings were held at which potential new clients and projects were discussed, and the benefit – or lack of – mutually agreed. The group would also take itself off for a long weekend of general strategizing every six months. The criteria for accepting a job into the studio were described as 'cheerfully unrigorous': a project had to be 'either profitable or interesting'. And as long as the books were balancing, the partners would actively encourage each other to do non-paid or poorly paid work in order to build a rich and unusual joint portfolio. For Crosby, for example, this would include substantial early planning work for Shakespeare's Globe Theatre, long before it became a high-profile initiative with appropriate funding; the months if not years of pro bono work that he clocked up on the project verged on becoming a point of concern for the other partners, but they recognized that Crosby's endless Globe fundraising lunches at Pentagram 'to woo the great and the good' did add a certain beneficial profile to the studio. Commercially, more than half of all project work coming in continued to be conducted as single-discipline jobs by individual partners. However, the unique multidisciplinary potential of the partnership did bring noticeable benefits, both in terms of partners finding support in each other and also in bolstering relationships with clients, who found the range of creative excellence under one roof compelling. Having proven their collaborative potential when working together on BP back in 1970, the Pentagram partnership worked on several significant shared projects in the early years including Reuters, for which Fletcher would bring in Grange; Shiseido and Maruzen, for which Grange brought in Kurlansky and later Pentagram partner David Hillman respectively; and Boots, for later Pentagram partner John McConnell and Grange.

Also unusual in the new organization's set-up were the catering arrangements, instigated by Grange and which came to be legendary and an effective way of tempting clients into the building for meetings. Grange had often experienced the workers' canteens and executive dining halls of his clients across the industrial sector, but for the other partners and for the wider design industry, which until now had seen only small studios, this was a novel concept. The partners introduced a culture of team mealtimes, installing substantial kitchen and dining facilities and employing a new in-house cook each year to keep things lively, the thinking being that not only was this democratic, sociable and good for team morale but commercially it also saved valuable time for the partners, who would otherwise be 'out for lunch with clients most days'. Everyone ate the same menu and ate together, from directors to junior staff. And clients and other high-profile guests, who Grange recalled 'loved the socialism' of this novel arrangement, would regularly be invited and were delighted to join in. Perhaps most importantly, it ensured that every member of staff had at least one square meal per day.

The 'excitement of the new' aside, there were naturally also teething problems with the new partnership arrangement, alongside the mutual respect, as the working processes of the partners' different creative disciplines came together under one roof for the first time. The main point of friction for Grange emerged from the other partners' realization of how much time he spent working out of the studio; this was by far the larger share of his time, because so much of Grange's consultancy involved visiting the

5. Grange at a meeting-room table in the Needham Road studios of Pentagram; visible are a Maruzen 800 sewing machine, a first-generation Reuter Monitor terminal and a Wilkinson Sword Retractor razor. Pentagram partner Alan Fletcher's poster artwork is displayed on the wall behind him.

5

manufacturing facilities of his clients to review the progress of his designs, leaving his team to progress various aspects of the projects for him back in the studio. This led to an early comment to Grange by Fletcher to the effect of 'we never see you, what do you do all day?' In contrast, the graphic design partners were rarely out of the office owing to the nature of their work and because their 'office-based marketing department clients' loved to visit and absorb the vibrant scene of the studio. Although his regular absence became a source of friendly teasing, Grange recalled that 'it had an effect. We had to work at it not being harmful to the partnership.' And he has always remained firm that he 'had no choice, [he] had to go to the factories' and that his business flourished because he 'turned up' for his clients, always putting in the time and effort to visit them, especially at a time when the concept of an industrial design consultant was still a new proposition and finding its place in the product manufacturing industry.

Meanwhile other minor early teething troubles with the other partners, which Grange would later describe with amusement, were due to some of his chosen employees. As part of his substantial existing team from the Hampstead office Grange brought with him his bookkeeper Miss Wallis, an elderly German Jewish refugee who Grange acknowledged 'saved my bacon on many occasions' with her meticulous records of his sometimes chaotic spending and receipts; but it seems her 'severe appearance', and the fact she would 'take her shoes off and put her slippers on' when she arrived in the office, did not sit well with the other partners' vision for the 'look' that suited a cutting-edge design studio. Similarly, Grange also brought with him his loyal and much-adored cleaning woman, Tamar Eburn, known always simply as 'the wonderful Mrs E'. Although North Wharf Road was far too big for her to continue in the same role, Grange found it 'unthinkable she wouldn't come with me' so a new role as the office housekeeper was created specially. She took to the new situation with gusto and went on to become a long-term fixture and rather a legend, bustling around the building each day; Grange, ever her favourite, 'could never do wrong' in her eyes, and she would 'cook forbidden treats' for the staff – mainly those that left a lingering smell in the studio. By all accounts she could also be 'quite ferocious', with new kitchen recruits having to run the gauntlet of her keen eye and close monitoring of valuable commodities, gaining fame through once exclaiming to the cook: 'Don't put out all those bananas, they'll only eat 'em!'

The year 1972 proved one of multiple moves for Grange, who in the spring got married for the second time, to Philippa Algeo, a whirlwind relationship

that would only last a few years, and simultaneously moved home to a new house in Hampstead. He had bought the property, a converted stables in need of renovation, some years previously but, preferring his flat and social life near the old studio, had only popped round sporadically to check on the building works and to mow the lawn in the courtyard garden; the latter activity he often conducted late at night, on his way past after working late or after a night out on the town. When he finally moved in, a formidable neighbour was inspired to comment 'Oh! *You're* the phantom gardener ... !'

His appointments diaries for these early years of the 1970s, and a comprehensive record of letters in the British Rail archives, show Grange spending substantial time working on the InterCity 125 train as the project gathered momentum (see pp. 132–147). On this 'life-changing project', one of the many remarkable pivotal points in his career, he would later reflect: 'I'd like to think I knew what I was doing, but I am positive that I had no idea this thing was going to be such an important event in my life and as it turns out in the history of the railways.' Regardless of whether he knew what he was doing, he relished every moment of the experience, greatly enjoying his visits to the Derby Works and always dressing the part – the decade brought with it plenty of opportunity for creative expression in men's tailored fashion. To this day he takes great pleasure in describing one particular scene where he strode through the gates of the Derby Works one morning, through the smoke and steel of the engineering site to reach the design office, sporting a pale pink suit with wide lapels that

6

6. The celebrated winged ankle boots worn by Grange were designed by Jim O'Connor and commissioned by the London fashion entrepreneur Tommy Roberts (aka Mr Freedom), *c*. 1970. The boots are now held in the permanent collection of the V&A's fashion department.

7. A memo issued by James Cousins, Director of Industrial Design at British Rail, to his Design Panel colleagues, recommending Grange for the job of developing the 'appearance design' for the prototype HST. As is now legendary, this 'small' graphic design project evolved into the redesign of a whole new nose profile for the power car, which became the icon of a new era of high-speed train travel.

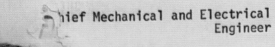

Chief Mechanical and Electrical
Engineer

Director of Industrial Design

Copy to G. S. Calder Esq.,
David McKenna Esq.,

171-6-54
30 November 1970

CLASS 41 LOCOMOTIVE

At the recent Design Panel meeting attended by Mr. Calder, it was agreed by the
Panel that the services of a design consultant should be made available to
co-operate with your staff on the finished appearance design as is now
developing.

I am sure that you would agree this can be a natural extension of the work
already in hand on the ergonomics side and the preliminary discussions and models
prepared with Mr. Hill of my department.

The design consultant I have in mind is Kenneth Grange, RDI, FSIA, a Royal
Designer for Industry, who is retained as an industrial design consultant by
a number of important companies at home and abroad including Japan.

In order to progress the wishes of the Design Panel in this respect, I would be
glad if an early meeting might be arranged between your staff and Mr. Grange
to investigate how his services might be immediately useful.

As a result of this discussion I would then be in a position to assess his
likely fee which should be met from Design Panel budget resources, but will,
I assume, be a charge on the Railways Business.

7

8

8. Grange (left) with John Bowers, founder of Bowers & Wilkins loudspeakers, and Antony Armstrong-Jones, who had introduced the pair, 1976. They are pictured here at the launch of Grange's first design for B&W, the DM6 loudspeaker.

'look just the same as cotton kimonos for men', after an accompanied shopping excursion to buy souvenirs at a Tokyo department store, where he had openly tried the garments for size on the shop floor. 'So, you should imagine an eight foot man, in the aisle of Selfridges, trying on ladies' nightdresses!' he would later crow with delight.

By the late 1970s the profile of Pentagram as an entity was reaching new heights on the international scene. Particularly on the graphic design side, there was appetite to expand and, having been comfortably handling 'a substantial chunk of American business in Europe', in 1978 Colin Forbes, ever the businessman of the original five partners, saw an opportunity: moving to the USA, he set up a New York office, in the early days generously hosted by the renowned US designer George Nelson. From here Pentagram began its second chapter as 'truly an international agency', and not long afterwards, back at home base, the London contingent moved to new and more prestigious premises in Notting Hill as the number of partners and employees continued to steadily grow. The renovation of the spacious former dairy building on Needham Road was painstakingly masterminded by the architect of the partnership, Theo Crosby, with Alan Fletcher, and continues to be the home of the London office today.

Meanwhile Grange was continuing to forge his own path within the studio; after the InterCity 125 burst onto the scene in 1975, and into the 1980s, his profile was reaching a peak. His early success designing loudspeakers for Bowers & Wilkins (see pp. 202–215) catapulted him into another new industry: the rarefied world of music recording studios. He seemed to be on every guest list as the design world jostled to host him, with a whirlwind of international speaking engagements taking him from Denmark, Finland and Russia to South Africa, Australia, India and Singapore. His attendance at trade shows was substantial too, the three biggest being Electronica, Domotechnica and Hannover Messe in Germany, which he visited every year in his roles with Kenwood, Kodak and other clients. He also navigated numerous requests to join judging panels and the advisory committees of design organizations. Behind the scenes, if the mass of neatly penned entries in the appointments diaries is anything to go by, it was an impressive and meticulous military operation on the part of his secretaries and assistants to keep everything seamlessly rolling.

The first years of the 1980s brought with them a maturing of the consumer goods industries as a wider understanding of 'how design can beneficially impact industry' was embraced and companies moved into an era of highly competitive, commercially

he had recently had made: the memory of the baffled looks on the faces of the rail workers has amused him ever since. The suit now resides in the Victoria and Albert Museum's fashion collection, alongside other of his wardrobe treasures, including a pair of Mr Freedom winged boots and a full-length bold red-and-green plaid coat in the style of Doctor Who – all pieces he could be spotted wearing on a Saturday morning pottering around the shops of the King's Road, alongside other figures of the time, including fashion designer Zandra Rhodes and Barbara Hulanicki of Biba. For comfort in the workshop Grange's distinctive look was more likely to feature rolled-up shirt sleeves under a much-loved knitted waistcoat, while public appearances late in his career would involve a dashing line in hats. His approach to fashion was similar to his attitude to the purchase of cars; he had an eye for style and understood its power to communicate, he had the means to dress well and could often be flamboyant, but his choices were 'always about having fun' rather than projecting status. His flair also made him a big hit in Japan, where through the 1970s his star as 'the European innovator' rose fast. He appeared in press photographs demonstrating his sewing machines for Maruzen (see p. 153), while other clients in Japan were also drawn by his combination of style and friendly personality. Always keen to host him and conscious of polite etiquette to the last, his client at Maruzen would only very reluctantly advise him of his error in purchasing women's *yukata* (cotton night robes), which Grange forever afterwards insisted

The Prince Philip Prize
for the
Designer of the Year
1990

Finalist
Mr Kenneth Grange CBE

9

10

9. One of many award certificates in Grange's archive, this one presented to him as a finalist for the Prince Philip Prize for Designer of the Year in 1990, a prize that he was first awarded in 1963 and went on to win again in 2001.

10. The partners of Pentagram on a strategy away-weekend at Leeds Castle, Kent, when the original five had become nine. Front (from left) the original five: Alan Fletcher, Theo Crosby, Mervyn Kurlansky, Colin Forbes and Grange. Back (from left): David Hillman, John McConnell, Peter Harrison and Ron Heron.

focused manufacturing and design processes. This is apparent in Grange's appointment to two consultant design director roles in quick succession – Wilkinson Sword and the Thorn EMI group, by then owners of Kenwood. A press release from Wilkinson Sword stated that 'directorships command respect within a company, and the hope is that this appointment will have a beneficial effect on the design departments within Wilkinson'. During this period, in recognition of his wide-ranging experience across both design itself and the industrial design management process, Grange was also appointed industrial design adviser to the Design Council (previously the Council of Industrial Design), which had done so much to promote him during his own early career years and to which he would give much support in the following years. In his SIAD (Society of Industrial Artists and Designers) Milner Gray Lecture at the beginning of the decade, the British Rail chairman, Sir Peter Parker, would credit Grange's part in embedding design in industry, stating that the successful InterCity 125 project showed that 'design management should insist in sharing the long hard look ahead; design management must be part of the strategic leadership'.

May 1983 saw his first solo show, remarkably the first complete show at the V&A dedicated to a designer during their lifetime, staged in the new Boilerhouse Gallery at the V&A, a project initiated by Terence Conran and Stephen Bayley, director of the Conran Foundation, which would later lead to the creation of the Design Museum. Titled 'Kenneth

Grange at the Boilerhouse – An Exhibition of British Product Design', the exhibition was designed by David Hillman, a second-generation Pentagram partner of whose work Grange was a great admirer. The show consisted of a selection of product designs – Grange bravely including those that had been less successful alongside his big breaks, as an honest review of his evolving career; and in the accompanying captions and catalogue he spoke self-deprecatingly about the driver of 'fear more than talent' behind his work. Bayley, who penned the introduction to the catalogue, stated that 'it adds strength to a designer's reputation when you hear him explain the reasons why some designs became lemons' and concluded that 'it would be a very dull person who was not moved by the evidence of what a directing mind can do on the empty canvas of industry'. To mark the occasion, renowned photographer Anthony Armstrong-Jones, Lord Snowdon, shot a striking black-and-white portrait of Grange, now in the National Portrait Gallery.

Following this first solo show, Grange would later be similarly honoured by the Japanese in 1989 with that country's first retrospective of the work of a British designer. In the UK the recognition through the V&A was followed by the award of a CBE in Queen Elizabeth's 1984 New Year's Honours list 'for services to design and British industry', and not long afterwards a flurry of honorary doctorates followed from a number of British universities. And in 1985 he was made Master of the RDI (Royal

11

12

13

11. Grange with his production team ahead of the opening of his first solo show, staged in the Boilerhouse Gallery at the V&A, 1983.

12 / 13. Glimpses of Grange's first solo show, 'Kenneth Grange at the Boilerhouse: An Exhibition of British Product Design'. The exhibition design was by Pentagram partner David Hillman.

14. The poster for Grange's first solo show, designed by David Hillman. The face profile of the walking figure is a likeness of Grange.

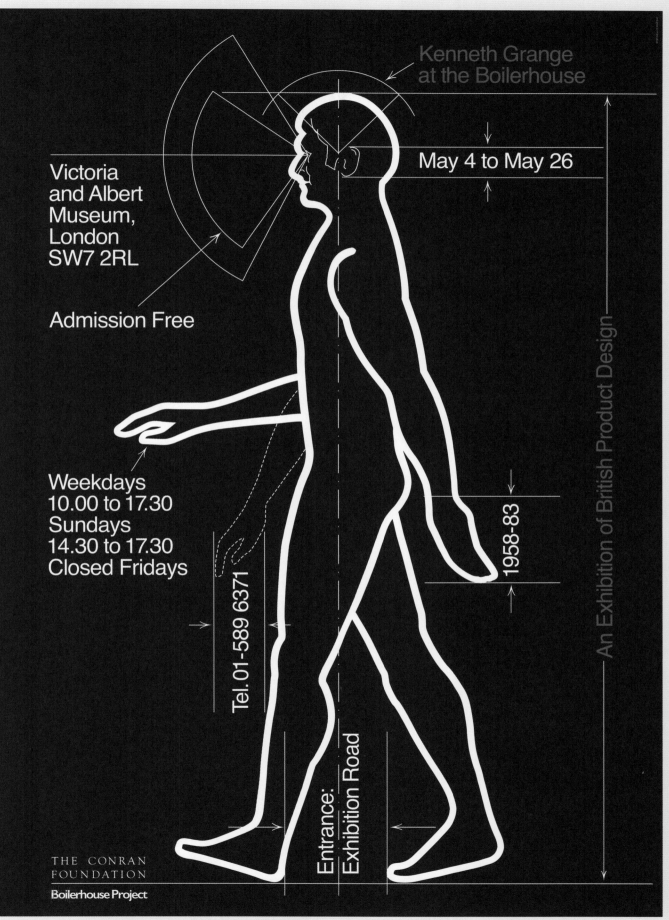

Kenneth Grange
at the Boilerhouse

Victoria
and Albert
Museum,
London
SW7 2RL

Admission Free

May 4 to May 26

Weekdays
10.00 to 17.30
Sundays
14.30 to 17.30
Closed Fridays

Tel. 01-589 6371

1958-83

An Exhibition of British Product Design

Entrance:
Exhibition Road

THE CONRAN
FOUNDATION

Boilerhouse Project

14

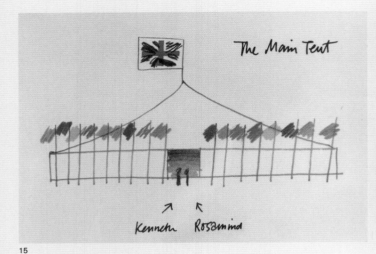

15

16

Designers for Industry) faculty for a two-year stint, during which he focused on promoting the Master's Medal to encourage young designers, a cause he continued to take up across other positions too, as well as encouraging a constant flow of student visits through the Pentagram offices.

Meanwhile, on a personal note, 1984 saw Grange marry Apryl Swift, his former secretary in the early years of Pentagram, who had since departed to try her hand at other creative activities. Their marriage was met with great celebration by Grange's team, many of whom remain close friends of the couple to this day. Grange often acknowledges with much gratitude and admiration the huge part Apryl has played in the success of his career from beyond the studio, and her exceptional care for all their life arrangements; a shared love of art, architecture and opera, and of hosting lively dinner parties, has seen them at the centre of a social whirl and a throng of friends for decades. They later embarked together on a substantial barn renovation project in Devon, which today remains a beloved second home welcoming friends from far and wide, where Apryl indulges her love of gardening. Often teasingly yet lovingly referring to her as 'her indoors', as does the witty and good-natured Apryl herself, Grange recognizes how valuable it has been that she 'understood where I was coming from' but that she also 'won't take any nonsense from me'. It certainly proved very fortunate that as his secretary Apryl had previously experienced Grange's frenetic diary and constant motion, and that they also share a love of travel: some of the busiest years of his career were about to land, starting with a three-week lecture tour around Apryl's birth country, Australia.

One might argue that a particular peak in Grange's profile was reached in 1986, which in the UK was dubbed by the government 'Industry Year' and saw a mass of activity to 'further promote understanding

of the role of design in industry'. *Design* magazine explained that 'as Britain attempts to reposition itself in world markets, there is a wealth of new opportunity for design'. Grange was involved in much of the activity, from speaking at the Design Commitment conference hosted by the Prince of Wales at Lancaster House to presiding over the 'Eye for Industry' exhibition at the V&A showcasing the work of the RDIs, as well as helping to promote the exhibition 'Thirty Years On' at the Design Centre, originally set up by the CoID in 1956, in London.

However, his activity that year was, in his mind, crowned by the results of a vast undertaking when, together with the renowned British furniture manufacturer Rosamind Julius, he co-chaired the annual International Design Conference in Aspen, Colorado. The 1986 iteration of this highly prestigious event was titled 'Insight and Outlook – Views of British Design', commissioned in response to a boost in overseas demand for British-trained design talent, and saw Grange and Julius bring together a host of top names from across the spectrum of the British creative industries to deliver talks and set up showcases. The workload was immense and involved employing a dedicated project manager: Grange appointed Mary Alexander, who would become a long-time friend and who, after the success of Aspen, later went on to organize other international design events and to lecture widely, crediting Grange's generosity for her career path. Two years of graft and planning culminated in a complex week-long event of great acclaim, and the extraordinary coming together of so many key figures was considered 'a unique coup' in the industry's history. Guest speakers ranged from David Hockney and Ralph Steadman to Norman Parkinson and Christopher Frayling; apparently the only person who turned down the invitation was the 'notoriously difficult' Malcolm McLaren. Grange described the flight out to Aspen, during which he

15. Postcard design by Pentagram partner Alan Fletcher for the prestigious annual International Design Conference staged in Aspen, Colorado. The 1986 event was co-chaired by Grange with his good friend Rosamind Julius of the British furniture manufacturer Hille.

16. By 1986 the partners of Pentagram had grown in both number and international reach, having opened offices in New York and San Francisco. Pictured here: (back) Alan Fletcher and Neil Shakery; (middle) Theo Crosby, John McConnell, Kit Hinrichs, Linda Hinrichs, David Hillman, Peter Harrison (who took this photograph with a timer); (front) Colin Forbes, Mervyn Kurlansky and Grange (sporting trademark eye-catching shoes).

17

18

17. On receiving his CBE in 1984, Grange was presented with a custom-made sword by his client Wilkinson Sword to mark the occasion. The hilt features a framed miniature of Grange. He is pictured being presented with the sword by the head engineer, Angus McCready.

18. The deep family bath with shallower seat for a child was designed by Grange as part of a complete modular bathroom solution for tile manufacturer INAX in Japan. On launch, the company shipped Grange a full bathroom set, which he installed at his home in Devon.

'worked the aisle', introducing everyone to each other: 'it was almost a plane-full and most of them had never met before. It was an incredible buzz.' The event attracted sponsorship from the Department for Trade and Industry, the British Council and leading manufacturing companies, as well as collaboration from the Design Council and the Society of Industrial Artists and Designers. As Grange also recognized, the project saw generous support from Pentagram to assist the sizeable production and logistics.

By the end of the 1980s more than fifty per cent of Grange's projects were based in Japan, where he found great satisfaction and pleasure in the work. Reviewing his comparative experiences of British and Japanese industry, when he later delivered the RDI Annual Address at the Royal Society of Arts on the subject of 'Twenty-one years in Japan', he said that 'our manufacturers do not have the expansive attitude to employment of resources, and by that I mean energy and enthusiasm as well as money, which you get in Japan. The result there is sheer elegance, time and time again, wherever you look. It's tremendously stimulating and I feel privileged to work in such a community.' And interestingly, following the great success of a meticulous, modular bathroom scheme for Japanese domestic tile company INAX (see pp. 258–61), his last years working in the country would see him return to the origins of his career in the architectural industry, consulting on a sophisticated new prefabricated housing concept for the Tokyo-based developer Sekisui Heim: a vision

to deliver design-conscious homes catering to the requirements of 'three generations of family under one roof'.

Although he was spending the largest share of his working time in Japan, Grange still retained considerable involvement in projects for the USA and Europe, though these were increasingly being handled by his capable team. Of this era he spoke with gratitude both for his team and for the growing ubiquity of the fax machine, meaning he could keep abreast of projects while out of the office and also speed up the process of gaining approvals from clients. He explained how 'we could chop up a drawing and post it through the machine in pieces' rather than having to wait days to see it if it was mailed or him having to 'forever exist on planes'. He reminisced about how 'it's extraordinary now to think back to the days when my secretary might say to a client, "Mr Grange is away on business, he'll get back to you in three weeks." The pace of business just wouldn't accept that now. You'd be out of the game immediately.'

By the early 1990s, while he was still ever prominent as a spokesperson in the industry, Grange was noticeably starting to hand the baton of responsibility for managing projects to his team, some of whom had been with him since the earliest days of the office in Hampstead. Notable among these shifts was the appointment of one of the senior designers, Johan Santer, to an internal design management role within Kenwood. With Grange's

19. Scale model of Grange's competition design for the nose profile of the Eurostar train; he lost out in the pitch to two of his former design assistants.

20. Grange's design for a new rural postbox was launched soon after his retirement from Pentagram. The prototype is pictured here attached to the gatepost of Grange's rural home in Devon.

21. Grange's reinvention of the classic aviator shape for a new sunglasses proposition for Polaroid Eyewear was part of a series of collaborations between the brand and top designers. Grange also devised the packaging and graphic solution.

agreement the company had by now set up an in-house design agency, rather than outsourcing consultancy as much as they once had – a move that was becoming increasingly common across the industry – and Grange handed the reins to Santer with his blessing. This brought to a close an exceptional client relationship that had seen him through from his earliest days as an independent designer back in the late 1950s.

Another sign of the evolving times, and a new experience for Grange, came in the form of the emergence of former employees in competitive roles at agencies elsewhere in the industry. One particular lesson he felt he gained late in his Pentagram years was when he was beaten in the pitch for the design of the Channel Tunnel train by two of his former design assistants. They had cut their teeth working for Grange on the InterCity 125 project, and having since left Pentagram and set up their own practice

had also been invited by British Rail to pitch for the job. Of regret to Grange for years afterwards, he felt it was a lesson to him in not acknowledging that things were no longer as they had been, and that he had been tied too much to the spirit of the 125. 'Because British Rail were custodians of the national railway system, everything went through them, so I went into the pitch thinking it was a British project, an evolution of the 125. But the reality was that it was also French and Belgian,' he would acknowledge. 'I misread the context, but the next generation recognized it and did a great job.'

The 1990s was also a time of radical change in the working processes of the studio at Pentagram and in the wider design industry too, with the gradual introduction of desktop publishing (DTP) and computer-aided design (CAD); for Kenneth's team particularly this change was driven by the requirement to keep up with the preferred practices

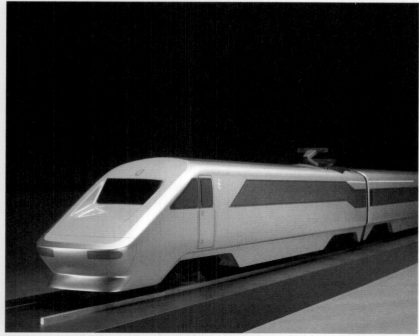

19

20

21

of their clients. Although he himself never felt that he needed to learn to use the software, and the investment in the Pro-E software for industrial design of that era was a very costly consideration, Grange accepted that the format of the studio's output needed to evolve and encouraged his team to take the steps needed towards meeting these requirements. At first a shared 'corral of technicians' was introduced into the centre of the studio, while later this was gradually replaced as young designers already proficient in the necessary skills joined the design team.

The changing technological times were also reflected in the later project commissions coming into the studio, which started to include early mobile phones and personal computing and other increasingly advanced digital products. Although these jobs excited him less than they did the younger designers in the team, Grange appreciated the value of his lifelong learning across the spectrum of technology, fabrication and working processes; when in 1996 he was awarded the inaugural Minerva Gold Medal in recognition of a lifetime's achievement in design from the Chartered Society of Designers, the body he had first been elected to join as a fledgling designer in 1955, he reflected: 'In my career I have found that pretty much everything I have learned has been given to me by my clients.'

The following year, 1997, brought round the twenty-fifth anniversary of Pentagram, and was a time of introspection and review as well as celebration for Grange. The studio had mourned the death of Crosby a couple of years previously, Fletcher had retired in 1992, and from its original vision Pentagram was becoming a more commercially savvy, competitive organization in a fast-paced global industry; the company now had a wide array of partners installed across multiple international cities. It was at this

milestone that Grange decided it was time for him to start his transition away from Pentagram and return to practising as a smaller, independent studio. Feeling a yearning to distance himself from the constant pressure and intensity of it all, he wanted to 'get back to simply focusing on making things'. It was also late in this time at Pentagram that he employed Daniel Weil, a product design graduate, and later tutor, of the RCA (Royal College of Art), whom he had happened to critique during his finals, and to whom he would eventually hand responsibility for the industrial design division of Pentagram along with a recommendation that he be made a partner.

Grange's last projects delivered while at Pentagram included a rural postbox for Royal Mail (see pp. 280–283) and, arguably a fitting swansong, an acclaimed design of the new-look London taxi cab, the TX1 (see pp. 276–279). The renewed fame this brought both in the industry and in the public consciousness were a well-timed boost to him on his way to reinstating Kenneth Grange Design as an independent practice. In early 1998, at the age of sixty-nine, Grange finally extricated himself from the 'Pentagram swim' and – taking with him just a few favourite clients and a couple of his closest Pentagram team – embarked on another new chapter in his career. Naturally, for Grange, there was to be no such thing as retirement.

5
No Such Thing as Retirement
1998–present

In the twenty-five years since he returned to practising independently as Kenneth Grange Design (KGD) – which incidentally equals the years he tallied as a partner of Pentagram – Grange has lived a rich and full career of the third age. Retirement never being something that occurred to him, he admits that owing to an unquiet mind and boundless energy he is 'useless at taking it easy'. True to his character, as demonstrated throughout his career, he has continued to embrace 'learning on the job' with an enduring appetite and curiosity for taking on new design challenges, explaining that 'being faced with something to solve is an absolute pleasure. You know somewhere out there is a solution, it's just a case of working out how you find it.' And in the design output for his most recent clients he has arguably demonstrated more exacting standards than ever.

Transitioning away from Pentagram in early 1998, Grange set up a new centre of operations for a small team at his home in Hampstead, just a few streets away from the location of his first office back in the early 1960s, though he describes the area as having 'changed a great deal' since those more bohemian

days up on the Hampstead hills. A small room above his garage became the studio – known fondly as the 'Wendy house' – with a modest workshop installed alongside in a brick-and-glass extension that he built specially; model making and prototyping have continued to remain central to his design process.

The first team member Grange engaged on leaving Pentagram was Ian Buchanan, a long-time employee and friend who had joined Grange back in the earlier Hampstead studio days. He had always held a valued role in meticulously organizing the records of Grange's studio projects, alongside his position as an engineering designer, and worked with him for a number of years after the move back to Hampstead. Of those years Buchanan recalled supporting on the delivery of projects including finalizing the details of the rural postbox for Royal Mail, ongoing work for AJ Binns, another of Grange's longest and dearest clients (see pp. 178–184) and completing work for More O'Ferrall on large-scale outdoor advertising billboards. Both were existing clients Grange had brought with him from Pentagram.

(see pp. 178–184)

1 / 2. One of many CAD drawings and physical mock-ups of design options for a range of lift interiors for Otis in 1998, one of the new clients Grange started working with on returning to practising as Kenneth Grange Design after his retirement from Pentagram.

3. A range of door handles for the brand izé, founded by writer, architect and designer Edwin Heathcote in 2001. Grange collaborated on designs for over a decade. Pictured is the first series he designed for the company on its launch.

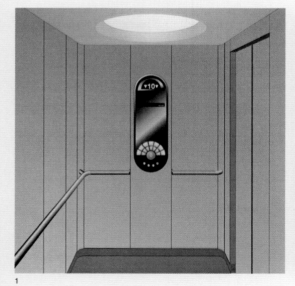

1

2

3

4

4. Small scale model (note the tiny paper figure) of a design for a large-scale billboard support structure for roadsides and roundabouts, for More O'Ferrall. Grange and a small team worked on this commission during his first post-Pentagram years, having previously worked with the company's bus stop advertising division, Adshel.

5. The Anglepoise Type 3 desk lamp, the first product designed by Grange after being appointed design director of the brand in 2003. He sensitively evolved the original iconic 1227 design by George Carwardine, including introducing a double shade to avoid the burning-hot surface of the original when in use.

Grange would also for a while regularly employ freelancer Gavin Thomson, another former designer from his team at Pentagram, who had left to set up his own practice. With new project commissions increasingly required to operate within the workflows of the fast-evolving digital era, Grange welcomed Thomson's 'hot-shot skills' with CAD, for example in his continuing consultancy for Wilkinson Sword on precision packaging, and in compiling the technical drawings of his design for a chair for new client Hitch Mylius (see pp. 296–299), in order that the team in the advanced workshops of the RCA could construct prototypes for him. Another talented former Pentagram designer whose experience Grange called upon in these later years was Peter Foskett, who had also earlier left Grange's team at Pentagram to set up as a freelancer; he and his wife, also a former Pentagram employee, had remained close friends with Grange and Apryl and were very supportive of Grange's return to independent working.

Alongside bringing a select few existing clients with him from Pentagram, Grange proceeded to work on project commissions for a number of new companies during the following two decades, across a wide span of industry and ranging from the interiors of lifts for Otis to refined door furniture for izé. However, the most enduring and acclaimed of his recent client partnerships has without doubt been with Anglepoise, the directors of which had the smart vision to appoint Grange as the brand's design director in 2003, a move that arguably led to the lighting company's renewed success (see pp. 284–291). This appointment came after a serendipitous seating plan at a design industry dinner, where Grange found himself beside Simon Terry, MD of the family-owned firm and grandson of the founder. The two talked at length about the industrial production of metal springs; perhaps not the usual dinner party conversation, but the origins both of Grange's early industrial experience, working with his mother in a spring factory, and of the Terry family's business in large-scale spring manufacture. Twenty years on, Grange remains closely involved with the brand's output, working on new product development and material innovations with the internal team and employing his discerning eye to constantly encourage the company to push for excellence.

Throughout these years Grange has relished being able to get back to being fully hands-on again with the practical detail of all his projects, while also finding space and time to conceive and deliver on his own personal projects; from small items such as a new banister rail for his Hampstead house to the largest by far – the Devon barn conversion that he and Apryl embarked upon together after buying a series of derelict farm buildings and surrounding land in 1991. The late Pentagram and immediate post-Pentagram years saw Grange spending substantial amounts of time, mainly weekends, on-site in Devon, honing his commute by taking the train to Exeter St Davids where he kept his trusty Land Rover parked, ready for an easy shuttle to and from the rural location of the barn. While there he could often be found happily engaged in moving earth and materials around with his 'single biggest toy', a Kubota digger. Of that time he recently recalled: 'Not only could I design everything in sight, but I could make it too, with one man to help and four years of time. Slow but efficient, and very satisfying.'

These days, years after the renovation was completed, when he and Apryl transfer from London for their regular stays at the barn, they prefer to drive because they 'always seem to have so much stuff'. Of the journey down, Grange says 'really it's always a very welcome scene. The landscape, and every yard of the road, just gets better and better.'

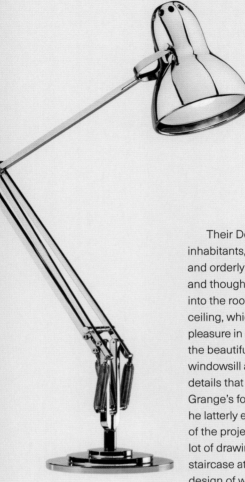

6. An early sketch by Grange for the design of a spiral staircase that features at the centre of his home in Devon. He had envisaged including a small lift platform, to rise up through the centre, for assistance in his later years. But following a knee operation, he was encouraged to stay as mobile as possible, so abandoned the idea.

7. A plan drawing from one of Grange's sketchbooks for the terraced landscaping along the front façade of his Devon home, featuring notes to the builder regarding cabling and avoiding cement falling into the plant troughs. The renovation of a dilapidated barn into a house was a major activity for Grange through his last years at Pentagram and into retirement.

Their Devon home tells you a lot about its inhabitants, and naturally also includes a sizeable and orderly workshop. One of its many interesting and thoughtful features is a large owl box designed into the roof above the first-floor sitting room ceiling, which Grange and Apryl have found great pleasure in over the years, especially when one of the beautiful, otherworldly birds perches on the windowsill and peers in at them. There are also details that are testimony to the care and skill of Grange's former employees at Pentagram, whom he latterly employed to help with certain aspects of the project – mainly those involving 'a heck of a lot of drawing work'. These include a striking spiral staircase at the centre of the house, during the design of which the exceptional skills of Grange's long-time head of workshop, Bruce Watters, were once again put to use with the construction of a full-scale model. Prominent too are signs of Grange's years of Japanese adventures: they can be found in the sizeable fitted bathroom designed by him for the

Tokyo-based company INAX, which was shipped to him in large crates as a thank-you gesture from the client; and in the pleasing experience of the 'slipper regime' whereby just inside the front door guests are presented with a rack of Japanese cotton slippers in every size, to swap into before stepping up onto the hardwood floors of the house – as Grange describes, 'a very sensible Japanese habit which saves your floor surfaces'. And as you head onwards up the staircase into the main living area, you pass one of his most ingenious personal projects of recent years, the Lifelong Bookcase: a unique coffin designed and sized for his own use, which 'until such a day comes when it might be required' stands tall and cheerful in the hallway, fitted with shelves containing art and design books (see pp. 306–309).

Meanwhile, in the industry, the awards and accolades continued to seek Grange out well into the 2010s. He has never shied away from using this recognition and profile to voice his opinions on the changing nature of the industry and to strongly

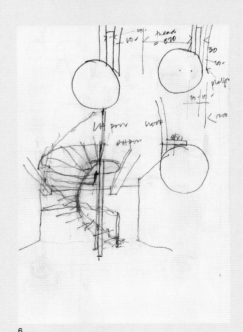

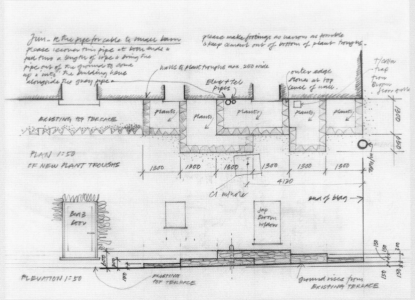

8

9

argue for greater appreciation of the value of design. More honorary doctorates were bestowed soon after he departed Pentagram, followed by the Prince Philip Designers Prize in 2001 for lifetime achievement. His communications with Prince Philip continued in 2003, when he staged a small exhibition in the Pentagram gallery titled 'Those That Got Away', spotlighting his favourite projects from across the decades that for various reasons never came to market, including the Hippo child seat and a 'glugging' sherry bottle (see pp. 268–269 and pp. 194–197). He sent an exhibition catalogue to the Duke and received a supportive letter in reply exclaiming: 'I think the exhibition might have been "brave" if they had all deserved to be failures!! They may have failed in the market place ... but they could hardly be described as "design failures".' Grange was later honoured with a full retrospective solo show at the Design Museum in 2011, at the invitation of then director of the museum, Deyan Sudjic, titled 'Making Britain Modern'; the Duke once again wrote to Grange, saying, 'it represents a massive contribution to good design in this country'. Grange's message at this large retrospective show echoed his first solo show, back in 1983 at the Boilerhouse; at the launch he spoke humbly of his acute awareness of his 'great fortune' in being in the 'right place at the right time' and of the lessons he had absorbed across his career through his failures as well as his successes. A lifetime of honours was crowned in 2013 when he was awarded a knighthood. It was bestowed upon him at Buckingham Palace by the Prince of Wales, with whom, even in the pressure of the moment, Grange managed to share a quip about not wobbling on one knee 'in case I lost my head to the sword'.

Grange continued to sit on various advisory committees for many years, including the board of the Globe Theatre, which he had taken on after the death of Theo Crosby. With more time now available to dedicate to mentoring, he also greatly enjoyed his decade as visiting professor on the Design Products course at the RCA from 2005, having been asked to take on the role by the then head of the prestigious department, Ron Arad. He would later go on to collaborate with one of his star alumni, Jack Smith, on a range of furniture pieces for Modus (see pp. 300–305), and also joined the judging panel of the James Dyson Award, which spotlights rising talent. He is quoted by the Chartered Society of Designers as saying that 'there is nothing more important to the design profession than young talent', and he was an enthusiastic participant in the RDI (Royal Designers for Industry) summer schools that ran for a number of years and brought together design students with the RDI's line-up of established industry names.

A new generation of talent has also coincided with the technological revolution in working practices across the design industry. Grange recognizes this to have been necessary, though he still believes adamantly that 'every designer should first learn to draw freehand' before they become restricted in exploration by the computer. He himself has amassed a rich collection of personal sketchbooks over the years, illustrating his lasting habit of 'seeing and capturing' details of the world around him. And although Grange once stated 'I'll be the last man on earth to get a computer', he has since been 'sucked in', greatly admiring the design of products by new industry greats such as Jonathan Ive at Apple, and appreciating the tools he now has at his fingertips through which he can stay connected. In most recent years this channel of communication, and even a new-found proficiency in video calling, has greatly aided Grange in continuing to share ideas and

8 / 9 / 10 / 11. Sketches from Grange's personal notebooks from his travels and holidays. He always carried an A4 sketchbook when travelling, and spotted details and subtleties in texture and colour wherever he looked.

10

contribute to industry discussion; while travel has become a less practical option, he thrives on firing off a constant flow of articles, thought pieces and letters, as well as keeping up email correspondence with long-time friends, ex-clients and colleagues, now scattered far and wide across the globe.

The physical nature of his involvement in the industry has gradually slowed, dimmed only by age and arthritis, never by lack of enthusiasm, curiosity or willingness. But his consultancy work continues to roll as clients take great pleasure in being the ones to travel to him these days, bringing prototypes for his review, rather than the other way around. Outings include regular lunch and dinner invitations, Pentagram board meetings and occasional industry gatherings, as well as milestone moments such as unveiling the refurbished original InterCity 125 power car – named the *Sir Kenneth Grange* for the fortieth anniversary – at the National Railway Museum in York, and visiting the V&A's new research centre in east London, where his archive, gifted to the museum, is now housed. Of this comprehensive archive, compiled across a lifetime, Grange has said: 'It is really fortune more than planning that has meant

11

12. A publicity photo, taken at his home in Hampstead, of Grange holding one of his Kodak Instamatic cameras and standing in front of a wall display of his collection of Japanese hair combs. Grange was endlessly fascinated with the handcrafted detail of many traditional products, such as lacquerware, during his years working in Japan.

13. A glimpse into the workshop at Grange's Devon home. A workshop has sat at the heart of Grange's practice at every stage in his career, both in his design studios for model making and at home for his house refurbishment projects. He would meticulously lay out these spaces with 'a home for every object' and 'a tool for every task'.

12

I've kept almost everything I ever designed. I hate throwing anything away, and it just so happened that every time I've moved home in my life it has been to somewhere with more space, so I just never needed to purge the night before I moved.'

The story told through his archive compellingly illustrates how Grange's career has been one of a rare few to span an entire era in 'the rise and fall of a golden age in British industrial design', and from a completely analogue to an almost totally digital world in terms of design practice. It is a journey that has afforded him a unique viewpoint across an extraordinary range of industries, from the privileged position of collaborating within those industries yet keeping an independent perspective. His biography also closely tracks the British manufacturing

industry's own story, from experimenting with material innovations to witnessing the pioneering production solutions that forged the modern age. He is ardent about the relationship between good design and commercial success, and a major aspect of his work has always been about 'a fundamental revaluation of the purpose, function and use of a product and not just about its styling', an approach that he appreciated right back in the 1950s as an assistant to Jack Howe and which is clearly visible throughout his decades of archival records.

At a one-day summit looking at the work of the celebrated German industrial designer Dieter Rams, held at the V&A in 1982, Grange delivered a speech in which he took the line that 'Rams is very much a designer's designer, who has managed

13

14. This large portrait that hangs in his home captures Grange in his workshop, wearing his trademark overalls, holding one of his favourite black A4 sketchbooks and seated next to one of his Anglepoise 1228 floor lamps. The painting, commissioned by the Design Museum and painted by award-winning artist Danny Howes, was presented to Grange in 2019 to mark his ninetieth birthday.

14

both to produce eminently purchasable goods as well as inspire the world's design profession simply by example'. Looking back at Grange's complete catalogue of work, it could be argued that his comment about Rams is also true of himself: he has similarly delivered functional products, imbued with a certain element of wit and considered tactility that give them a distinctive personality unique to Grange.

Much has been written and celebrated by the industry about Grange's work over the decades, and his role in shaping the last decades of the analogue era and the first decades of modern consumer culture as we know it today. However, despite his devising, developing and improving the functionality and style of hundreds of products – which millions of people have experienced, enjoyed and benefited from across seven decades – public awareness of the sheer volume of his work in shaping modern Britain has remained relatively modest: a sign both of the man and of the nature of the industrial design world. Sometimes over the years his name, in conjunction with one of his most iconic, industry-changing designs, such as the nose of the InterCity 125, has broken through into mainstream public consciousness, but for the most part his product

designs have spoken for themselves. He has always been 'more interested in the job than the promotion'.

He himself is quick to acknowledge that he has been part of a vast collaborative and evolutionary process, involving innovations and expertise drawn from across industries to bring each new product to market; but arguably his unique understanding and position in this has been that he witnessed it all from the inside – a rare if not impossible position to hold in today's world. A giant among designers, he recognizes that he in turn 'stood on the shoulders of giants' and that other giants have followed and built on his path; his enduring presence is a combination of boundless enthusiasm, curiosity, a complete lack of cynicism and the determination to 'have fun with it'. And although he might muse self-deprecatingly that his success comprised 'odd moments where I happened to be on the right bandwagon', he undoubtedly blazed a trail as an exceptional force for good through a critical early era in the evolution and awareness of design. Remaining Britain's most distinguished industrial designer of the modern age, Grange has truly lived *a life in design*.

Kenneth Grange
The Designs that Shaped the Modern World

UK Atomic Energy Authority

Previous. Close-up of the front of the Instamatic camera that Grange designed for the European market, focusing on the grip and pointer details of the dial and the tiny graphic icons for daylight and flash settings, which he also designed.

1 (opposite). A pop-up modular exhibition stand for the fledgling UKAEA as part of an international initiative to promote Atoms for Peace, on a tour of UK cities in the summer of 1955.

During the latter period of his employment with Jack Howe through the mid-1950s, Grange and his fellow assistants were encouraged to take on small freelance design jobs on the side to expand their experience, skills and contacts. It was in this capacity that Grange first worked for the UK Atomic Energy Authority (UKAEA), after being recommended to the newly formed government organization by Howe, the initial brief from UKAEA being too small for Howe to take on as a commission.

That brief, a travelling outdoor exhibition called Atoms for Peace, had been touring a number of European countries and was now coming to the UK. Sponsored by the United States Information Service following the Second World War, its aim was to inform the general public of the peaceful applications of nuclear energy, such as in the generation of power and the role isotopes could play in medicine, agriculture and industry. The design brief to Grange was to devise a small, portable, weatherproof display stand as an addition to this US-led exhibition, to introduce the mission of the UKAEA within this international picture.

Referencing the geometry of atomic structures, Grange conceived a stand featuring a simple, lightweight ball-and-pole framework that he had first seen used at the Festival of Britain and which offered flexibility of scale and ease of assembly; modular printed information panels could be easily produced and clipped onto the structure. Proving an effective piece of public engagement, the exhibition stand was first situated on the South Bank in London in June 1955, before touring to other UK cities later in the year.

Late that year the outcomes of the inaugural United Nations International Conference on the Peaceful Uses of Atomic Energy, which took place in Geneva, escalated the focus on developing the UK's nuclear research programme and communicating this strategy at a national and international level. And so it was that, into 1956, the small PR team at the nascent UKAEA asked Grange if he could visit their offices during his lunch hour, where they proceeded to ask him if he would consider taking on the design of all the exhibits for a large exhibition stand for the second United Nations International Conference on the Peaceful Uses of Atomic Energy, at which the UKAEA would be requiring a major visible presence. Set to take place in Geneva in September 1958, this huge event would mark a pivotal moment not just in the history of nuclear energy policy but also in Grange's career.

Having accepted the job with enthusiasm, then realizing the magnitude of what he had agreed to deliver over the coming months, Grange brought the project back to Howe and proposed the office take it on. But Howe declined, stating in characteristically straight terms that this was Grange's opportunity and it was 'better he leave and do it on his own'. And so Grange found himself 'at the biggest turning point in my life', leaving full-time employment with Howe to set up his own practice, the Kenneth Grange Design Office, in the spare room of his marital flat. The job was far beyond the scale of anything he had previously worked on and, with other jobs starting to roll in too, within a few months he found himself employing a small team of assistant designers. By the latter stages of the project they found themselves often working through the night, with 'typesetting and pieces of exhibits spread across every floor and surface' in the flat. And for the final six weeks leading up to the conference Grange booked out a hotel room in Geneva from which he could more easily work while overseeing the on-site exhibition build.

The resulting substantial exhibition stand, built on two levels with numerous themed displays, was very well reported at the time, presenting the UK in a strong light at the forefront of early nuclear research. The exhibition as a whole, which ran alongside the main UN conference, welcomed tens of thousands of international visitors across two weeks.

During this same period, with momentum now rolling and increased funding for the organization,

2

2. Front façade of the substantial UKAEA trade show stand at the second United Nations International Conference on the Peaceful Uses of Atomic Energy, Geneva, 1958. This was the project that launched Kenneth Grange Design.

3

4

3 / 4. Early sketches for ideas for UKAEA exhibits on the theme of Atoms for Peace, to help exhibition visitors interact with the exhibits and better understand the science behind the topic.

5 / 6. Original presentation perspective drawing and the final result of Grange's interior design of the information centre and library for the UKAEA in central London.

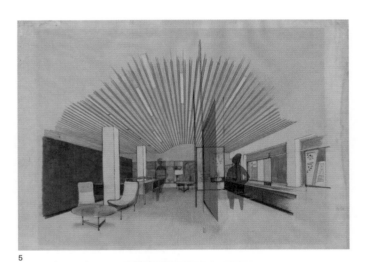

5

the UKAEA team also asked Grange to take on a third commission: this time the interior design of an information centre and photographic library at the UKAEA offices in central London. For this Grange considered everything from the architectural specifications to the furniture and decor – the most comprehensive architectural interiors project he had yet taken on as a solo designer.

6

Venner

1 (opposite). The distinctive Grange-designed parking meter for Venner, installed on a street in Westminster, central London.

2. A copy of the weekly guide *This is London* from 1983, featuring the Venner parking meter on the cover as part of promoting Grange's exhibition at the V&A's Boilerhouse.

2

Grange's very first industrial design commission as an independent designer also marked his first experience of the benefit brought by the Council of Industrial Design (CoID) and its Design Selection Service. Not long after Grange left Howe's full-time employment in 1956 to set up his own independent studio, Howe recommended that Grange be added to this professional listing; Howe himself was already on the list and well recognized by the CoID. Soon afterwards Grange was placed on a shortlist of three designers put forward by the CoID for consideration by the British manufacturing firm Venner Ltd.

Venner was on the cusp of installing the first coin-operated parking meters in London, as a pilot scheme for Westminster Council. However, the design of the meter that Venner had obtained a licence to import – a US model called the Park-O-Meter – had been recently rejected by the CoID, which had been asked by the Ministry of Transport to advise on good design standards for British street furniture. The introduction of parking meters was a particularly contentious issue, and while the mechanism of the meter was considered reliable and well constructed, it was deemed the outer casing 'needed a facelift' to give it a suitably refined profile and presence within the London streetscape. Consequently Venner had turned to the CoID to request advice on a solution.

The Venner team met and briefed the three recommended designers and, under pressure to deliver on manufacture and installation, set a very short timescale to submit proposals. The preparation period for this pitch deadline happened to clash with his summer holiday plans so – keen not to miss the opportunity – Grange would subsequently be found modelling the body shape for his proposed new meter casing while sitting on a beach in Italy with his wife, having bought up all the local supplies of plasticine he could find.

Presenting his proposal to the Venner and CoID teams back in London, his distinctive 'inverted teardrop' design was considered to capture a 'modernist lightness in the styling' that the CoID was seeking to encourage, and Venner appointed Grange for the job. He later described the view of modern design in Britain at that time as aspiring towards 'European restraint rather than the American theatre of that era of consumerism', but without such a 'ruthlessly simplistic' approach as continental modernism might apply. And he also acknowledged that considerations for the design of public-facing products during that time needed to enable the public to 'join the modern world' through 'simple, graceful everyday encounters'.

The first Venner parking meters were finally installed in Grosvenor Square, Westminster, in July 1958 and inaugurated by Richard Nugent, the parliamentary secretary to the Minister for Transport, with a quote from the seventeenth-century English poet John Milton: 'They also serve who stand and wait.' By the mid-1960s more than 25,000 meters had been introduced across Britain, and, additionally, more than fifty countries would go on to import and install the meters worldwide, resulting in a substantial source of overseas revenue for Venner.

The meters became a ubiquitous feature of city streets in the UK for more than three decades, but by the 1980s these enduring totems were starting to be replaced with electronic, card-reading versions; Grange himself worked on a design for an early electronic parking meter for GEC, but for various administrative reasons it never went into production in the UK.

Despite being such a widely produced item for so long, by the time of Grange's retrospective exhibition at the Design Museum in London in 2011 all the original Venner meters had been removed from service and not a single salvaged one could be sourced for display anywhere in the world. However, an immaculate model was made for the exhibition.

General Post Office /
British Telecom

1 (opposite). Grange's secretary posing with a model of one of many concepts Grange conceived for business telephone devices for British Telecom during his years of consultancy for the organization.

2 / 3. An exhibition stand by Grange for the GPO (likely pictured at the Ideal Home Exhibition), created during his early years of consultancy, explaining to the public the organization's products and services.

Grange first worked on a design project for the General Post Office (GPO), the nation's main provider of postal and telephone services, in early 1952 while in the employment of Gordon and Ursula Bowyer. That brief had been for a portable exhibition stand, his diary entries describing it as a 'pleasant job' and noting that it was also his first opportunity to 'conduct a high-level client presentation on my own'. His diaries also record that he continued to work on the delivery of that project for the Bowyers during his evenings once he had transferred to the employment of Jack Howe.

During the later 1950s, once Grange had set up his own independent practice, the GPO began to engage him on a range of design briefs of his own, recommended onwards by Gordon Bowyer. These early jobs were mainly modest exhibition stands to explain to the public the history and updated services of the GPO, as well as the occasional small graphic design job, including a version of the small paper disc in the centre of the dial of the rotary telephones provided by the GPO telecommunications service. But over time the design commissions Grange received from the GPO grew in scale and expanded across disciplines, from graphic and exhibition design to product design and even the interior design of broadcast studios, as the GPO itself evolved.

The GPO became the Post Office in 1969 and the telecommunications division eventually split away to form British Telecom (BT) in 1981; Grange would continue to receive design commissions from BT throughout his Pentagram years, keeping his workshop team busy with concept development of prototype desk phones in the 1980s and early hand-held personal computers into the 1990s. Photos of concept models in Grange's archive show variously a 'short-range radio telephone', early 'hands-free telephones', a 'flush-mounted kitchen phone', an 'outdoor phone on a pedestal', a 'new business telephone' and an 'advanced personal computer' or APC. However, none of these directly came to market.

But the most significant and prescient project Grange worked on was a futuristic studio space for video conferencing services launched far ahead of its time. This extraordinary, visionary project brief arrived on Grange's desk in 1969 from Richard Stevens, design manager at the GPO. The organization was itself tasked with promoting a cutting-edge technological future for Britain and during the 1960s had been experimenting with early picturephone technology, defined as 'a telephone receiver which can also transmit and receive television pictures of the callers', and by the turn of the decade the system was ready to launch commercially.

2

3

4. A glimpse of the space-age-styled reception area of the Confravision studios in London on the occasion of the launch of the radical new video conferencing service in 1971. The Confravision logo was by Banks & Miles

5. A scale model of the interior of a Confravision video conferencing suite. The set-up was conceived to be modular so it could be integrated into a range of venues.

6. A view of an original Confravision suite, featuring five seats for conferees facing the cameras and monitors, and two seats at right angles for a secretary and production assistant.

The first application of this technology, to be called Confravision, was presented as a service unique to Britain that would enable 'conferences by television'. The system, it was explained, would be housed in purpose-built studios in key UK cities, allowing conferences to be held between two groups of people in complete privacy over Post Office video circuits. The target audience was senior business executives, who it was promised could save valuable hours of travelling time and therefore not need to be away from their office teams for too long.

Basic demonstration studios had already been set up in London in the late 1960s, but Grange was asked to design a modular interior scheme that could be applied to the rollout of the final commercial studios, combining consideration for technical layout and user design with a visual look and feel that would be 'fitting for the premium, futuristic customer experience' on offer.

Each studio complex would comprise a reception area, restrooms and the main studio and back-of-house technical rooms. For the reception area Grange opted for bold yellow walls referencing the corporate identity, combined with 'postbox red' upholstery. Within the broadcast studio itself, where *Design* magazine noted 'Grange's influence is strongest', he opted for a bright white space-age environment featuring one continuous working area incorporating a length of floating conference table for the conferees; upholstered wings at either end ensured the line of chairs would not shift out of the video camera's field of view, while a raised edge on the front of the table held microphones and the chairperson's controls. The other end of this L-shaped surface offered two further seats, each with small playback monitors and controls; with one seat for a secretary to sit within eyeline of the conferees, and one for a further assistant, with a camera mounted overhead to enable the display of physical materials or a 'video blackboard'.

Facing the main attendee line-up was a central display wall incorporating: a two-turret camera within a black rectangular cone recessed into the wall, focusing on either the central three or all five conferees; two screens below, presenting a view of the remote attendees as well as any displayed materials; and above all this the necessary spotlighting to highlight the attendees. Transmissions were specified to be solely in black and white, as colour would have demanded an excessively high level of lighting to achieve a quality stream.

Grange commented of his scheme that it was 'essential the system be friendly, comfortable and simple to operate, since these studios would mostly be used by non-technical people'. The business model envisaged the Post Office securing space within existing host buildings in prime city locations and constructing 'sound-proofed, floating rooms' to house the studios; this advanced fit-out would result in substantial expense, but with the

4

5

confident forecast of recouping costs through rentals of the service.

In late 1971 the first commercial Confravision studios fitted out in Grange's modular scheme launched in London, Birmingham, Bristol, Glasgow and Manchester, with other UK locations gradually following. And Grange also designed a compact interior solution for a large trailer, fitted out as a mobile studio option. The magazine *Industrial Design* reported that 'Confravision is the first British intercity conference service for two-way speech, vision and display ... allowing discussions between groups of people as if they were in the same room', while the *Financial Times* predicted that 'transmitting vision as part of an ordinary telephone call economically is,

technically, a formidable problem but experiments using Viewphones are continuing. Before the end of this decade we are likely to see this facility available on in-house installations.'

Alongside the launch of Confravision, Stevens and Grange also worked together on a future-gazing GPO exhibition – Project 1990 – which, as reported by *Optima* magazine in 1971, imagined 'the perfect work space of 1990'; in his explanation of the project, Stevens predicted the return of 'cottage industries' and 'more and more individuals working from home'. According to *Optima*, the duo's solution – a vision for an office for a civil engineer – was 'completely self-contained, modular, and highly automated. He is linked by two-way screen with his colleagues in

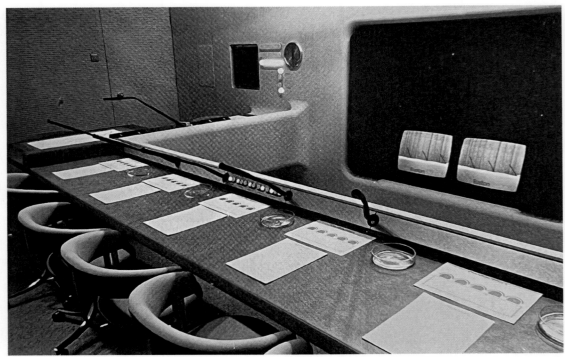

6

7 / 8 / 9 / 10 / 11. The photographs on these pages show a range of models of concepts for telephones and intercom systems – some for office and some for home use – demonstrating the prolific nature of Grange's design concept work for British Telecom during his years of consultancy for the organization.

other offices: he is equipped with a machine that can reproduce his plans, documents, data sheets, letters etc. in any office he dials. He has a cordless pushbutton telephone, telex, visual display unit with a large screen, used in conjunction with a keyboard and a light pen to provide access to a complete hierarchy of computers.'

By the mid-1970s Confravision was being celebrated as the world's first video-conferencing network for business, attracting global interest with a successful link-up to Australia, deals on the table with Japan and Canada, and a first European trial with Sweden. The service continued to expand slowly for a few more years, but ultimately the vision was too expensive and too far ahead of the customer adoption of technology of the time. It would take decades of network standardization, improved interoperability, cheaper connectivity and higher definition to finally create enough demand and trust in the service to conclusively cement the future of video conferencing as we now know it.

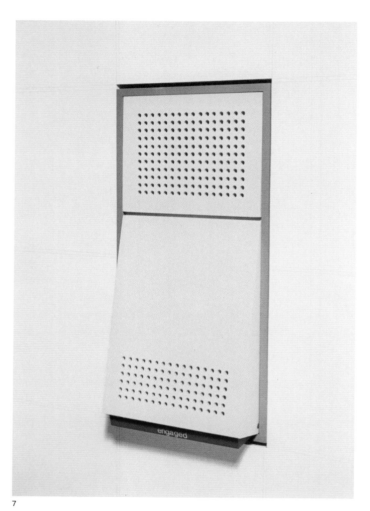

7

8

9

10

11

Kodak

1 (opposite). The Kodak Brownie 44A viewfinder camera, which won Grange his first Design Centre Award from the CoID, in 1960. The groundbreaking design introduced a moulded plastic body and plastic lenses, which reduced manufacturing costs.

2. The original Kodak Brownie, with down-facing viewfinder. At the time Grange began working with the company, Kodak was in the process of transitioning its Brownie product development to the more desirable horizontal viewfinder style.

Grange's first encounter with Kodak as a client came through his mentor and previous employer, Jack Howe, who had been commissioned to design the Kodak pavilion for the Brussels World's Fair of 1958. Howe in turn brought in Grange, who had recently left Howe's full-time employment to start his own small practice, to design the interior exhibition area of the pavilion for the camera displays.

During the on-site installation of the show in Brussels one evening in April 1958, Grange by chance briefly engaged in casual conversation with a representative from Kodak, who was there unpacking boxes of catalogues. Grange, having 'no idea who this relaxed gentleman in shirt sleeves was', happened to remark that the displays would 'look a whole lot better if the cameras were not so damned ugly'. The gentleman politely asked Grange how much he might charge to design a better-looking camera, Grange responded with 'a rather vague figure' and the two went their separate ways. Having thought no further of this interaction, a few days later back home in London Grange was startled to receive a phone call from one Dr F. H. G. Pitt, head of the Developments Department at Kodak Ltd, the European division based in the UK. Pitt explained he had 'been told by his Sales Director in Brussels' that Grange was going to design a camera for him. Confirming this commission, Pitt said that they required a camera specifically targeted at the European market, a first for the UK division of Kodak as, until this point, all new product designs were overseen by the US office.

The first camera for which Pitt commissioned Grange's input was to be an updated Brownie. The brief was to style a new body to better appeal to European tastes, working with existing functional components. At that time the professional Leica camera – with horizontal viewfinder, meaning the user held the camera up to their eyeline, rather than looking down into the top of the camera – was seen as highly desirable, so Kodak was keen to develop affordable products that offered this same

experience. Additionally, Kodak had for a while been investigating new material options for its cameras, and Grange's design would become the first to introduce a body made entirely of moulded plastic – and also, most notably, lenses made of plastic – meaning that both the manufacturing costs and price of the product could be much reduced.

Pitt was impressed with Grange's 'enthusiasm and diligence' during the initial development work, and in January 1959 Grange was appointed 'consultant for appearance design', a role that would endure for the following two decades. The Brownie 44A was launched later that year, to be met with instant popularity, and the following year was selected from over 3,000 entries to win Grange his first Council of Industrial Design (CoID) award. As a result of Grange's careful consideration of the material used, the 44A also became the first Kodak camera to make a profit for the company; previously the cameras produced by Kodak had been viewed by the company as 'a loss-making product in order

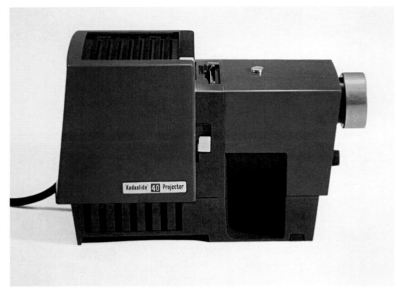

3

4

to sell film'. Sales of film and the corresponding print processing services would continue to remain by far the biggest and most lucrative part of the business, but Grange's designs, combined with smart use of materials and innovative manufacturing, sparked awareness internally at Kodak that the cameras could be profitable products and a marketing opportunity in their own right.

Quickly following this initial success came a brief to transform the look of another of Kodak's existing products for the increasingly design-conscious consumer market, the Kodaslide 40 projector. Grange's design solution was recognized with a second CoID award in 1961 and the product appeared on the front cover of the organization's *Design* magazine, while Kodak's own industry magazine proudly reported that 'the design embodies a number of refinements not normally available in a

projector of this price. The judges liked its compact and expressive shape and were impressed by the slide mechanism.'

Also in 1961, his design contributions having attracted the attention of the US parent company, Grange was invited to visit the New York offices and tour the factory, as part of Kodak's international sales conference that year. His first-time crossing of the Atlantic brought with it an important career moment for Grange as he witnessed the 'evidence of modernity' presented by the American dream. This visit further cemented his profile at Kodak and from here he started to build up a trusted relationship with the team that enabled him to suggest new concepts. While the Brownie 44A and Kodaslide had been design updates of existing Kodak products, Grange's next camera would be a completely new concept: the Brownie Vecta. From his visits to the print processing

3. The Kodak Kodaslide 40 slide projector, for which Grange won his second Design Centre Award from the CoID, in 1961. The product was already in existence, but Grange transformed the look of the body, giving it a modern forward-tilting elegance that made it a popular seller.

4. The award-winning Kodak Kodaslide 40 on the cover of *Design* magazine. The projector was featured in the Design Centre's 'designs of the year' in 1960, winning a Design Centre Award the following year.

5. A large-scale drawing by Grange in coloured pencil of a design concept for the body of a Kodak cine-film home projector. The design never progressed further.

6. The front cover of Kodak's newspaper from the company's participation in the Ideal Home Exhibition at Olympia in 1961, carrying news of its second win at the Design Centre Awards with Grange for the Kodaslide 40.

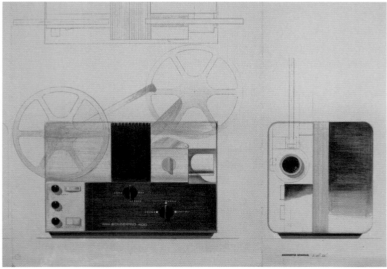

5

Kodak PHOTO-FANFARE

OLYMPIA LONDON 29 MAY — 3 JUNE 1961

TREBLE TOP!

3 major Kodak triumphs

★NEW KODACHROME FILM PAGE 3   ★WHAT PRICE MOVIES? PAGE 4   ★REPORT ON RETINAS PAGE 2

MODEL PUZZLE! No wonder she looks puzzled. Who wouldn't be, when invited to choose from such a wonderful array as the current range of Kodak cameras?

DRAMATIC PROOF THAT KODAK STILL LEADS THE WORLD IN PHOTOGRAPHIC DEVELOPMENT has been given in three different ways recently.

For the second year in succession, a Kodak product has been honoured with a Design Centre Award. In 1960, the 'Brownie' 44A gained one of these coveted awards—first camera ever to do so. This year, the distinction goes to the 'Kodaslide' 40 Projector.

Triumph number 2 is in the field of colour, with the introduction of new, faster 'Kodachrome' II film. (In strictly limited supplies of 25 ft 8 mm. spools to begin with. 'Kodachrome' film will of course continue to be available.)

The third success story is a 'moving' one, with Kodak introducing a 'Brownie' Movie camera at the amazingly low price of under twelve guineas.

These achievements are dramatic—almost sensational—but they are only a small part of the Kodak story . . . only three of the feast of good things on the Kodak stand at Photo Fair.

And if you happen to be reading this on your way home from the Fair, and come across something which you missed—your Kodak dealer will be happy to put you in the picture.

QUICK ROUND-UP

Kodak Films

especially . . . new fast 'Kodachrome' . . . High Speed 'Ektachrome' . . . superfast 'Royal-X' Pan, new improved 'Tri-X' Pan.

Kodak Cameras

especially . . . the latest Retina Automatic models . . . the amazing 'Retinette' IB . . . the superb 'Retina' Reflex S . . . the versatile but inexpensive 'Brownie' 44B and the popular 12-on-120 Cresta 3.

'Kodaslide' Projectors

especially the award-winning 'Kodaslide' 40 . . . and the 'Kodaslide' 50, with armchair control.

??? DID YOU KNOW ???

The majority of motion pictures—for cinema and T.V. (colour and black-and-white)—made in British studios are shot on film stock made in the Kodak factory at Harrow.

Over 5,000 people work there. Throughout the U.K. Kodak Limited, largest photographic manufacturers in the Commonwealth, employ over 9,000 men and women.

DESIGN CENTRE AWARD
FOR THE KODASLIDE 40 PROJECTOR
Styling, easy operation praised

'**T**HE design embodies a number of refinements not normally available in a projector of this price. The judges liked its compact and expressive shape. They were impressed by the slide mechanism which made it easy to operate . . .'

This is what the judges said of the 'Kodaslide' 40 Projector when they chose it to receive one of the coveted Design Centre Awards. Only 13 of these

Leading designer Kenneth Grange F.R.S.I.

awards were given throughout the whole of the industrial manufacturing world. The projector was designed by Kenneth Grange in association with Kodak Developments Department—the same successful team that gained a similar award last year for the 'Brownie' 44A camera.

The 'Kodaslide' 40 takes all 2 × 2 slides (including superslides). It has a 4-in. 'Ektanon' lens f/3·5, with fingertip focusing; 150-watt projection lamp and aspheric condenser system. Slides are fed in vertically, and

as each new slide is inserted, it pushes its predecessor out, to be stacked automatically in a chamber at the base of the projector. Elevation up to 6° can be obtained, and there is a retractable carrying handle. The projector is finished in striking blue-green and grey.

A Rapid Slide Changer—a manually operated slide magazine is available as an additional refinement.

'Kodaslide' 40 Projector
£12 17s. 6d.
150-watt lamp 21/9d.

'Kodaslide' 50 Projector

For those who want the ultimate in projection quality, there is the new 'Kodaslide' 50 Projector. Similar in design and styling to the award-winning 'Kodaslide' 40, this *de luxe* model is a fan-cooled projector, with a 300-watt lamp.

The projector can be made semi-automatic with the clip-on Rapid Slide Changer—or for real luxury and press-button armchair control there is an accessory Remote Control Unit.

'Kodaslide' 50 Projector . . . £16 2s. 6d.; 300-watt lamp 33/-. Rapid Slide Changer (optional extra) £3 17s. 6d.; Remote Control Unit (optional extra) £11 12s. 6d.

Tip-top value
If you want quality projection at a really rock-bottom cost, the 'Kodaslide' Home Projector is for you. It has the same optical and illuminating systems as the 'Kodaslide' 40.

'Kodaslide' Home Projector £9 10s. 0d.; 150-watt lamp 21/9.

7. A page from one of Grange's notebooks from 1970, documenting a meeting at Kodak and featuring quick sketches of two potential styles of grip moulding for a camera dial.

8. Cross-sectional diagram, longways through the centre of the Vecta camera body, highlighting the plastic moulded body components.

9 (opposite). The Kodak Vecta camera with its futuristic styling was the first complete product Grange had conceived for the company and earned him another Design Centre Award.

centre in Harrow, London, Grange had noted that the great majority of photos taken by customers were of people standing; however, because the traditional position in which to hold existing cameras meant the film was in landscape orientation, this resulted in 'a small human subject in the centre of a wide empty frame'. Grange therefore proposed a camera that would present the film in portrait orientation, enabling the human subject to be featured larger in the frame. The Kodak team approved his design proposal – an excellent demonstration of the strong, collaborative and trusted relationships Grange developed with his clients – and the Vecta was duly produced and launched in 1963, winning Grange and Kodak a third CoID award in 1964. The judges noted the smart feature of a single-piece moulded plastic body that 'in styling terms is well ahead of its time', as reported in *Design* magazine. But the camera had limited chance to prove itself in the market; the existing spool film type was soon to be superseded by Kodak's introduction of the easy-load 126 cassette format, which profoundly influenced the future development of cameras worldwide. Although the magazine *Design Week* later celebrated the fact that 'without such original pioneers who act on instinct ... the world would be bereft of glorious mistakes', Kodak's marketing focus at the time moved on, and not long afterwards came the launch of the groundbreaking Instamatic camera, introducing amateur photography to a whole new audience.

Setting to work on the Instamatic project, Grange collaborated closely with the engineering team to devise 'a completely new look' for this radical new amateur camera, one that hinted at the style of professional cameras, while remaining light, agile and affordable. Grange was dispatched to New York to present his design to the US team but, though they warmly welcomed him and approved of his design, they would go on to launch their own alternative version of the Instamatic for the US market, with Grange's design launched into Europe.

7

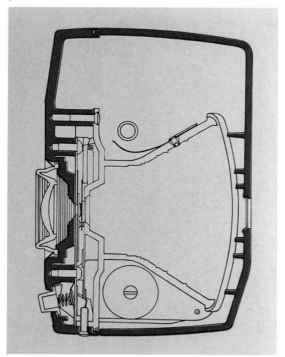

8

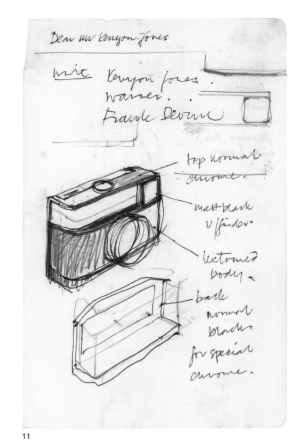

10

11

His original Instamatic design, the 33 series, launched in September 1968 – followed by the 55 series in 1971, and all with various specifications of flash, lens quality and telephoto ability – became an immediate sensation and thereafter a pop culture icon. The Instamatic sold more than 30 million units across Europe during the production lifetime of the product. The extraordinary business impact on Kodak in Europe was first recorded in November 1969 by the *Financial Times*, which stated: 'more than 1 million Instamatic cameras worth GBP 2.2 million were exported from the UK in the 12 month period to October 1969 – the first time British-made Kodak cameras have passed the million mark in exports. The immediate acceptance in export territories

led to the installation at Stevenage of automated assembly lines which raised production by 25 per cent'.

Market research increasingly played a central role in the product development process at Kodak, perhaps more so than at any other of Grange's clients; into the 1970s it was reported that the amateur camera was increasingly being viewed as a statement of personal style, so looks mattered equally to functionality and handling. Once the Instamatic was established, Grange was redeployed to develop a range of experimental designs in anticipation of a new camera series that would feature the next film innovation from Kodak: the smaller, slimmer 110 cassette. As with all his client

10 / 11. Pages from Grange's notebooks documenting one of many meetings at Kodak, and recording an early sketch of the Instamatic camera, which Grange was commissioned to refine for a European sensibility.

12. Grange's design for the Instamatic 33 series, which launched in 1968 and became an overnight sensation, rocketed Grange to new levels of design fame.

'The Instamatic – that really set me up. You need a few good mountains in your career and that was one of them for me.'

Kenneth Grange

13. A page from Grange's sketchbooks showing an early sketch for a series of slimline Pocket Instamatic cameras. Upside-down through the paper can be glimpsed a quick sketch of the prototype British Rail HST, with its distinctive bull-nosed profile.

14. A page from one of Grange's later sketchbooks, listing the many prototypes he had developed for the Pocket Instamatic during market research testing for the product.

15 / 16 / 17 / 18 / 19 / 20. A series of initial wooden models exploring form, next to later plastic prototypes exploring texture and colour, developed during market research for the Pocket Instamatic and showing the comprehensive development work undertaken by Grange and his team.

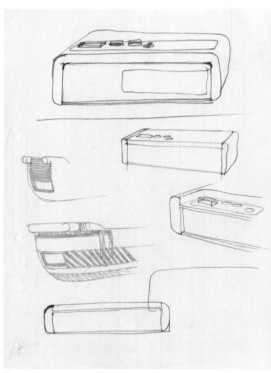

13

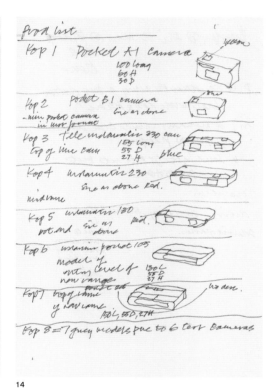

14

projects throughout his career, Grange and his team would proceed to make a comprehensive series of scale models – rather than simply relying on drawings – which could then be used more actively in market research for realistic handling. None of this experimental series ever came to market in the forms presented by Grange, but learnings from the research study were applied more widely. And in the end, the UK production focus shifted to a new product that the USA had developed for the 110 film cartridge: the Pocket Instamatic. So a new brief came to Grange to transform the look of this latest product for European tastes, while at the same time also taking into account

new techniques in mass production that would streamline UK production. Launched in 1975, the Pocket series would be Grange's last realized camera for Kodak.

Not long afterwards, faced with an increasingly competitive market, the Kodak business undertook a review and made the decision that the UK base would become assembly only, handing all responsibility for product design back to the US office. Papers in Kodak's archive record that the Development Department in the UK, along with Grange's position, was dissolved in 1979.

15

16

17

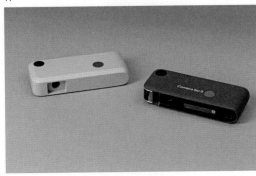

18

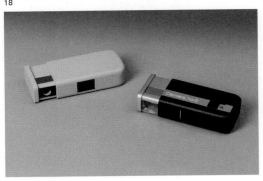

19

20

'It is a generally accepted truism that the smaller the product, the greater the refinement. It is fastidious attention to detail that marks out the superlative from the good. This requires effort, which consumes time.

'The temptation to concede to a quicker, clumsier solution is seductive and sometimes even politic. Despite such commercial pressures, the giant manufacturer can afford to put the effort into these details.'

Kenneth Grange about the Kodak Pocket Instamatic

21

22

23

24

21. Alongside cameras, Grange worked on a range of other projects for Kodak including, here, the interior of a Visitors Centre in Harrow, designed in collaboration with Grange's former employer, the architect Gordon Bowyer.

22. Packaging designs by Grange for a range of Kodak products.

23 / 24. Livery designs for Kodak delivery vans by graphic design studio Fletcher/Forbes/Gill, with whom Grange collaborated at Kodak.

25 / 26. Painted wooden models exploring the forms and volumes of concept designs for two different handheld cine cameras.

Grange later recalled that 'for a while there I would design everything for them, whatever they needed', which included not just cameras but also packaging, graphics and even the interior of Kodak's UK visitors centre. He would also comment on how influential his time with Kodak had been to his personal development, in terms of his early understanding of 'the power of mass production to enable good design and style to be truly affordable and accessible'.

It was also through Kodak in the early 1960s that Grange would first come to work with the renowned design office of Fletcher/Forbes/Gill, which had won a pitch to design packaging and graphics for Kodak's UK division. During the pitch presentation Grange, as design consultant to Kodak, was 'sat across the table on the side of the client' and was greatly impressed with the trio: the resulting working relationship between the four at Kodak would lead to further collaborations on projects for other clients and, within a few years, to the founding of Pentagram.

'I became very well entrenched at Kodak – so that almost anything they could think of a designer doing, I did – be it an exhibition or an interior, and all this packaging for the cameras.'

Kenneth Grange

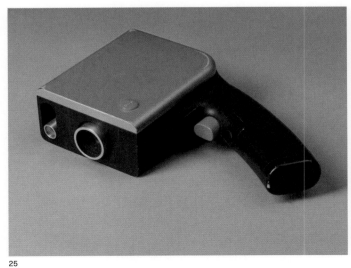

25

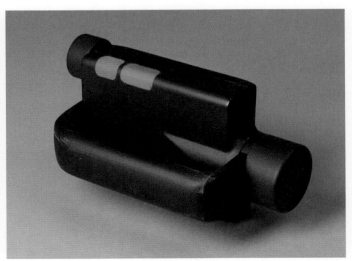

26

Hope's

Henry Hope & Sons Ltd (Hope's), founded in 1818, was a major British manufacturer of pressed and extruded metal structures and components, including horticultural buildings, window frames, roofing, ventilation systems and architectural ironmongery. The business reached a peak after the Second World War when the postwar housing boom favoured rolled-steel metal over timber as the quickest and most cost-efficient solution for prefabricated window frame construction.

In the late 1950s, following his work on the Venner parking meter, Grange came to the attention of Michael Hope; then managing director of Hope's, and on the board of the Council of Industrial Design (CoID), he would shortly after appoint Grange as a consultant designer to his family firm. This was Grange's first retained consultant position, a role that initially saw him working on exhibition stands for Hope's annual presence at influential industry shows including the Building Trades Exhibition and the British Industries Fair, which Hope's asserted in its newsletter to be its 'major advertising effort' each year. Grange later warmly recalled the experience of spending 'a very enjoyable three days a month', over several years, at the Hope's factory in Birmingham, where the family and team were very generous and 'taught me acres', both about British manufacturing and about the 'good values of independent business'.

But one of Grange's most publicity-attracting design commissions from Hope's actually came about as a result of Michael Hope's association with the CoID. During the late 1950s, littering of public spaces had started to become a significant issue as plastic packaging was increasingly introduced to consumer goods. The government-backed Keep Britain Tidy campaign was initiated and in 1960 the CoID responded by organizing a competition for 'well-designed, robust, cost-effective litter bins for

2

5

3

4

public spaces'; Michael Hope immediately commissioned Grange to devise a competition entry for his company. Able to draw on his experience working with Jack Howe on street furniture for clients including the British Transport Commission and Spun Concrete, Grange developed two designs: the more traditional Ironclad A, a vitreous enamelled cast-iron bin with removable steel basket for wall or post mounting, which drew directly on the company's expertise in metal manufacture; and the modernist Waterloo, a ground-standing circular design in concrete with removable steel basket. Grange later noted with admiration Michael Hope's 'strength of character' in agreeing to introduce a material into their competition entry in which his company did not have manufacturing expertise.

Successful competition submissions were presented for public critique in October 1960, with the awarded designs subsequently displayed in a permanent exhibition of street furniture on the South Bank later that year. As noted in that month's issue of the CoID's *Design* magazine, particular praise was given by the judges to one of Grange's designs, the lower, wider-diameter Waterloo D, noting it to be 'teddy boy proof' when it came to vandalism and serving the needs of a sporting public that was apparently 'fond of throwing their litter in from a distance'. The Waterloo bin went into production and featured in Hope's advertisements in industry media for the following few years.

Following this positive media exposure, Grange turned his attention to new designs for window and door furniture for the company; he initially worked on refining the design of the handles and peg stays of the metal window frames that were a staple of the company's manufacturing output. He worked in

5 / 6. Two of the distinctive Myron range of door handles. Developed by Grange as a complete project from concept to launch, they were produced in aluminium and moulded plastic at the company's factory in the West Midlands.

7. The trade catalogue for the Myron range, featuring characteristically stylish graphic design input from design studio Fletcher/Forbes/Gill/Crosby, which Grange recommended for the job.

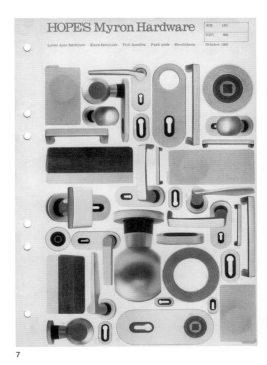

7

6

close collaboration with the company's engineers on introducing Delrin, a new plastic that promised to achieve greater economy and therefore efficiency; and the trade press recorded that 'often the fittings remain the most important mark of distinction, a point of vital importance in a highly competitive market'.

Later Grange developed a stylish new range of aluminium and plastic door hardware for the firm, called Myron. When it came to presenting the collection in a marketing brochure Grange recommended the skills of the renowned graphic design trio Fletcher/Forbes/Gill, whom he admired and with whom he had recently become acquainted when they worked on a packaging project at Kodak.

Grange later recalled that the Myron range, launched in 1965, had been in the running for a CoID award, but at the last moment Hope's decided to shelve production as part of a restructuring of the company when it merged with Crittall Manufacturing Co., another leading metal window manufacturer. Grange angrily described how not long afterwards the newly formed Crittall Hope Ltd, of which Michael Hope was chairman, became one of the first high-profile casualties of 'corporate asset stripping', a practice subsequently recognized as unlawful, and through which the notorious Slater Walker Securities conducted a hostile buyout and gradually demolished the heritage and identity of a 150-year-old mainstay of British manufacturing in the Midlands.

Kenwood

Woodlau Industries, later to become Kenwood Electrics and then the Kenwood Manufacturing Company, was founded in 1947 by entrepreneurial salesman Kenneth Wood and engineer Roger Laurence, who manufactured early electrical kitchen appliances. They launched the business with a toaster and a food mixer, both imitations of existing products Wood had seen in the USA and Europe. Then, having carefully studied the competition and defined a niche for a much-improved food preparation machine – with a vertical motor and more features combined in one unit – Wood unveiled the company's first original product at the Ideal Home Exhibition of 1950: the Kenwood Chef. Laurence had by now left the business and Wood, who was known to be an engaging salesman, himself demonstrated this new machine at a small booth – to the great excitement of the visiting British public, who increasingly sought efficient, labour-saving solutions to domestic chores. This was the start of the company's investment in technical innovation, and from here began its phenomenal rise.

During its first decade Kenwood became renowned for commitment to product quality and an excellent after-sales service, which gave it notable competitive advantage. However by the late 1950s the company's flagship product was starting to look outdated; its Americana-inspired style was falling out of favour, and some maintenance issues were proving too difficult to fix. The company was fast losing market share to the increasingly tight competition, so Wood turned to the Council of Industrial Design (CoID) for advice on engaging a designer to help them turn things around and create a distinctive-looking product of their own. Having initially experienced the benefit of the CoID's Design Selection Service in bringing him the Venner opportunity, Grange would later acknowledge that this subsequent introduction to Wood in 1958 was 'by far the most influential' of his career and also signalled 'a step change in the company investing in design'.

One of a shortlist of designers recommended for the job, Grange travelled to meet Wood at his office and manufacturing facility in Woking, Surrey, where the brief was straightforward: give the Chef 'a new suit of clothes' to renew customer demand. However, he was given just four days in which to respond with a proposal. Working in his father-in-law's garage, crafting a model of his proposed design, Grange realized there was no way he would finish it in time, so he proceeded to shape just half of the symmetrical form, in wood and plaster, and added a mirror borrowed from the bathroom to complete the whole.

2

3

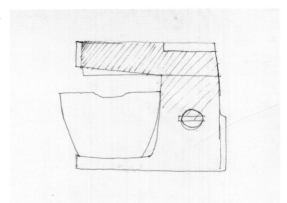

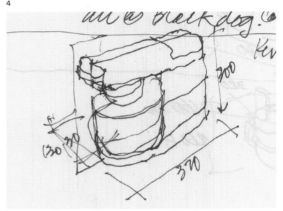

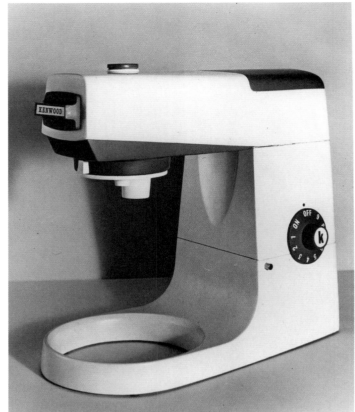

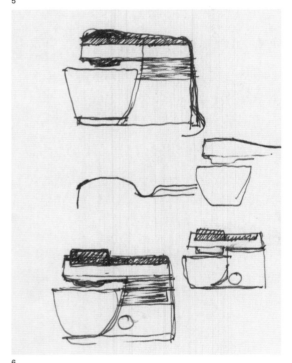

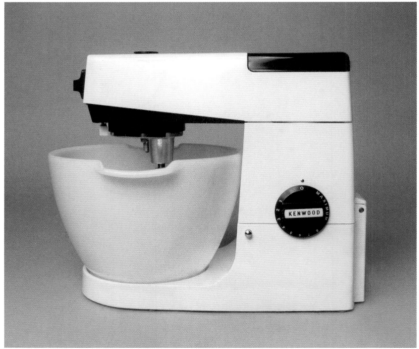

4 / 5 / 6. Various sketches of the Kenwood Chef from Grange's sketchbooks during further development of the product after his appointment to the company.

7. An early model of the complete revised body shape of the Kenwood Chef, made by Grange after winning the initial pitch with his half-model.

8. The first production model of Grange's revised design for the Kenwood Chef, introduced to great acclaim in 1960.

9

9. A later model of the Kenwood Chef, refined by Grange after two decades of continuous production of his original design. The updates mainly focused on improved mechanics and additional accessories.

10. The graphic design from the front of the original packaging for the new Kenwood Chef, also designed by Grange, featuring an outline of the highly recognizable Chef silhouette.

11. A delighted-looking couple on the cover of the product manual, with their brand new Kenwood Chef.

Now recounted as a much-celebrated tale, this inventive solution was greatly appreciated by Wood as 'a creative sales technique' and Grange believed it was 'this problem-solving approach as much as the design itself' that made Wood decide to appoint him for the job.

Throughout his career, model making would always sit at the centre of Grange's design approach; some of his earliest employees notably were tool makers rather than designers, and the workshop in his studio and later at Pentagram was always the heart of activity. So refined were Grange's presentation models, and made with such precision, that the engineers at Kenwood were known to often reference these models rather than scale drawings when producing the tools for manufacture.

Grange's redesign of the Chef introduced a sharper, modern silhouette with a streamlined body and arm, softly curved at the corners. The maintenance issues of the previous model were resolved, introducing a separate gearbox, upgraded motor, improved attachment fixings and a new hinge solution. The handle on top was removed as Grange considered this to 'give a negative visual impression as it demoted the product to a tool' and, cast in aluminium alloy, the machine was necessarily too heavy to lift in that manner anyway. On its launch in 1960 the machine immediately became hugely popular, selling millions of units over the following years, more than doubling previous sales, and changing kitchens forever. The food writer Caroline Conran captured the consumer's delight with the

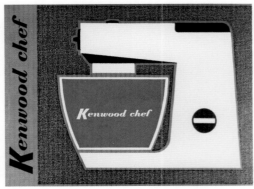

10

11

> **'When a cartoonist draws a kitchen, a few lines suffice to indicate the ubiquitous kitchen mixer – and it is sure to be a Kenwood Chef. For the designer there is a special pride in having shared in the fame of such a design.'**
>
> **Kenneth Grange**

product when she described its solidity and 'efficient hum' in place of other models that 'clattered about all over the room'. In the industry press coverage of the time it was reported that initial designs had been produced by the company's staff, but had not had the impact the firm was seeking, and Kenwood's press release stated: 'Mr Grange arrived at a time when the basic design was well under way, but this did not stop him querying the many limits he soon found himself up against.'

When in later decades Kenwood and Grange considered introducing design upgrades, the Chef had become such an icon of domestic modernity that there was considerable pushback from the market and hence the shape was barely altered. The updates focused instead on improved mechanics and the addition of a multitude of additional accessories – from juicers and shredders to coffee mills and even a wheat grinder – to feed the appetite of the booming foodie culture in Britain and in response to good reviews in the USA.

Following the huge success of his first design for the Chef, which saw sales expand to 140 countries,

in 1961 Grange was appointed consultant designer to Kenwood, a role in which he became instrumental to the design direction and commercial success of the company across nearly four decades. So began the longest and most celebrated client relationship of Grange's career, demonstrating not just impressive longevity but, as was noted in reports, also the great benefit to a manufacturer of long-term dedication to shaping a coordinated look for a complete family of products. A few years later *Design* magazine reviewed the company's output, saying: 'Kenwood has been strikingly successful, returning a profit of £924,211 for the year ending January 1966. This is an impressive figure by any standard and provides eloquent testimony to the fact that good design – the company has Kenneth Grange as its consultant designer – and commercial success are compatible.'

After reviewing the designs of various larger domestic white goods for Wood, including dishwashers and a short-lived venture into the business of refrigerators, Grange turned his attention to his next notable product design brief:

12. One of many presentation drawings by Grange and his team, proposing options for a Kenwood Chef design evolution; this one features a spout that fitted into the side column.

13. An immaculate model of a later proposal for a more compact Chef, made by the team in Grange's studio workshop.

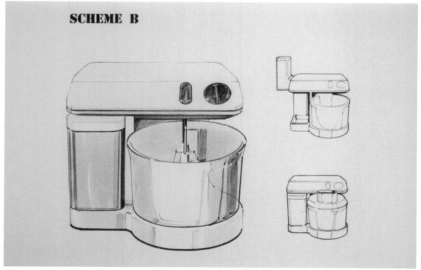

12

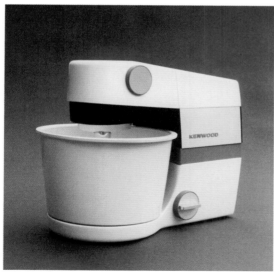

13

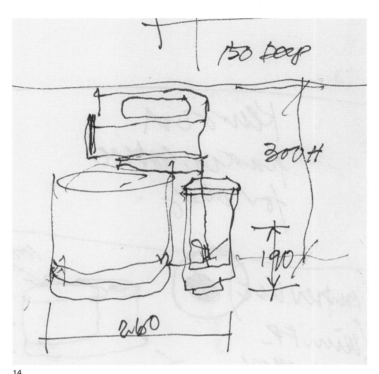

14

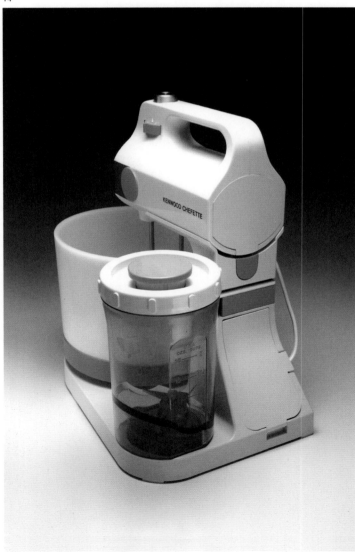

15

14 / 15. Sketch and final design for the popular and accessible Kenwood Chefette, the design of which Grange was commissioned to review after the company's first iteration did not perform well against the competition. Grange's revised design caused the product to fly off the shelves.

16–23 (overleaf). Full pages from Grange's sketchbooks featuring comprehensive lists and sketches, including Kenwood product codes, documenting just some of the vast range of products designed by Grange for the brand over the course of three decades.

another redesign, this time for the Chefette, a small handheld mixer that the Kenwood engineers had first developed and launched in 1959. Again, the product had seen early success and had also contributed to cementing the reputation of the company. However, as visibility on the shelf in electrical appliance shops became more competitive the Chefette too needed a new look to regain market share. Grange's brief also included the reworking of an accompanying blender accessory; this was not usually displayed with the product in the shops, and neither was an optional bowl and stand that were sold separately. He queried this, and was told Kenwood might in the future look to 'bring all the pieces together in one product', but not yet. Grange explained of his subsequent strategy that there is 'little that is more frustrating to the engineer or designer than to complete a job to the brief given, only to be faced with the belated intervention of the marketing man wanting this or that added after the product has entered production'.

So he set about devising a new Chefette proposition, featuring a squarer profile aligned with the Chef and including a blender, bowl and stand in one complete set. This could, he said, be more effectively displayed in shops and would be perceived to be a 'richer product'. When he presented his solution to the Kenwood team it was very well received, 'with no mention of the fact this was not what had been asked for'. It went into production in 1966 and Kenwood found they sold far more units than the earlier model that had not related the parts. It was considered 'the most successful mixer Kenwood had ever marketed', and would also be exported in increased volumes to Europe. This, Grange felt, demonstrated that 'regardless of how perceptively a brief is written the designer is employed to be creative and, provided he meets the brief, he must always have the audacity to push an opportunity that bit further'.

Grange's early work with Kenwood also became as much about the engineered functionality of the

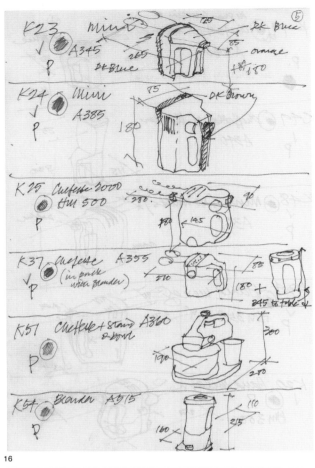

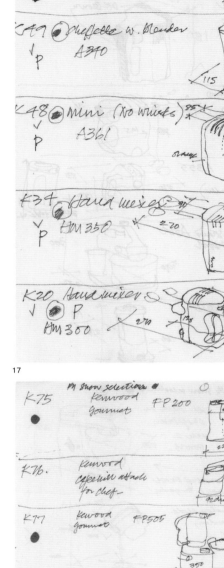

16

17

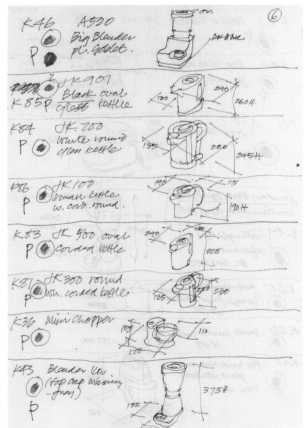

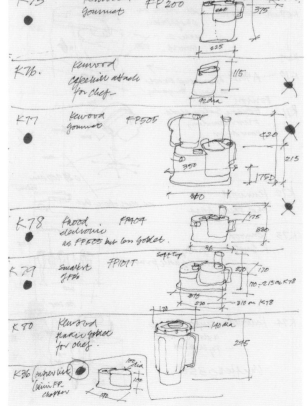

18

19

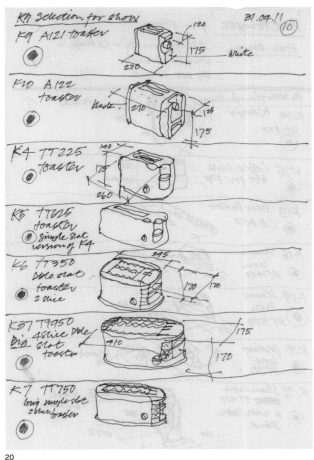

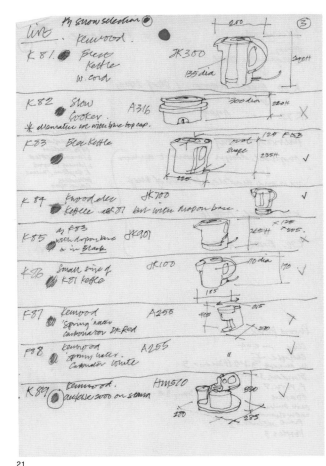

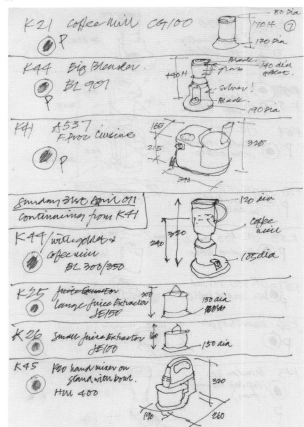

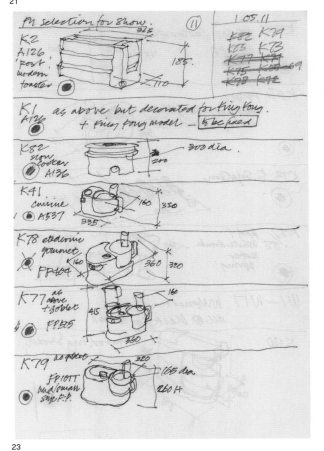

20

21

22

23

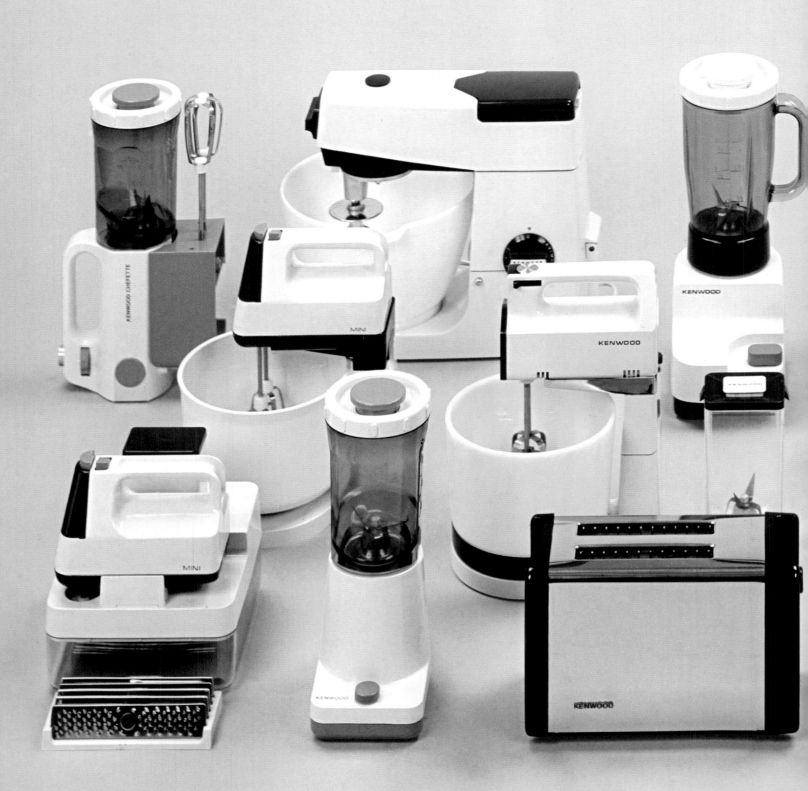

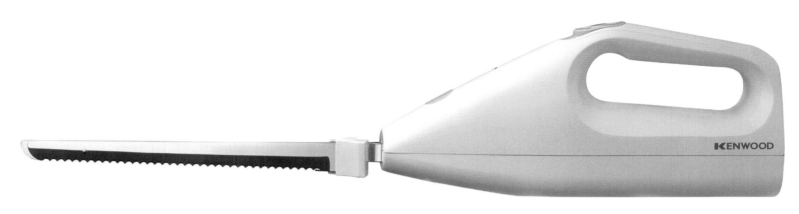

25

product as about the style, as demonstrated by the Chefette blender goblet accessory. This was devised to plug into the rear of the body of the handheld machine, and Grange evolved the design to improve the function as well as the look. The action of liquids on enclosed propellers was closely observed by Grange and his team, and improved over a number of models; sharp cutters revolved off-centre and asymmetric walls 'swept the liquid down and back into their path', making it highly efficient. The issue of the cable and plug was also given careful attention, being considered 'a visual sore'. For the wall-mounted version of the mixer, a special compartment was devised to accommodate the cord and plug, enabling ease of insertion; as explained in an article Grange later wrote, 'generous allowance for the impatient user was considered an essential design criterion; there is no merit in an elegant solution if the user has to work extra hard to use it'.

Following the positive response to the Chefette came a brief for a cordless electric carving knife, the only British product of its kind at that time, the design of which well demonstrates Grange's keen awareness of user design and 'how the user might

most comfortably hold the object', first learned in the office of Jack Howe. The meticulously honed wooden model of the product made by Grange with Bruce Watters, who oversaw Grange's workshop, is a good example of a model that was used by the Kenwood engineers to tool the final product for manufacture.

It was in the early 1970s that Grange would conceive one of his personal favourite products for Kenwood, an idea sparked while on a factory visit with another client working in the commercial food sector. While inspecting a production line for cake mix the manager happened to mention to Grange that their consumer business was limited by the type of mix they could sell, because they knew 'the only suitable tool for whisking which the housewife would reliably have to hand was a fork'. Grange took this insight back to Kenwood and the lightweight, mini electric cake whisk was born, enabling light and airy cakes to be whipped up with ease.

The 1980s and early 1990s saw Grange complete the design of more than one hundred products for Kenwood, from food processors, jug kettles and the award-winning High Rise toaster to irons, hairdryers and microwave ovens, with an ever-growing team

24 (previous). A promotional photograph of the growing 'family' of Kenwood kitchen appliances designed by Grange through the 1970s, featuring orange detailing on some of the products.

25. This cordless electric carving knife demonstrates Grange's careful consideration of the ergonomics of the hand holding a product while in use.

26 / 27. Two toaster designs by Grange, both featuring Kenwood's innovative 'cool wall' technology. The earlier model (right) is metal and melamine. The Post Modern toaster (left), pitched by Grange in an 'enthusiastic but misguided attempt' to move Kenwood into the realms of high-design kitchen equipment, proved a rare commercial failure in his portfolio for the brand.

26

27

28. The compact Kenwood Whisk, a favourite product of Grange's, was proposed by him after a visit to a cake-mix factory, where he learned that most home cooks used a fork to whisk cake batter because a dedicated tool did not exist.

29. Two iterations of the electric jug kettle, a product for which Grange developed many designs during his three decades with the company.

30 / 31. Sketch and final product in-situ on a kitchen wall. This prophetic innovation, introduced a while before cordless chargeable appliances became the norm, was one of the few full concept-to-production projects that Grange developed in his latter years with the company.

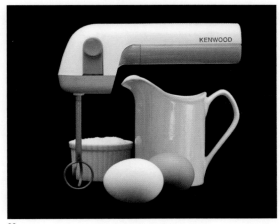

28

29

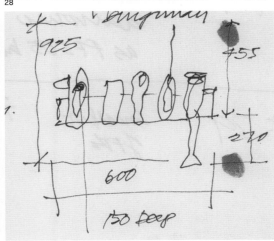

30

31

32

33

32 / 33. Grange honed a pleasing, simple profile for this coffee bean grinder (left). The base of this product, and of the lemon squeezers (right), reference the smooth, angled profile of the base of his original Chef and the later Chefette and Mini mixer, and allow for the cable to be wound securely.

around him both at Kenwood and at Pentagram. Later briefs predominantly responded to an insatiable consumer appetite for the 'new look' year-on-year, and involved less new product development and less engineering input from Grange and his team. However, in the late 1980s one prophetic innovation Grange did work on was an early wall-mounted rechargeable unit for cordless electric appliances, called System K, which paved the way for today's increasingly battery-powered tool market.

Additionally, in 1982, Grange was made consultant design director of Thorn EMI's domestic appliance division; Thorn Electrical Industries had taken over Kenwood back in 1968, with the departure of Ken Wood, and over time had brought the brands Tricity, Bendix, Parkinson Cowan, Moffat and Thorn Lighting under one umbrella. So Grange's last decade at Pentagram until his retirement also saw him consulting across the group of companies, though this was never as plentiful in output as the golden age of Kenwood. When latterly DeLonghi bought Kenwood, his contact at the company confirmed to Grange that just one product had indeed been the mainstay of the business for the past four decades: Grange's design of the Chef. Grange would explain that the 'ethos of always over-engineering the product', so it would last generations and could be easily serviced, was of huge value to the company and a 'testament to the personalities of both Wood and Laurence'.

Worth noting also is that these years of Grange's career developed in parallel with the growing dependence of UK product manufacturers on sourcing and production in China, this being a more efficient and cost-effective solution for the production of parts. So this era saw Grange visiting factories and suppliers in Hong Kong with Kenwood's engineering director Michael Lapham, with whom he struck up a long-time friendship and whom Grange would later recommend to bring his expertise in the Chinese manufacturing scene to benefit Anglepoise too.

In 1995, a couple of years before he retired from Pentagram, Grange worked with Kenwood's directors to set up an in-house design studio at Kenwood to take on the day-to-day design management of all future product developments; and with his approval, his long-serving and highly valued assistant designer Johan Santer was installed to run the department. But such was the enduring relationship between Grange and Kenwood, and so famous was his story within the company, that he kept in touch long after his retirement, and his colleagues there even made him a trophy in the shape of the legendary half-Chef model on the occasion of his knighthood in 2013.

A note about colour

In 1972 when Grange and his team dismantled the spray booth where models were painted, to move from their Hampstead studio to the new studios of Pentagram, they discovered a pleasing detail of 'modern archaeology'. On the back panel they could see 'a real thickness of solid cellulose' around 50 mm (2 in.) thick, which, when they sawed through it, revealed layer upon layer of 'a history in colour' of every model they had sprayed over the past decade. Recent among the layers was a notable stripe of orange: a record of the couple of years when Sweden had particularly requested orange kitchen products.

34 / 35. As the years went by the Kenwood kitchen product range became increasingly sophisticated: two of the sleek later iterations of the Gourmet food mixer with additional accessories.

36. After Grange received his knighthood in 2013, the team at Kenwood produced this award to mark the occasion, featuring a mini version of his famous original half-model of the Chef from 1958.

37. A later iteration of the Kenwood Chef.

34

35

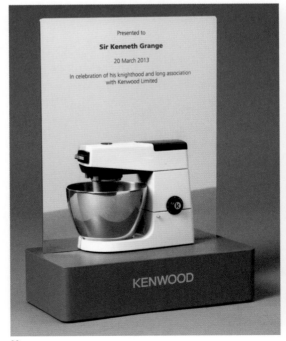

36

37

Needle Industries

Needle Industries Ltd was the holding company for a number of manufacturing businesses, including Henry Milward & Sons, which had led the UK in the industry of fine sewing needle manufacture since the mid-1700s.

Two hundred years on, in the separate industry of shaving products, by the early 1960s plug-in dry electric shavers were widely available; however, cordless electric models were still nascent. Seeing an opportunity to diversify through applying the precision skill of the Milward needle business in 'making perfect, tiny holes in steel' to the challenge of piercing the foil of the cutter screen of a rotary-style shaver, Needle Industries decided to enter the shaving market with a cordless product offering.

The directors approached the Council of Industrial Design (CoID), later the Design Council, to request a recommendation from its Design Selection Service for an industrial designer to consult on the complete design of this new proposed product. After a pitch meeting process with a number of candidates Grange was appointed design consultant to Needle Industries by the company's production director, Norman T. Sanders, whom Grange recalled as 'unquestionably the finest creative engineer' he has known, stating that 'it was a privilege and a major milestone in my life to work for him'.

Grange's visits to the Needle Industries manufacturing base also left a lasting impression. He was endlessly fascinated by the needle-making process, and he credited these factory visits as being among several such that honed his passion for 'appreciating the physicality of how objects are made'. He described the 'beautiful machines' and the immaculate factory where they would 'pile thousands of needles into a great heap, wrap them in sacking,

2

3

4

5

4. The plastic carry-case for the shaver featured a steel loop that covered two functions: it held the lid in place for travel, clipping into a groove in the moulded plastic, and doubled as a way to hook the case onto a bathroom wall for storage of the shaver.

5. The cutter screen features hundreds of impeccably pierced holes, made by the manufacturer using the same expertise as that applied to making the eyes in needles.

6. A cross-sectional diagram longways down the centre of the shaver body, illustrating the ingenious nature of Grange's design for the moulded plastic body, which minimized the amount of material used.

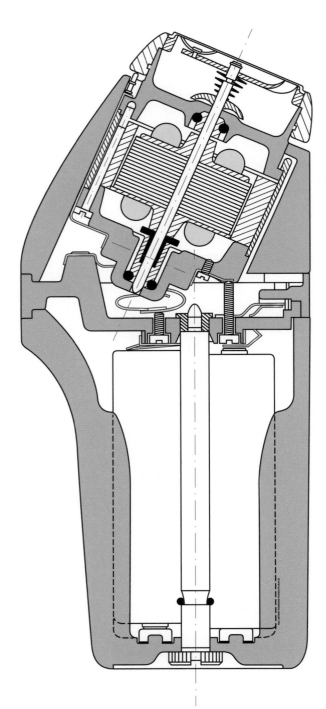

6

pour in sand and oil, tie it all into a great sausage and roll it for ten hours'.

Grange worked closely with Sanders throughout the year-long process of developing the shaver: while Sanders oversaw development of the internal components, for which he registered a number of patents, Grange was responsible for designing the sculpted body and angled head of the shaver, alongside consulting on other elements including the premium material specifications, functional details such as the battery-saving switch mechanism, and even the typography for the new brand.

He later recalled of the final product that it was 'immaculately made' and that Milward took his advice and used compression-moulded melamine for the body. Grange described it as the 'Rolls-Royce of materials' for its ability to be compression moulded in such thickness without showing sink marks on cooling; the technique gave a high-gloss finish and a 'nice, sturdy weight'. And he praised Milward's ability to pierce the tiny holes in the foil of the cutter screen 'to a degree of accuracy unknown in the industry at that time'.

Launched under the Milward brand in 1962 and named the Courier, the shaver was recognized in the Council of Industrial Design awards in 1963; selected from over 10,000 entries via the council's Design Index, it proceeded to win Grange the coveted Duke of Edinburgh's Prize for Elegant Design (the fifth year it was awarded), for which it was selected from a shortlist of thirty products. The judges, including the Duke, noted it to be 'an exceptionally economical and elegant product' while the esteemed Paul Reilly, at that time head of the CoID, enthused that he 'took one round Russia on a lecture tour as it is really well designed and small enough to carry in a pocket. It's a real Rolls-Royce of a shaver.'

The award brought Grange widespread publicity and a significant boost to his fast-rising career in the burgeoning industrial design sector; and the product initially flew off the shelves. Unfortunately, despite

'The judges, including the Duke, noted it to be "an exceptionally economical and elegant product" while the esteemed Paul Reilly, at that time head of the CoID, enthused that he "took one round Russia on a lecture tour as it is really well designed and small enough to carry in a pocket. It's a real Rolls-Royce of a shaver."'

The Duke of Edinburgh's prize for elegant design and the design centre awards 1963

7

The Council of Industrial Design

awards this certificate to mark the presentation of

THE DUKE OF EDINBURGH'S PRIZE FOR ELEGANT DESIGN 1963

to Kenneth Grange FSIA

Designer of the 'Courier' cordless electric dry shaver
manufactured by Henry Milward & Sons
a branch of the Needle Industries Group Limited

THE DESIGN CENTRE, HAYMARKET, LONDON, S W I

8

the exceptional product manufacturing, the limited product marketing capability at Needle Industries was not able to deliver the necessary cut-through for a new entry in the highly competitive, established shaving products market, and sales of the product gradually faded. Needle Industries eventually sold its stake, along with the tooling and knowledge, to the large competitor Wilkinson Sword, which later shelved the product.

Nonetheless, the Courier shaver launched Grange into a new consumer industry and led to later high-profile work with Wilkinson and also with Ronson. And through the Wilkinson connection, Needle Industries would later be commissioned to manufacture Grange's first razor for Wilkinson, the Royale, in 1969, because its engineering capability in steel was recognized for its 'exceptional quality'.

Duke of Edinburgh's Prize
for Elegant Design

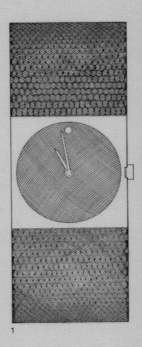

The award given to the winner of the Duke of Edinburgh's Prize for Elegant Design (later the Prince Philip Designers Prize) comprised a brief to design and have manufactured a trophy or personal item, funded to a value of £100, which would be presented by Prince Philip at the following year's ceremony. Grange chose to design a gold wristwatch, happily commenting at the time that since he was a consultant 'he would never be given one as a gift for long-service upon his retirement' so he 'had better make my own'; plus, he added, it presented a rare opportunity for him to work on a product in precious metal.

His design specified an Omega women's movement to benefit from the slim profile, and was the first wristwatch to his knowledge to feature no markers on the dial, save for a small marker at the 12 position to ensure the watch was worn the correct way up. This initially came about because it was too difficult to fashion just one dial 'as elegantly as those that are carefully tooled for production by the thousand'. But it then became a research project for Grange, who for a few weeks, proceeded to wear tape over his current watch so he could only just see the hands; 'contrary to expectation he could tell the time to a high degree of accuracy' simply by the angles of the hands, describing it as quite natural to simply 'look rather than read'.

For the manufacture of the watch he found a goldsmiths' shop in Chesham, recalling later they were 'wonderful engineers', who introduced him to the expert technique of finely machining the tiny links of chainmail to create a smooth, supple surface akin to fish scales – a finish Grange much admired and chose for the wrist strap of his watch.

The finishing touch was producing a presentation box, which was 'expertly crafted by my brilliant German design assistant' at the time, Klaus Lehmann, in the workshop at the studio in Hampstead. Fashioned in solid ebony, with suede lining, it featured an ingenious hidden hinge mechanism devised by Lehmann, which Grange still admires to this day. On presenting Grange with the watch the following year Prince Philip, with a keen eye for quality and expensive craftsmanship, quipped that he 'hoped he had not had to pay for the box too'.

Grange described this project as a good example of his ambition, and that of most designers, to always strive to make a product as 'exceptionally good' as it could be by ensuring that 'even the smallest details lived up to the same promise of quality', thus creating the complete effect. He had brought this ethos to the Milward Courier shaver, which had, of course, won him the prize in the first place.

1. Original drawing on tracing paper by Grange for the gold watch with distinctive strap that he opted to have made as his chosen trophy object.

2. Cross-sectional drawing through the slim-profiled watch face, which Grange presented to a goldsmiths' shop in Chesham.

3. The final, beautifully elegant watch with its supple chainmail strap.

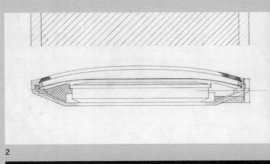

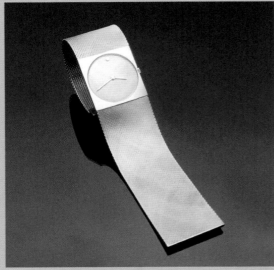

Short & Mason /
Taylor Instruments

1 (opposite). The award-winning Mariner range of instruments – barometer, thermometer and clock – for Taylor Instruments, which was recognized with a CoID Award in 1971.

2. The original Ranger barometer, Grange's first commission from Short & Mason, bringing a refined modern style to a traditional product. His remit also included the packaging and graphics.

Founded in 1864, Short & Mason Ltd was a leading British manufacturer of precision measuring instruments including barometers, compasses and aviation instruments. Grange was introduced to the company in the early 1960s – as with other significant early clients including Venner, Hope's and Kenwood – through the influential Design Selection Service run by the Council of Industrial Design (CoID). Following some introductory product discussions Grange was appointed the manufacturer's consultant designer and, during his eight-year tenure, would work on two notable generations of instruments, between them neatly demonstrating the evolution of manufacturing, and the awareness of materials and styling, in the production of modern consumer products in Britain during the early span of his career.

Grange's first commission was the Ranger barometer, later followed in the same series by a thermometer and a clock; his design responded to a brief from the sales director, Bob Fitch, to 'bring the barometer firmly into the twentieth century' so that it would 'better fit into modern domestic and office environments'. Substantially more compact than the instruments that came before it, the Ranger still had a presence when on display. The barometer coil set the dimensions for the scale of the overall product at nearly thirteen centimetres (five inches) in diameter, as the coil was an existing component and required a certain volume of airflow in the back of the instrument. The thermometer and clock were then designed to fit the same casing. Each product was housed in an individually turned drum of zebrano hardwood, with a twist-on steel-framed face with slightly concave glass to reduce light reflection, which doubled as the cover to access the internal components. Grange also designed the graphic styling of the dial face, a notably modern look and easier to read compared to previous products.

2

3

4

3 / 4. The Ranger barometer, alongside a clock also introduced to the range. The barometer shows the original zebrano hardwood body while the clock sports the all-steel option that was introduced a few years later. The steel ring around the glass front could be unscrewed for maintenance.

Launched in 1965, the Ranger series opened up a new style-conscious domestic market for the company in the UK and the design was acclaimed, but commercial success was limited by the relatively low volume of units that could be produced owing to the traditional manufacturing processes employed for the wooden body. An all-steel version was launched in 1968, which grew sales further.

However, it was the merger of Short & Mason with the US manufacturing group Taylor Instrument Company in 1969 that brought the opportunity to build commercially on the initial success of Grange's work. Fitch was offered the role of managing director for the new Taylor Instrument Companies (Europe) Ltd and, now with substantially more US capital at his disposal for further modernization of the company,

he set about commissioning Grange to devise a brand new product range.

The resulting three-part Mariner range, comprising a barometer, a thermometer/hygrometer and a clock, would be distinctively different in the marketplace, the choice of material having a profound influence on the design. Drawing on his knowledge of aluminium extrusion previously gained while working on window frames with Hope's, Grange specified an extruded body of set dimensions that could then house a variety of components across the family of instruments. The aluminium would be anodized, in silver and black versions, to a standard marine specification as these modern precision instruments were intended for use at sea as well as on land. Red, blue and white colour details were introduced for

5. The full Mariner range of instruments, in silver or black powder-coated aluminium, with an acrylic face replacing traditional glass. This solution was cost-effective and simplified manufacture while making the products more portable and robust.

5

6

6. CoID Award certificate presented to Taylor Instrument Companies (Europe) Limited, for the Mariner instruments range, with credit to Grange for the design.

7. Close-up of the detail of the typography on the face of the Mariner barometer, showing the detail of the red marker line (bottom right) embedded in the plastic face, which could be adjusted by turning the whole disc.

8. Detail of the back of the Mariner instruments, with a black polystyrene back panel. During manufacture a hollow, extruded aluminium length was sliced into individual units – a technique of which Grange had first become aware during his time working for Hope's.

7

8

the pressed metal hands, with the scale of the dials marked in millibars and millimetres 'in recognition of metrification and the practice of meteorologists and seamen'. A transparent acrylic injection-moulded front cap, again slightly concave to reduce light reflection, slotted into the extruded body and could be rotated to move the barometer marker. The back panel covering the internal components was also injection-moulded in durable black polystyrene.

The combination of material and structural specifications resulted in both a stylish profile and relatively economical manufacture, so, although initially aimed at the UK market, the instruments went on to sell profitably in substantial quantities internationally, with the company finding that it was challenged to keep up with demand.

The Mariner range won a CoID award in 1971. A corresponding feature in the CoID's *Design* magazine highlighted that 'the barometer in particular represents a breakthrough in the way information is presented' in the sophisticated design, explaining that care had been taken over details such as 'putting 60 per cent humidity at the six o'clock position' because acceptable humidity in Britain is between 50 and 70 per cent, while the magnification system was designed 'so that the whole dial is used for 2.4 in. (61 mm) of barometric pressure', as it is unusual for this range to be exceeded.

Despite the positive momentum around the Mariner range, the wider industry was in flux and Taylor Instrument Companies Ltd subsequently closed in the UK. Fitch went on to become CEO of the parent company in the USA, where Grange would visit him, and the two maintained a long friendship. More than a decade later the UK retailer Habitat, under Terence Conran, picked up the Mariner clock and reproduced it for a while, in collaboration with Grange, recognizing the enduring modernist design quality of the original.

The Ronson company originated in the USA, but for three decades from the early 1950s operated a production facility in the UK, under Ronson Products Ltd, which quickly became the largest subsidiary outside America. First and foremost a household name as a manufacturer of quality cigarette lighters, by the mid-1960s the company was diversifying into small personal electrical products. Recognizing a niche for modern products with a European sensibility, a senior director at Ronson in the UK, Alan Forrest, approached Grange, who had come to the company's attention following his award-winning 1963 design for the Milward Courier electric shaver for Needle Industries.

Grange's first commission was the design of a small handheld hairdryer, the Rio. Ronson had initially introduced a US model to the UK market but it had made little impact and so Grange was tasked with rethinking the form and style of the product. He worked around a standard set of internal components for the tangential fan system: this greatly determined the final shape of the body, which behaved as a small electric heater, but was held in the hand like a brush with circular recesses for finger holds. Drawing on his experience of the economical use of materials in production, Grange worked closely with the Ronson engineering team to resolve the smallest details of the design for efficient manufacture and usability, recalling that 'the purchaser knows little of the scope of intellect and invention in these seemingly mundane everyday products'.

The Rio hairdryer launched in 1966, an era that was starting to see greater importance placed on the colours of consumer products: it was launched in a distinctive powder-blue option alongside a simple black version, and later in a hot-pink limited edition. The product quickly became known for its good performance and good looks, and moved Ronson rapidly from no market share to leading the market in portable hairdryers, for both the UK and export markets. The Rio won the Daily Mail Ideal Home

Blue Riband award in 1967 and went on to sell well over a million units.

This success would lead Ronson to commission further hairdryer designs from Grange during the late 1960s and into the 1970s: the Escort 2000 and the Rapide. The first was an evolution of the Rio, bigger and more powerful, featuring what was claimed to be the world's first infinitely variable heat control, and with additional accessories that reflected hairstyle changes and mimicked hair salon equipment. To launch the Escort 2000 for Christmas 1969 Ronson mounted what *Electrical & Electronic Trader* called the 'biggest ever advertising campaign for any of their products' across print and television. The Rapide was considered the company's budget model, offering a pistol-grip style that required the most economical assembly of components and minimized the volume of plastic material required in the mould; but, as Grange described, he was still able to include 'a minor witticism' in the design detail, without adding cost, through introducing a pattern of small ventilation holes 'which trace the spiral of air as it is sucked in, around and out'.

Alongside the hairdryer designs, and after also considering both an electric shaver and an early electric toothbrush – the latter being described as demonstrating his awareness of the German style of quiet engineering – Grange was employed by the cigarette lighter division of Ronson to bring a 'refined sensibility' to their products. He first reviewed the design of the Varaflame Comet, a popular product that had originally been designed by the research and development division of Ronson in the UK in 1965, but which by 1967 was losing market share. Grange was asked to refine both the form of the lighter and the use of materials; the result was an eloquent example of his understanding of material wear in relation to the impact of relentless everyday use.

Until the introduction of the Comet lighter the Ronson brand had been strongly identified in the public mind with top-quality metal products, often in

2

2 / 3. Grange later followed the Rio with two larger home hairdryers: the affordable Rapide (top) and the Escort 2000 (bottom), a bigger and more powerful version that mimicked professional hair salon equipment.

ornate silver. But as the industry evolved the company had determined that this new mass-produced product could only be economical if moulded in plastic. The material selected by the development team was black Delrin, chosen for its strong resistance to impact, abrasion and fatigue, while the injection moulding process introduced, in Grange's words, the 'eye-opening phenomenon of vast numbers' on the production line. But it quickly became apparent that the visual and tactile nature of this material was not in keeping with the quality expectation of the brand. The answer, Grange believed, was to invest the surface of the plastic with the kind of tactile quality of finish that 'distinguishes an ivory from a plastic comb'. Grange knew of a technique being employed by Braun in Germany to treat the plastic surfaces of their shavers to give them a warmer, softer feel. This technique, which he described as 'crudely simple', involved the moulded plastic bodies being tumbled in

a rotating drum with thousands of pieces of walnut shells; the shells hammered and texturized the plastic surface, while the nut oil soaked into the body. The resulting effect was 'a fine surface looking like alabaster' that no matter how often it was handled would never show the fingerprints of oily hands. Grange reflected that although this effort could be seen as 'nonsensical in a modern mass manufacturing process' the perceived value to the consumer was beneficially heightened through 'an appreciation, very rarely articulated, of the fine sense of quality that our hands give us'.

The relaunched 1968 product, featuring Grange's subtle interventions in shape and material – and with a new packaging design by Grange too – became Britain's top-selling lighter through the 1970s, with the product lasting in use for years and 'illustrating the fine degree of quality that can be brought to a commonplace article'. Its success soon led to Grange

3

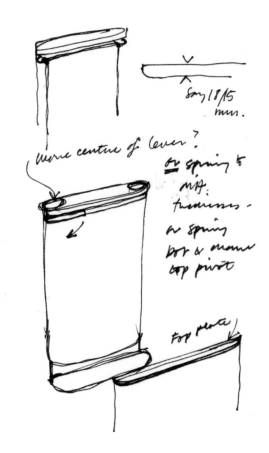

4

5

6

being commissioned to consider a range of small table lighters: the outcome was the square Quadrille, the round Piccolo and the triangular Tricorn, for which he designed both the product and the packaging.

Table lighters had long been seen as status objects for display, and therefore commanded a higher price tag; reflecting this, the standard lighter components would traditionally be set into a weight of marble or a chunk of fine hardwood. But seeking to introduce a modern look to the sector, here again Grange's material specification was central to the impact of the products; as with the Milward Courier shaver a few years before, he suggested the premium compression-moulded hard plastic melamine. As the Council of Industrial Design's (CoID) magazine *Design* explained in its review of the lighters in 1968, 'when moulded in bulk, melamine has the weight and surface hardness of porcelain without its chipping properties'; the resulting range of lighters was 'reasonably priced' while at the same time being 'both tough and attractive'.

Following the good publicity, in 1970 Grange was commissioned to create one more product; a limited-edition, premium table lighter, the Egg – featuring a base and lid in solid, perfectly smooth white melamine. The resulting object felt 'cold, solid and weighty in the hand', creating a perceived value

4. A cluster of early notebook sketches in which Grange explores the impact of the geometry of the spring mechanism under the top steel plate on his reworked Comet lighter for Ronson.

5. The new Comet lighter, re-released to market after Grange's subtle refinements, featured an injection-moulded black Delrin plastic body that was finished in a drum with walnut shells.

6. Grange also designed the packaging for the new Comet lighter, which featured the graphic of a flame that grew taller as the box was lifted up to open it.

7

7. Following the success of the Comet, Grange designed a set of stylish modern table lighters, the Piccolo (circular), Quadrille (square) and Tricorn (triangular), all compression moulded in melamine for a weighty, premium result.

8. Grange was also commissioned to design the packaging solution for the range, in this case sturdy premium white boxes with simple modern typography and simple overhead photos of the products to highlight the profile shapes.

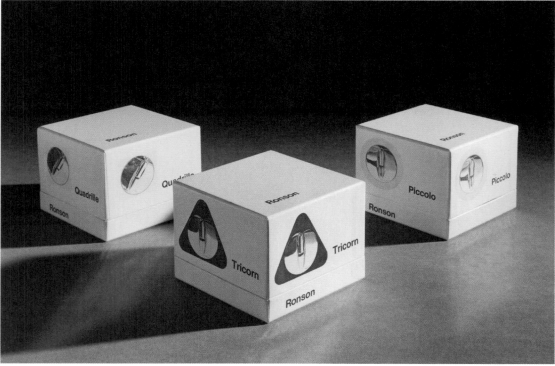

8

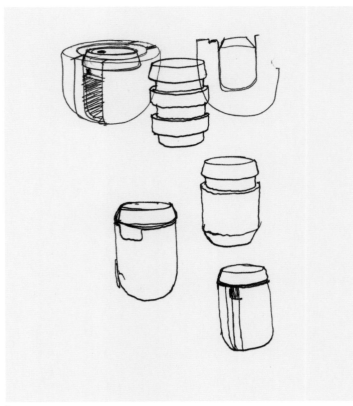

9

9. A page of early sketches from Grange's sketchbooks shows him exploring options for the form of his last, limited-edition, premium table lighter design for Ronson.

10. The endlessly pleasing, sculptural Egg table lighter made of solid compression-moulded white melamine. The lighter component is housed in the top half of the egg.

'greater than the sum of its parts', and is one of the very few of his designs that Grange has openly stated as being a fond favourite. Referring to the overtly sculptural shape, he later explained that 'wit in products' was something he greatly admired, though he advised that 'it is only occasionally appropriate, so the opportunities are few'. He described the chosen egg shape as 'a familiar, ever beautiful form, which when placed on the table gave a touch of humour without risking absurdity'.

The Egg lighter would be the last realized product that Grange designed for Ronson. Under ever-increasing pressure across its core lighter business through the 1970s, with the competitive introduction of Japanese and French disposable lighters and a general decline in the habit of smoking, the UK division finally closed in the early 1980s.

10

Imperial Typewriters

1 (opposite). The brief
to design the Model 80
typewriter for the US-based
Royal Typewriter Company,
which had bought the British
typewriter brand Imperial,
offered Grange one of his
first opportunities to travel to
the USA, where he attended
design meetings with his client
in New York.

2 / 3. Working sketches for
the Model 80 from Grange's
notebooks and studio
archives, exploring profile
and panel divisions.

The Imperial Typewriter Company was a leading British manufacturer of typewriters, founded in 1911, and renowned for sturdy, reliable machines used daily around the world – for a while predominantly by offices across the British Empire. By the early 1960s, however, the industry was in flux, with the entry of electric typewriters and a market demanding easier, more efficient solutions for increasingly fast-paced office life.

Grange was approached by the company in 1965 – records suggest through a connection made by the Council of Industrial Design (CoID) – with a commission to design the next generation of the Imperial standard manual typewriter. The brief asked that the design solution make it a more manageable machine and give it a 'modern form to suit a new era'. However, not long after he undertook the job, in early 1966, Imperial was acquired by the US company Litton Industries through its Royal Typewriter

Company division; Grange recalled that almost overnight his client 'became a US company'. The new owners employed noticeably different working processes but asked him to continue to consult and deliver a typewriter for the European market, within weeks summoning him to New York for meetings.

Launched in Europe in 1968, Grange's design for the Royal Imperial Model 80 was seen by the industry as the heir to the Imperial Model 70 of 1962, which had been widely considered the heavy workhorse of reliable office use. Made in all metal but lighter and more easily handled, and with a distinctly modern profile, the Model 80 would be the last of the Imperial typewriter family to be entirely made at the company's Leicester factory. The industry press of the time described it as 'embodying all the traditional qualities associated with Imperial machines, plus valuable new refinements, all enclosed within a striking modern exterior'. The CoID's *Design*

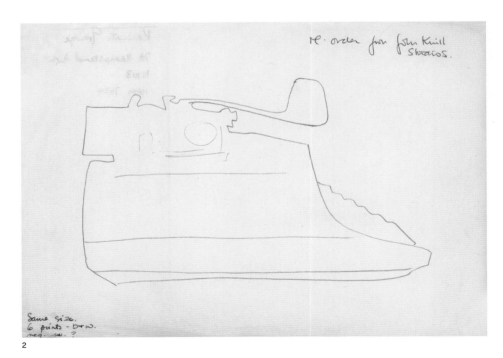

2

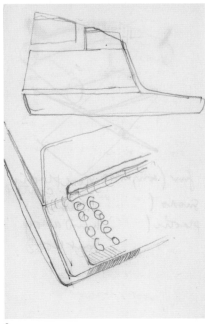

3

4. The angular Messenger manual typewriter gained strong early orders in Europe. It was Grange's second and last product under the Imperial brand, before the US owners closed operations in the UK.

5. A full-scale model, built in Grange's Hampstead workshop, for a proposed evolution of the Model 80 featuring automatic carriage and more angular casing, as also seen in the Messenger.

6. As with other client projects around this time, Grange was also commissioned to design the packaging for typewriter consumables such as ribbons and carbon paper for the Imperitype brand.

4

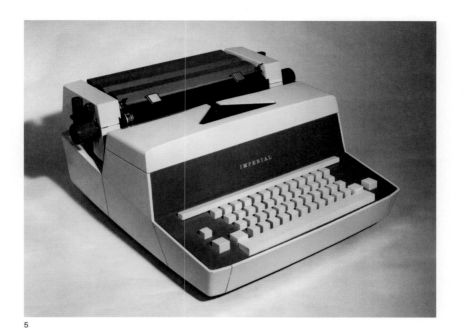

5

magazine described the machine as 'quiet, light and easy to use', featuring easy dismantling for servicing. Users were also offered 'five sizes of carriage length and a wide range of typefaces'.

The Model 80 proved highly popular and durable over the years that followed; Grange delighted in spotting the machines sitting on desks in offices and 'still in working order two decades later'. Following the machine's success Grange soon designed an electric version with an automated carriage, the Messenger, which launched in 1970. On its launch, the *Financial Times* initially reported that 'large

domestic orders coupled with lively interest from North America and Europe bode well'. But this came just before all manufacture finally moved to the USA and Grange's consultancy to the company came to an end.

Into the 1970s Grange went on to apply his experience to designing typewriters for his client Maruzen in Japan, under the Jaguar brand, for which he first worked in the late 1960s in its capacity as a manufacturer of sewing machines for the US and European markets (see pp. 148–155).

6

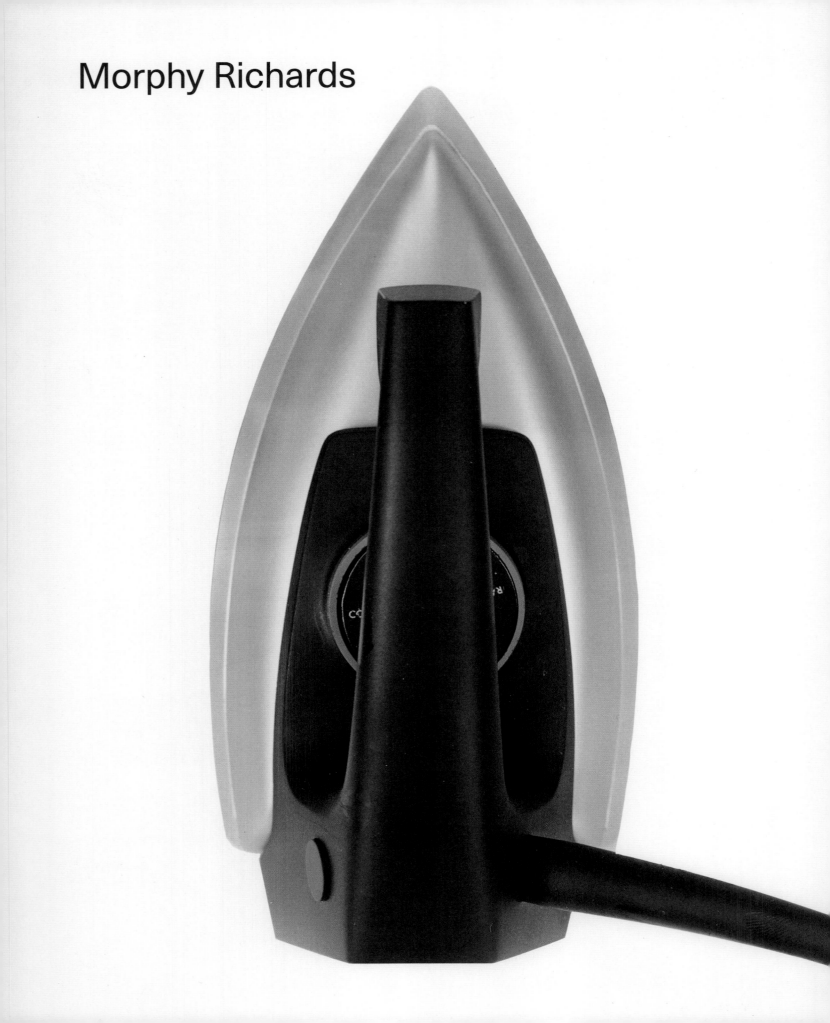

Morphy Richards

1 (opposite). Full-scale model of the dry iron, Grange's first design for Morphy Richards, a product that had not been reimagined in almost three decades.

2. Side profile of the same full-scale model, showing the open handle, which Grange pushed to introduce following market research determining that this European style was becoming popular.

3. Presentation sketch as part of the final design package for the dry iron, illustrating how the power cable and lamp lens could be easily swapped over by a left-handed user.

Founded in 1936 when electrical appliances were starting to be introduced into the domestic market in the UK, initially at a restrictive price point, Morphy Richards was an early pioneer in the design and manufacture of affordable modern appliances. After launching with a portable radiant fire, in 1937 the company introduced its first electric temperature-controlled iron. The factory was then brought under government contract during the Second World War to produce aircraft components. But by the late 1940s it returned to developing new products – including hairdryers, toasters, vacuum cleaners and its first heat-controlled steam iron – as the postwar domestic market began to surge and competition grew rapidly through the 1950s.

By 1964, in a sign of the insatiable demand for Morphy Richards electric irons, the company had manufactured a staggering 20 million units, predominantly of the dry iron model, which had barely changed in design in three decades. But constantly looking to innovate, and recognizing that it needed to introduce a design vocabulary that would give new distinction to the brand name in a now crowded international market, the company finally considered that it was time to bring in an external design perspective.

And so it was that Morphy Richards approached Grange, through a Council of Industrial Design (CoID) connection – probably after noting the impact of his recent redesign of the Chef for Kenwood, another client introduction that had been made for Grange by the CoID. Similarly to Kenwood, the brief from Morphy Richards to Grange was to modernize the look and feel of the existing dry iron product, working closely with the company's engineering team.

This period in the commercial industries saw increasing value placed on market research to give weight to decisions regarding substantial investment in new product development and manufacturing techniques, and in the hope of finding the 'magic formula' that would predict what the customer wanted to purchase. His commission to redesign the dry electric iron came to Grange just at the time when market research was reporting that the Scandinavian market was adopting a radical new model – an iron with an open handle at the front, to 'better reach into pockets and cuffs'. This look appealed to Grange's eye as it gave the design a more refined, streamlined profile; however, market research in the UK uncovered that this open handle was not perceived to offer a product that was 'physically robust'.

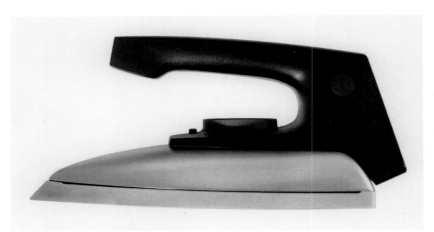

2

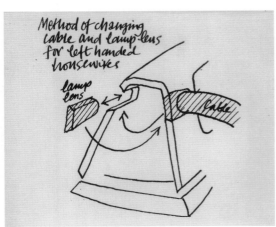

Method of changing cable and lamp lens for left handed housewives

lamp lens

cable

3

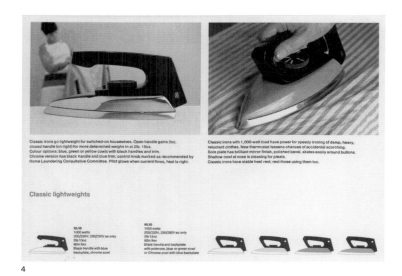

Classic irons go lightweight for switched-on housewives. Open handle gains 2oz; closed handle (on right) for more determined weighs in at 2lb. 15oz.
Colour options: blue, green or yellow cowls with black handles and trim.
Chrome version has black handle and blue trim; control knob marked as recommended by Home Laundering Consultative Committee. Pilot glows when current flows, heat is right.

Classic irons with 1,000-watt load have power for speedy ironing of damp, heavy, reluctant clothes. New thermostat lessens chances of accidental scorching.
Sole plate has brilliant mirror finish, polished bevel, skates easily around buttons. Shallow cowl at nose is pleasing for pleats.
Classic irons have stable heel rest; rest those using them too.

Classic lightweights

CL10
1000 watts
200/220V, 230/250V ac only
2lb 13oz
90in flex
Black handle with blue
backplate, chrome cowl

BL10
1000 watts
200/220V, 230/250V ac only
2lb 15oz
90in flex
Black handle and backplate
with primrose, blue or green cowl
or Chrome cowl with blue backplate

4

4 / 5. A page (top) and the cover (bottom) of the brochure for Grange's lightweight dry iron, with open or closed handle in urea formaldehyde, and available with shiny chrome or pastel-coloured options for the body.

6 / 7. Grange's design for the reimagined lightweight dry iron with open or closed handle, showing the final plug-in socket for swapping the power cable from one side to the other. The products are shown here with no power cable attached.

Grange therefore designed two models, one with a closed handle for the home market and one with an open handle for European export; to ensure economy in manufacture these two models were designed to be identical in every way except for the front detail of the handles. The new products were also designed to be noticeably lighter and more comfortable to use, with Grange and the engineering team bringing their knowledge of desirable modern materials to the project, including new compression-moulding techniques for manufacture of the handles in urea formaldehyde, alongside chromium-plated steel soleplates. And as a thoughtful additional detail, which helped differentiate the product in a competitive marketplace, both models offered the ability to swap the cable across to the other side of the unit to aid a left-handed user.

Launched in 1966, Grange's modern, affordable dry iron designs greatly boosted sales for Morphy Richards against the competition, going on to sell many further millions of units internationally over the following seventeen years and giving Grange a significant boost in profile. And *Design* magazine recorded that in fact, despite the market research, once launched Grange's open-handled design also went on to sell well in Britain alongside the more traditional closed-handle version.

Following this success, market research then dictated that 'although at the moment the majority of homes have dry irons, steam irons are becoming more popular, particularly with the younger generation'. So Grange hastily embarked on the design of a new steam iron, the Easisteam, launched in 1968. The design integrated the 'sophisticated technical development' by the Morphy Richards engineering team of a new innovation, the push-button spray nozzle. The new Easisteam reached the market just as the popularity of steam irons was overtaking that of dry irons.

Looking back on this chapter in his career, Grange described the lack of design evolution of the original dry iron product over thirty years as being of huge benefit to him personally, saying that 'anything I designed was going to be viewed as modern and relatively sensational'. And although he did not design any further products for Morphy Richards, which was soon afterwards merged into the British Domestic Appliances group and later sold to GEC, Grange has always recognized that 'designing the early market leader of a truly commonplace product makes for a lasting visibility which is particularly rewarding'.

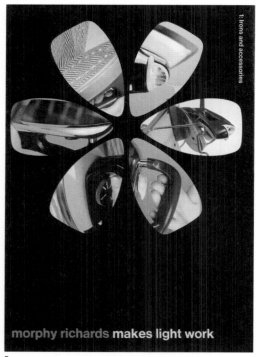

morphy richards **makes light work**

5

6

7

British Rail

1 (opposite). A dynamic promotional image of the HST as if in motion, created for use on British Rail posters to promote the energy and excitement of 'the age of the train'.

2. The new-look departures indicator board, made user-friendly for passengers for the first time, was an early job for Grange working with BRB design officer Jack Bloomfield. It is seen here installed for a trial at Marylebone Station.

The environment at British Rail into which Grange entered when he received his first small design commissions from the organization in the mid-1960s was one of optimism and belief in the vital role design could play in reinvigorating industry. This attitude and the huge investments being made in design and new material technologies were the legacy of George Williams, one of the first industrial officers at the Council of Industrial Design (CoID) and a determined champion of design in industry who had coordinated the transport exhibits for the Festival of Britain in 1951. After leading the design panel set up by the British Transport Commission in 1956, Williams was then appointed the first Director of Industrial Design at the British Railways Board (BRB) in 1963. His widely respected influence was critical in bringing all parts of the organization together – from engineers to marketeers – to back a strategy for modernizing and revitalizing the nation's faded railway system. Although they only ever briefly met in person – Williams died unexpectedly in 1965 – Grange would later clearly recall the 'early generosity' Williams showed towards him, and he went on to work closely with Williams's successor, the dynamic James Cousins, across the following decade.

The initial job Grange delivered for Cousins was a redesign of the departures indicator board for station concourses. In order to streamline the system and avoid the requirement for constant printing and distribution of revised timetable posters, BRB design officer Jack Bloomfield had devised a concept for a modular system of perforated plastic panels into which letter and number tiles could be plugged; Grange was commissioned to refine the final design of this system, called Infomatrix. First trialled in 1968 at London's Marylebone Station, the location of the BRB design office, the design solution also introduced the first ever timetable

2

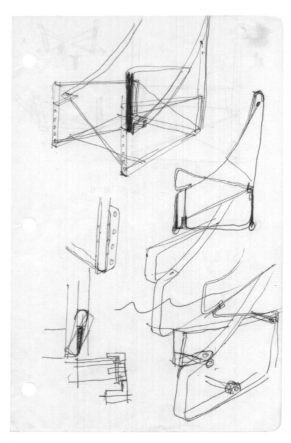

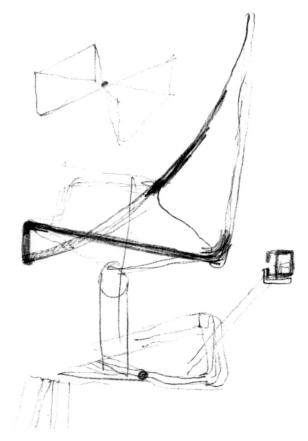

3

4

layout to be designed 'with the passenger in mind', rather than the railway worker: destinations were listed alphabetically in the first column, followed by departure times in the second, rather than the other way around. Grange also took the initiative and pushed the whole concept a step further by considering the concourse surroundings in which passengers would be consulting these boards. Having listened to one of the BRB team grumbling about how difficult it was to see where the cleaners had swept, he proposed that instead of the dirty black asphalt surface that was ubiquitous across stations at that time, the area around the timetables should be relaid with an island of pale, hard-wearing marble. His suggestion was taken up, signalling the beginning of the passenger-friendly experience offered by the bright, spacious city station concourses of today.

This first job delivered by Grange gained some pleasing publicity for British Rail as the organization focused on transforming its image, so it was soon followed by another small commission later in 1968. This time the brief was to refine a passenger chair design that the BRB engineering team had been working on ready for the coming era of high-speed travel, where lightweight interior solutions were required to make the overall economics work. The 'suspension seat' concept was inspired by technology being applied in the Apollo space programme to comfortably and safely support the astronauts: the BRB engineers had sourced an aerospace-grade nylon–polyester netting sling from NASA as part of their research and development. Grange's task – again in collaboration with Bloomfield and, radically for the time, also working with an ergonomist to advise on passenger comfort – was to refine the design of the aluminium frame over which the netting was to be stretched, in such a way that the seated passenger would not come into contact with the frame and would therefore be insulated from vibration. Although the project was never brought to market because, in Grange's words, the netting 'simply wouldn't face up to the anticipated attention of vandals', the radical design was displayed as part of the CoID-hosted exhibition 'The Next Train ... Into the 1970s with British Rail' in 1969, which promoted British Rail's forward-looking investment in design. By the end of the 1960s British Rail was feeling the pressure of dwindling passenger numbers owing to the glamorous travel freedom offered by private cars and the UK's growing motorway network, and the competition of newly launched national air travel options from city airports. So the exhibition aimed to raise public awareness of the potential of 'a whole new look and new experience for rail travel' in the

3 / 4. Various sketches from Grange's notebooks during the process of considering structural options for a 'suspension seat' concept for train passengers, which he was commissioned to explore with the BRB design team.

5. The first prototype 'suspension seat' chair design, made in the Hampstead studio workshop and modelled by Grange's secretary, featured an open lower back to relieve pressure and keep the passenger cool on long journeys.

6. The final prototype for the 'suspension seat' chair featured an aerospace-grade nylon–polyester netting sling inspired by NASA innovations for astronaut seating.

5

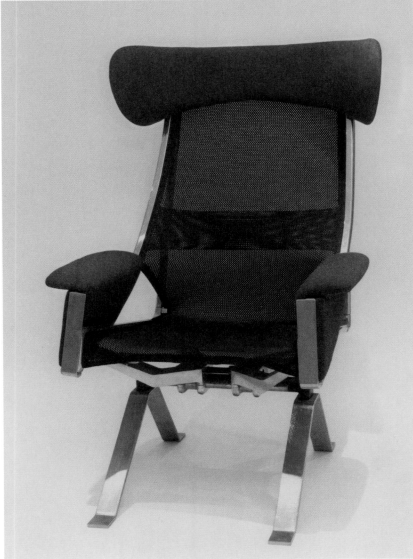

6

coming high-speed 'intercity' era, a strategy for networking the country first conceived in the early 1960s. However, to deliver on this vision British Rail would need a new train.

Late the following year Grange was asked to take on another design job, after Cousins had recommended him to his fellow directors on the design panel. The brief might have been larger in physical scale than the timetable and chair, but in Grange's words 'it started very modestly', with a brief to devise the 'appearance design', or exterior livery, of the power car (a single-ended locomotive) of a proposed new high-speed train. By the turn of the decade the development of the much-anticipated electric (originally gas-turbine-powered) Advanced Passenger Train (APT) was proving a highly challenging project, so an alternative diesel express solution was being developed by British Rail as a nearer-term solution. Built with existing technology, this option promised to be more cost-efficient and could be brought to market on more routes sooner because there was no additional requirement to

install overhead electric power wires. Initially called the High Speed Diesel Train (HSDT), it would later be known simply as the High Speed Train (HST).

On receiving the commission Grange was provided with drawings and a model of the then-proposed HSDT locomotive prototype; his task was to conceive a design to 'improve the visual impact of its rather primitive ball-nose shape'. However, as is now a legendary tale in the industry, Grange's resulting design explorations led him down the route of considering not just the two-dimensional livery but also the three-dimensional form of the nose around which the livery would wrap.

Curious about the physical impact of the shape of the cab on the aerodynamics of the power car and therefore the performance of the train, Grange set about making models of various amended forms. Working after hours with a consultant aerodynamicist at Imperial College London, he would take these models to be tested in the university's wind tunnel in order to 'gradually develop a cogent argument for a revised shape'. As he later explained, the HSDT

7

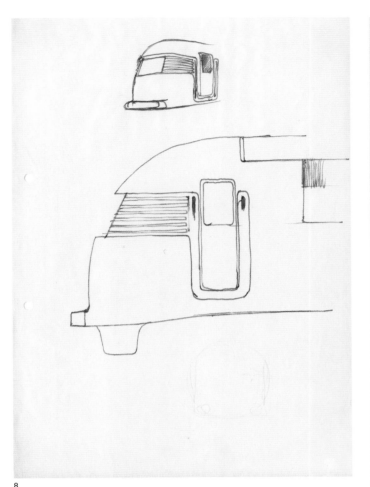

8

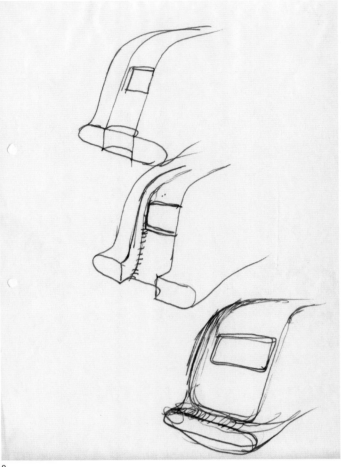

9

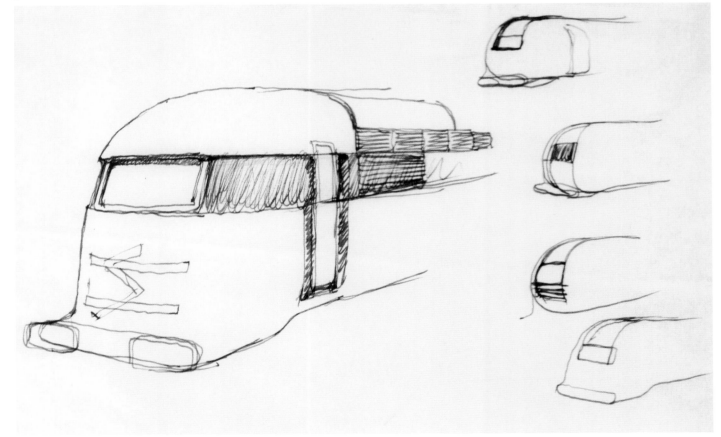

10

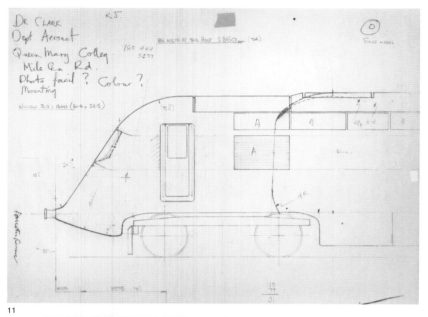

11

12

13

14

11 / 13. A side-profile drawing of the power car, and associated scale model, showing Grange's evolving attempts to streamline the buffer section of the nose.

12. A larger half-model, using a mirror, showing a further-refined profile and the distinctive final shape of the power-car nose starting to emerge from behind the still mandatory buffers.

14. Another scale model of the power car, this one recording the point at which Grange's design to date was translated into the full prototype HST that went on to set a new diesel rail world speed record.

15. An early sketch from Grange's portfolio during the same period as the initial exploration of streamlining the buffers (11 and 13), here working out a first solution for the alignment of a colour scheme along the side of the power car.

16. An intricate technical sketch of the profile of the power-car nose, calculating the optimum angle at which the window would meet the lower body. The page also features a quick overhead sketch view of a driver's chair.

already used proven engineering technology, but what was not proven was how the aerodynamics of the nose could beneficially impact 'the economics of regularly running at high speeds, where the power needed escalates steeply with every additional 10 mph [16 km/h]'.

When it came to delivering his presentation to the design panel directors a few weeks later – they were expecting a proposed new livery design – Grange, sick with nerves at having far overstepped the brief, but confident that his proposal 'at least put forward a well-founded argument', meticulously laid out photographs of the whipping lines of smoke trails in the wind tunnel, alongside models and drawings of a new nose. His nerves were unfounded: his argument was met openly and with positivity and he was subsequently given the green light to conduct further refinements of his proposal in collaboration with the engineering team. The subsequent operations moved fast and the first two power cars for testing, modelled on Grange's design,

went into construction at the Crewe Works in 1971, and, coupled either end of a rake of newly developed Mark 3 carriages, became known as the prototype HST. Two years later, while undertaking successful main line testing, to everyone's thrill the prototype HST set a new diesel rail world speed record of 230.5 km/h (143.2 mph).

Until this stage the construction of the power car had been kept strictly within the original technical parameters of an existing specification derived from traditional locomotives: it was required to feature buffers, a window made of 25 mm (1 in.) armoured glass and a single, central driver's seat. However, once the prototype had demonstrated speeds of over 160 km/h (100 mph), the train drivers' union ASLEF took note and demanded greater safety precautions through provision for two drivers side by side. During further wind tunnel testing the wider window width required for visibility from these two seats was shown to considerably throw out the aerodynamics that had delivered the speed record; the necessity for a

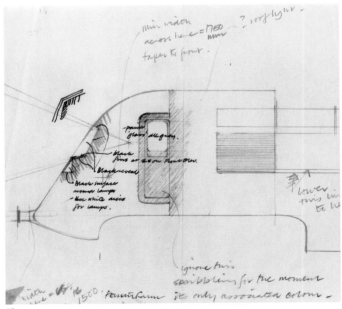

15

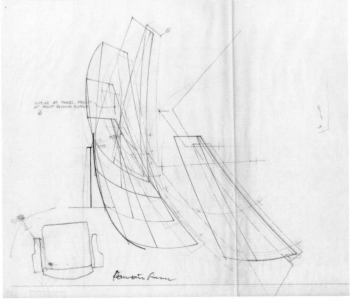

16

'The High Speed Train – in reality only a small part of the vast efforts made to improve British Rail – reawakened some of the old railway pride. British Rail now use the image of the train everywhere and anywhere as a symbol of progress. For the chance to take a small part in this venture, I am grateful.'

Kenneth Grange, Boilerhouse exhibition, 1983

wider window resulted in a sharper meeting of the glass with the body of the cab on each side, and also required a visually obstructive central bar to hold two separate panes as the armoured glass available at that time was restricted in size. After working through a range of unsatisfactory solutions, Grange met with his 'first stroke of luck'; a few months later the armoured-glass manufacturers devised a method of producing larger panes, so Grange could dispense with the central bar. However, this did not immediately solve the issue of the aerodynamics.

The other feature of the original design that Grange considered 'unsatisfactory' was the buffers; the wind tunnel tests had shown that these were highly disruptive to economically reaching an optimum speed. Still grappling with this problem in one of the latter prototype HST review meetings in 1974, Grange had a 'second stroke of luck', which

occurred when he asked, with 'great trepidation', if the engineers could remind him why it was that the power car required buffers. The respondent admitted that in fact it would have no need of buffers, since unlike traditional engines these power cars would never be used to shunt other vehicles around, as they would always be paired – one at the front and one at the back of whole trains. With this revelation Grange was handed his 'major breakthrough', and following this revelatory meeting he rapidly dispensed with the buffers, which, in turn, enabled him to smooth out the nose profile and place the front window on a greater slant, improving the airflow around the sides. And so the subsequent highly recognizable shape of the nose was refined, with final details integrated such as the embedded formation of horns and lights and a compact hatch on the underside to access the towing mechanism.

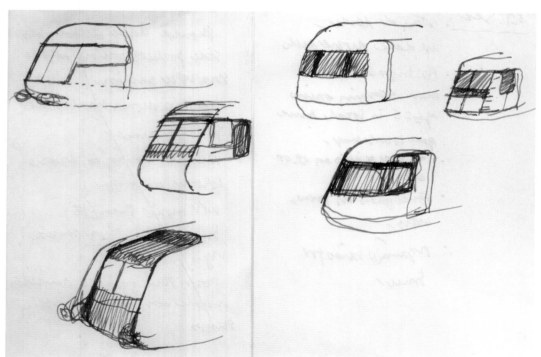

17. Pages of sketches from Grange's notebook where he is starting to dream about how the nose of the power car might look if the buffers were no longer required.

17

18 / 19. Scale models of the next iteration of the power-car nose, once Grange was advised that he was required to widen the front window to allow for two drivers to sit side by side in the cab. The glass could not be produced in wide enough panes, leading to this dual-panel solution with central column.

20 / 21 / 22. Another scale model of the power car with dual-panel front window shown here with smoke trails during aerodynamic testing in a wind tunnel (20 and 22), with – for comparison – the original wind tunnel testing image from Grange's very first trial with the ball-nosed prototype.

18

19

20

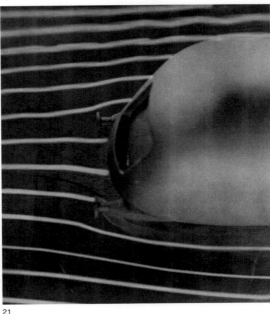

21

22

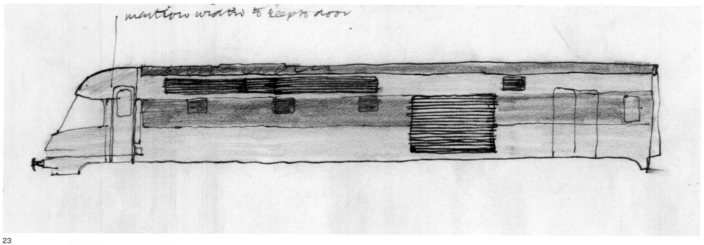

23

24

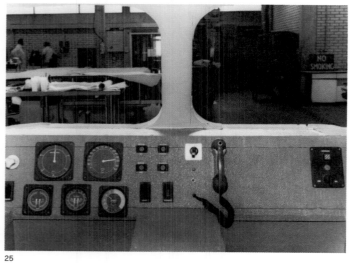

25

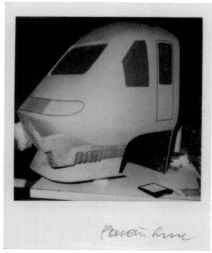

26

23. Final sketch by Grange of the prototype nose with buffers, as he works on the visual styling down the side of the power car.

24 / 25. Full-scale carbon-fibre mock-up – external and internal – of the shell of the prototype driver's car while it still featured a split front window with central column. Made at the Derby Works.

26. Large-scale model of the final form of the production HST, with single wide front window, from which Grange is finally removing the buffers once it was deemed they were not needed.

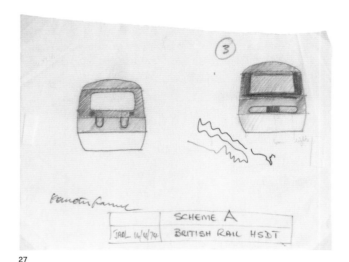

27

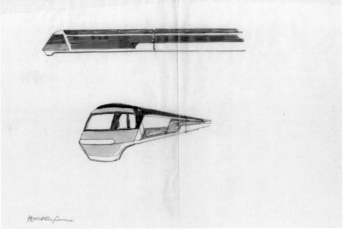

28

To aid the aerodynamic and therefore economic efficiency of the power car, the nose of the final production model was specified in moulded glass-reinforced plastic to a thickness of 50 mm (2 in.), making it lighter-for-given-strength than steel and highly streamlined through only requiring minimal joints. The unique ability to introduce this innovative material solution within the rail industry was due to George Williams and others, who had spearheaded the set-up of a visionary plastics laboratory at the company's Derby Works back in the early 1960s. The shell of each nose was manufactured as a complete unit with all the ducts and pipes integrated within the thin wall; this also ensured maximum space,

insulation and ergonomic comfort within the driver's cab. The general spatial design of the cab was also looked at by Grange as part of his remit and, interestingly, it was later noted that the consideration that went into ensuring the driver's comfort was what gave the power car design its final seal of approval.

Finally, in 1975, Grange's finishing touch was to return to considering the livery – five years after it was first commissioned. His striking, streamlined graphic arrangement is particularly notable for how much yellow is introduced along the sides of the power car; previously the distinctive bright yellow had been applied only as a visual warning sign on the front face of earlier locomotives. Grange transformed the use

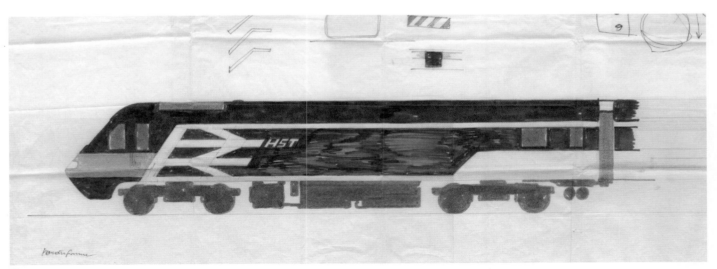

29

27. A sketch sheet from Grange's portfolio showing two possible design solutions for the headlamps on the front of the production HST power car.

28 / 29. Sketch sheets from Grange's portfolio showing geometry and colour explorations for the final production HST livery design.

'When the HST first launched, it was the only modern thing in sight. There was nothing else that approached it as evidence of the future.'

Kenneth Grange

of this colour into a highly effective and memorable stylistic statement in combination with British Rail's standard blue, grey and white.

The resulting 'production HST', presented to the public as the Inter-City 125 service (later rebranded InterCity 125) went into manufacture in 1975 with an initial government-authorized order for fifty-nine sets of power cars coupled to seven or eight Mark 3 carriages. Intensive testing and crew training began in April 1976, followed soon afterwards by the first passenger services. The introduction of a limited number of trains into regular service in October 1976 marked the beginning of 'the age of the train' – an era, Grange often remarked, when 'the HST was the only modern thing in sight, there was nothing else that approached it as evidence of the future'. While reviewing the project a few years later in his SIAD Milner Gray lecture, Sir Peter Parker, chairman of British Rail, would say of the huge impact the train had made on the company that 'good design management pays dividends'. Citing the HST as an outstanding example, he claimed that 'it has transformed our fortunes on the intercity routes'.

From 1976 the HST rapidly became a symbol of national pride and progress, uniquely reinvigorating the image of the nation's rail network and starring in many advertisements and posters. In November 1987 the power cars 43102 and 43159 set a new world speed record of 239 km/h (148.5 mph), a record still held for rail diesel traction. The much-loved fleet, in production until 1982, has since transported passengers far and wide across the UK for nearly five decades, sporting a wide variety of liveries, and the power cars are only now gradually being retired from main line service.

The very first production class power car, number 43002, manufactured in 1975 and retired in 2019, has since been fully restored to its original livery and sits at the heart of the National Railway Museum in York; it was named *Sir Kenneth Grange* and unveiled by Grange himself to mark the fortieth anniversary of the train. The museum, which opened in 1975 just as the HST was coming into service, also owns the original prototype HSDT locomotive, number 41001, which achieved the initial speed record and is also the power car that brought VIPs from King's Cross

30. Final display model for the production HST Inter-City 125 with its launch livery design.

31. The team at the Derby Works apply the Inter-City 125 logo vinyl sheet to one of the first, newly painted production HST power cars off the production line in 1975.

32 (opposite). A technical drawing of the final proposed profile for the cab of the HST power car, drawn by Grange's assistant designer on the project, J. A. D. (Tony) Lowe.

30

31

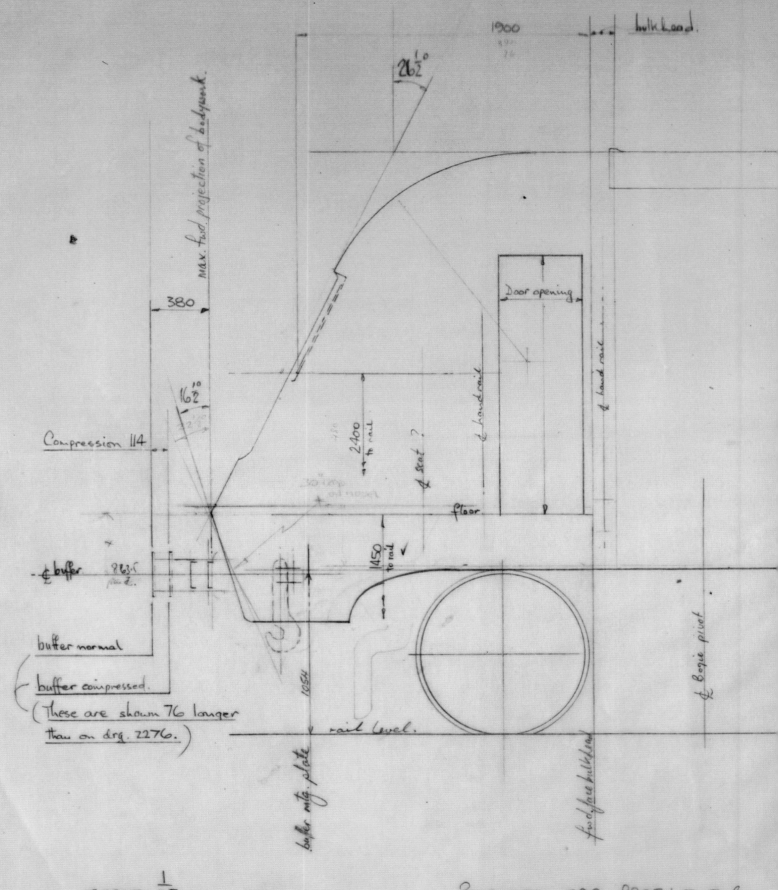

1900

bulkhead.

$26\frac{1}{2}°$

max. fwd. projection of bodywork.

380

Door opening

℄ handrail

℄ handrail

$16\frac{1}{2}°$

Compression 114

2400 to rail

℄ seat ?

floor

-℄ buffer   863·5

1450 to rail

buffer normal

buffer compressed.

(These are shown 76 longer
than on drg. 2276.)

1054

rail level.

buffer mtg. plate

fwd. face bulkhead.

℄ Bogie pivot.

SCALE: $\frac{1}{25}$

PROPOSED CAB PROFILE FOR
H.S.D.T. POWER CAR.

JADLowe. 15/3/71.

B.R. - 490 - sketch

Mister– Im going on Holiday on your Train cos I know its The quickest.

⇄ Inter-City 125   Have a good trip!

33

34

to the opening of the museum in 1975, and then transported the Duke of Edinburgh from York to his other appointments following the official ceremony.

Power car 41001 was meticulously restored from static exhibition piece to fully functioning order by the dedicated volunteer 125 Group, and from 2014 operated on heritage railways for five years, to the delight of railway staff, engineers and enthusiasts. The group has since acquired four production power cars – numbers 43044, 43048, 43089 and the record-breaker 43102 – plus nine Mark 3 carriages, all of which are maintained and still capable of running at 200 km/h (125 mph) on UK main lines. In recent years

Grange was invited to become honorary head of the group, a gesture he cherished as recognition of his 'favourite project' and of the 'small part he played in a very big national story'.

35

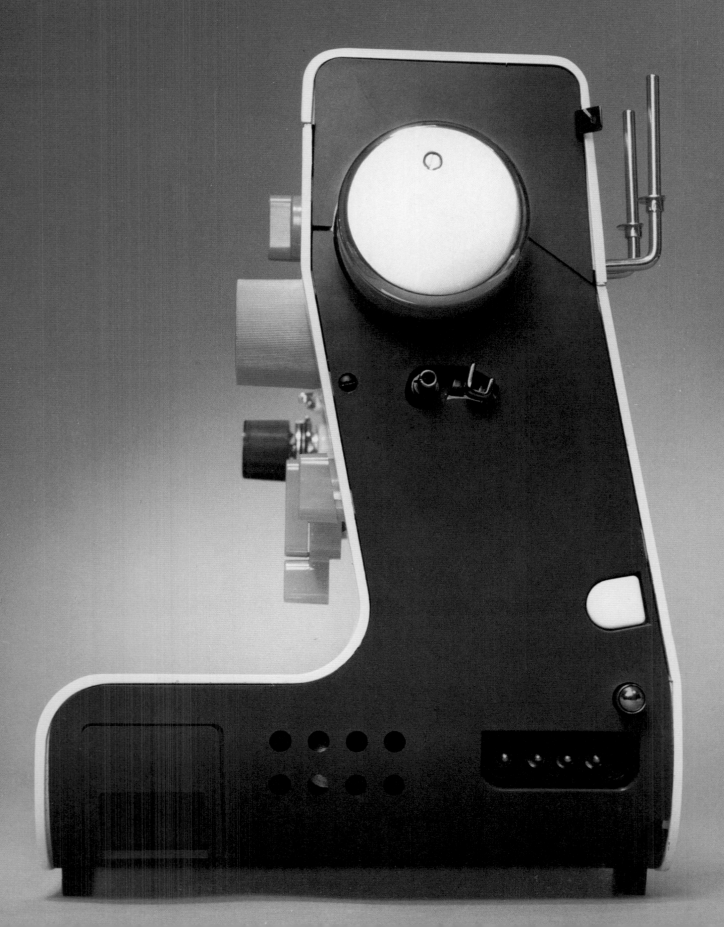

Maruzen

1 (opposite). Side profile of the 800 series sewing machine, showing how Grange shifted the sewing arm backwards (towards the right in this image) to create more working area on the flatbed at the front of the machine (on the left in this image).

2. Sketch of a sewing machine in which Grange is exploring the idea of extending the flatbed work area.

The Maruzen Sewing Machine Company of Osaka, Japan, was founded in 1949, initially as a distributor of sewing machine parts. By the mid-1950s the company had evolved to become a leading manufacturer of sewing machines, launching the domestic zig-zag sewing machine into the Japanese market for the first time and landing a long-term export contract with the huge US retailer Sears Roebuck & Co. This resulted in Maruzen swiftly scaling up to export more than 350,000 machines annually, and by the mid-1960s, following trade liberalization, the company was looking to expand its overseas business in Europe.

The Maruzen directors viewed the UK as a substantial potential market but, in a narrative similar to that of the early Kenwood Chef, they also recognized that the style of the machines they exported to the USA would not agree with modern European domestic tastes. So they appointed their European agent to seek out a design consultant to refine their machines accordingly. This agent was Derek Quitmann, director of his family's long-standing business Frister & Rossmann, which distributed sewing machines across Europe. And so it was that late in 1967 Grange received a call from Quitmann – Grange believes probably via a contact at Kenwood – explaining the requirement from Maruzen. And soon afterwards, in February 1968, he found himself on a plane bound for Osaka – the 'Manchester of Japan', as the *Financial Times* referred to the city in a report later that year – to meet with the Maruzen team; this was Grange's first long-haul trip beyond the USA, and a journey that marked the beginning of a happy, energetic and extraordinary three decades of working with clients in Japan.

After three days touring the factory and facilities and being 'hosted impeccably' by the Maruzen team, including meeting the company's owner, Yoshio Mikuni, Grange returned to his team in London and embarked on responding to the brief: to refine the form of the company's existing bestselling

US machine to better fit a European aesthetic. In answering the brief he opted to take things further than requested, making two different concept models to present back to the directors. The first offered a revised form of the existing machine, following the brief precisely and altering neither the basic mechanical layout nor the geometry. However, the second model was 'quite unlike the standard sewing machine'; most notably, based on his own experience of using sewing machines with his mother, this design proposed that the sewing arm be moved further away from the user to give more assembly working space on the nearside of the flatbed. This was a radical move as the machines were traditionally symmetrical for weight distribution. Another thoughtful variation Grange suggested was a curved base edge to enable the machine to be rolled back and propped on its end to keep it stable and safe while conducting maintenance and cleaning away lint; as *Design* magazine later noted, 'most other machines simply pivot in the rear edge and have no built-in balance or support'. This innovation gave the proposed machine a very distinctive shape.

Flying back to Osaka a few months later to present his proposals, Grange felt 'sick with nerves', anxiously wondering if his deviation from the brief might be viewed as bad etiquette and lose him the

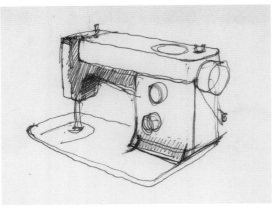

2

3. A full-scale model, made and photographed in the Hampstead studio, of a proposed carry-case with integrated accessory boxes for the 800 series sewing machine.

3

job before he had even begun. And his nerves would not be soothed by the fact that the cellulose paint with which his team had painstakingly finished the models had melted inside the sealed carrying cases while on the plane – his first experience of travelling with a precious model, and 'a lesson learned'. Grange finally convinced himself to present the more radical design only as he left his hotel in Osaka on the morning of the presentation. In the event, he recalled that the directors were impressed and had been 'very understanding of the painterly mess of the model' and highly appreciative of his efforts. His reputation in Japan as 'the European innovator' was launched.

This successful follow-up meeting is documented in a letter sent by the sales director, Osamu Nakamachi, to Quitmann in June 1968, describing their overwhelmingly positive impressions of Grange's 'professional talent' and explaining their intention to employ him more widely. Grange subsequently refined his design, introducing further features including a sliding drawer for storage in the flatbed; bright, solid, playful orange controls making operation clear and easy; and an additional accessory that later became commonplace – a carrying case with two storage boxes that could ingeniously double as an extension to the working surface, clipping onto the flatbed.

The radical 800 series machine initially launched in 1970 and was marketed to substantial success in Europe under the Frister & Rossmann name and also in Japan under Maruzen's own label, Jaguar. As part of this 'new look' for the company Grange also designed a new identity and logotype – featuring a stylized zig-zag graphic device – which was displayed both on the machines and in the marketing materials.

And so began a strong twenty-year relationship with the Maruzen company, and an enduring friendship for Grange with Tomio Nishigami, the company's project engineer, with whom he would keep in touch for decades afterwards. Grange would quickly gain respect owing to the great importance

placed on the sewing machine in every Japanese home; notably it was called a *mishin* (based on the Japanese pronunciation of the word 'machine'), which in his mind showed its high status, as 'above all other machines it was the only one to take on this universal word'. He was also admiring of the working practices of the company; he described how the team would quickly develop working prototypes based on his models – a sophisticated approach compared to his European experiences at that time – in order to rapidly gain feedback from their international sales representatives.

Grange learned much too about the 'expectation of excellence' in the manufacture of products in Japanese industry; used to over-engineering the products they delivered for the US market – a demand placed on them by their huge client Sears Roebuck to ensure robust products that minimized the numbers of returns – the Maruzen team 'patiently listened' to Grange's suggestion of applying a one-coat paint finish to his designs, as was used on typewriters in the UK, to reduce production costs. They would then politely counter that they would 'put nine coats of paint, that way getting a good finish'. Grange was endlessly impressed when visiting the factory and watching 'dozens of ladies at work with wet and dry glass paper', resulting in a deep gloss finish to the products that truly set them apart.

Variations of the 800 would follow over the next few years, as new innovations in the mechanics were developed, including the 804 in 1971, which was labelled 'the most beautiful sewing machine in the world' by the *Sewing Machine Times*.

However, concurrently, Grange was also working on a completely new model of machine as tastes in domestic appliances were maturing and it became apparent that slimmed-down, lightweight machines were also required in order to grow the market. Noting that the existing lightweight option developed by Maruzen was made of aluminium rather than cast iron but was still a substantial weight, Grange

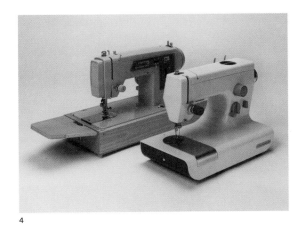

4. A photograph showing a traditional Maruzen sewing machine (left), the design of which Grange evolved to create the modern 800 machine, which sits next to it.

5 / 6 / 7 / 8. Views of the 804 sewing machine, the second release in the 800 series, taken from a product photo shoot for press use on launch of this machine in 1971. Image number 7 appeared on the cover of the *Sewing Machine Times* trade magazine.

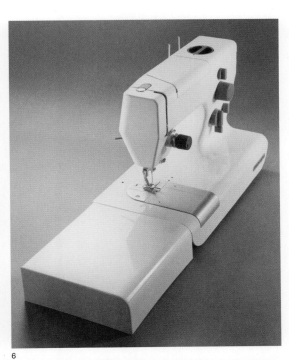

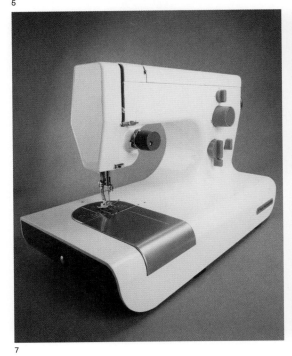

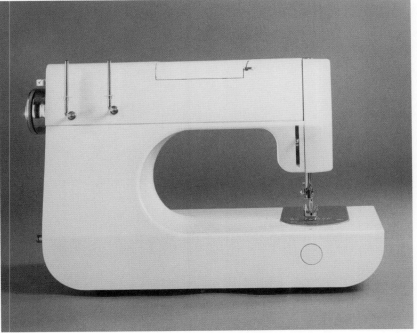

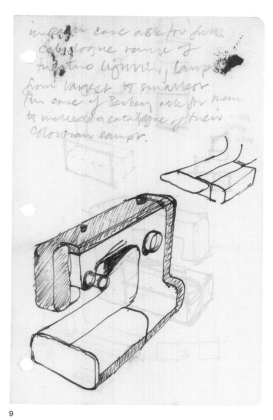

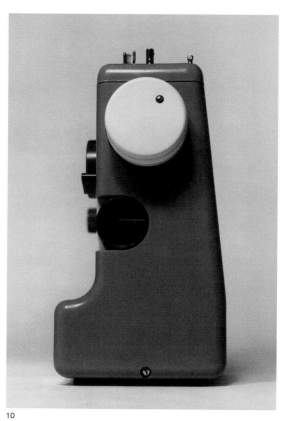

9. Working sketch from Grange's notebooks during his development of the Cub series sewing machine, showing his early thoughts on how a storage box would integrate into the flatbed.

10. Side-profile view of the Cub 3 sewing machine, showing its slim volume and lack of wide flatbed: this was compensated for by a fold-out surface integrated into the machine.

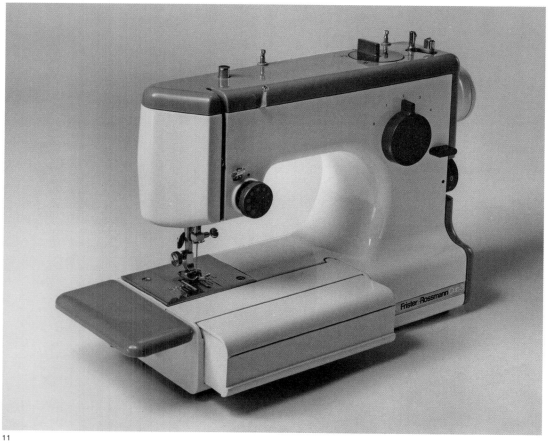

11. This photograph of the Cub 3 sewing machine demonstrates the fold-out surfaces, with the front segment also doubling as storage for accessories.

9

10

11

12

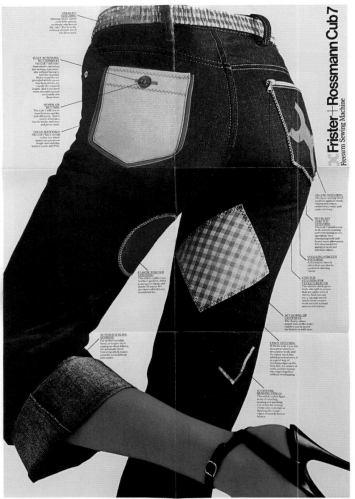

13

12. The selected publicity photo from a PR photo shoot with Grange, taken at the headquarters in Osaka, to launch the Cub (see also contact sheets on pp. 13 and 44).

13. A fold-out poster supplied with the Cub 7 sewing machine, to explain all the features and capabilities of the machine's functions. Designed with customary wit and style by Pentagram partner David Hillman.

suggested that a real weight reduction could be made by 'reducing the overall size of the machine'; to achieve this, nothing would need changing mechanically and therefore the performance would be as good as a full-sized machine, but he stressed that it would require physically shortening the driving shafts. This presented a sizeable engineering challenge and the team were not convinced, but duly took on Grange's suggestion and developed a prototype. This proved highly successful in testing, and the small, nimble Cub machine was born, the name suggested by Grange to align with the Jaguar brand. The final machine featured an ingenious flip-out storage compartment and fold-up wing to ensure there was still plenty of working surface on the flatbed, and the final weight was reduced by almost half by using tough injection-moulded ABS plastic alongside aluminium die-cast components.

The Cub launched in 1971 and quickly became the most successful original machine developed internationally by Maruzen. Offering everything you would expect from a much larger machine, Grange's 'friendly little machine' opened up new markets, brought prestige to the company and offered real benefit and a pleasing experience to users. It even became the only European design to successfully enter the US market.

The *Sewing Machine Times* called the machines 'small miracles of design, compactness and lightness', while in terms of the refined functionality the *Sunday Mirror* raved that 'previous designers of sewing machines seem to think that the average housewife wants to embroider a Hungarian peasant's blouse and run off a pinch-pleated smocked dress or two in her spare time. Not so Mr Grange. He has restricted the Cub to practical extras like a couple of embroidery stitches, a buttonholer, blind hemmer and an appliqué stitcher.'

While reviewing a talk given by Grange at the press launch, the *Sewing Machine Times* would report that 'Mr Grange made it sound easy to his lay

14. Early working sketches for an electronic calculator, one of a few other product design briefs given to Grange by his client at Maruzen, when the company expanded into other areas of product manufacture alongside sewing machines.

15. The final electronic calculator, manufactured by Maruzen and marketed in Japan under the brand name Jaguar.

audience, but he was too modest to say that it takes a very special design skill to do all that and come up with a result that looks as good and performs as well as the Cub.'

Grange's face appeared in numerous press photographs in Japan, making him more recognized there than in the UK. Continuing the thread of creative ingenuity running through the project, when it came to the design of the promotional materials for the later refined Cub 3 model, he brought in David Hillman, by then a partner at Pentagram, to give the graphics a desirably European 1970s pop flair.

Grange continued to work with Maruzen into the 1980s on the manufacture of further professional sewing machines for the Frister & Rossmann brand name, alongside other products including typewriters and calculators. The company changed its name to the Jaguar International Corporation in 1989 and is today still one of the largest internationally recognized sewing machine manufacturers; to this day it continues to use the same zig-zag graphic identity designed by Grange in the 1960s, as does Frister & Rossmann.

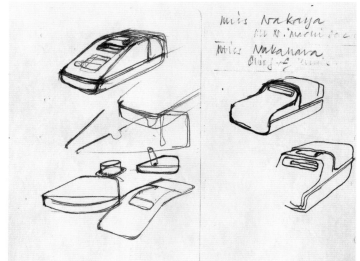

14

15

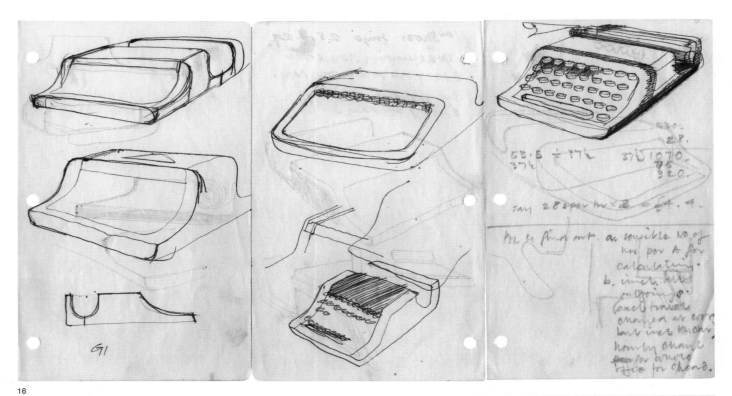

16

17

16. Pages from Grange's notebooks where he is exploring early shapes and volumes for a typewriter for Maruzen, building on his earlier experience working with Imperial Typewriters.

17. The final typewriter for Maruzen, marketed under the Jaguar brand, as part of the company's manufacturing expansion outside of sewing machines.

Wilkinson Sword

As the name suggests, the origins of Wilkinson Sword date back to weapons production in the eighteenth century, when the company specialized in metal manufacturing and blade crafting. In the twentieth century production diversified through commercial areas such as garden equipment, kitchen utensils, scissors and most prominently shaving products. The brand's first double-edge razor product launched as far back as 1898, but it would not be until well after the Second World War, and through the emergence of stainless steel as an alternative material for razor blade manufacture, that the Wilkinson Sword shaving products division really entered the market. The story of the company's development since then, and Grange's portfolio of work with it, is also the story of one of the biggest and most ruthlessly competitive sectors of the modern fast-turnover consumer goods industry.

In the early personal shaving sector Wilkinson Sword was dwarfed in scale, particularly in terms of the all-important marketing budgets for new products, by the giant competitor businesses of Gillette and Schick; but through investment both in its manufacturing technology and in design expertise the company was able to stand its ground and compete at milestone points through the sector's evolution.

Since producing its original double-edge razor, Wilkinson Sword had focused predominantly on the production of the blades rather than on further razor models. In 1956, to strengthen its production capabilities and gain a bigger share of the market, Wilkinson Sword formed a partnership with Osberghaus, a German manufacturer of razor blades, licensing it to provide technical knowledge and substantial manufacturing facilities. Soon afterwards Wilkinson Sword, with its German partners, brought a key new product to market: the stainless steel razor blade. Offering a cleaner cut and better durability than the previous rust-prone carbon steel blades, the blades immediately made an impact in the UK market.

Wilkinson Sword rapidly built on this opportunity to reinforce the company's position by further advancing its manufacturing technology and developing arguably the most important innovation in the company's history: the patented PTFE-coated razor blade. Called the Edge, this highly durable blade launched in 1961 and was an immediate game-changer for the industry, for a while enabling Wilkinson Sword to lead its competitors in sales of blades.

However, owing to the business focus on blade manufacture, Wilkinson Sword held hardly any market share in terms of the razor products themselves; until now customers of the blades had been obliged to

2

3

4. An original pen-and-ink presentation drawing of Grange's design for the Royale, the razor that revived his consultancy work with the company and which became Wilkinson's flagship product in the 1980s.

5. A promotional product photograph, taken by Grange's team in the Pentagram photography studio, of the Royale razor from three angles, showing its refined profile.

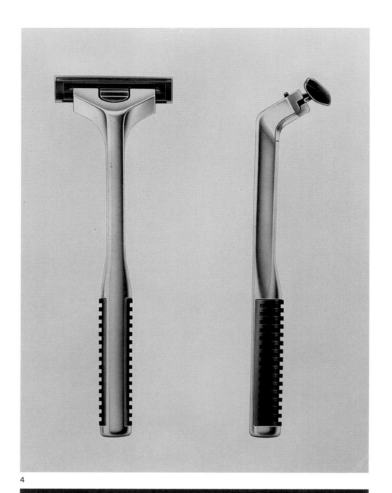

4

buy razors from rival manufacturers. This presented an untapped opportunity for the business, which being a relatively small player could also be nimble. So, during the latter part of the 1960s, under chief executive John Bloxcidge, it was decided to start controlling the application of its blades in the market by investing in the design of its own new razor products. It was not long before Wilkinson Sword came calling at Grange's studio in Hampstead, having noted his earlier award-winning design of the Milward Courier electric shaver for Needle Industries (see pp. 108–112) and recent products for Ronson (see pp. 118–123).

Launched in 1969, Grange's first design for Wilkinson Sword was a high-quality, conventional double-edge safety razor, a modern take on the company's original razor, this time with the central twisting core housed inside an injection-moulded plastic handle with metal detailing, while a little duct in the plastic case drained away water. *Design* magazine would announce that 'Wilkinson Sword have twice previously reached the point of tooling up to produce a modern double-edged razor. Yet each time they abandoned the project because they were not satisfied their product was of a sufficiently high standard in this very exacting market.' Not so with Grange's solution. Grange himself would later critique his design as 'unremarkable, except perhaps in that it makes the ubiquitous product more elegant, and more easily cleaned'. Interestingly, on this project, through Grange's recommendation, his previous client Needle Industries was commissioned to manufacture the razor since, in his words, 'they made metal parts so beautifully'.

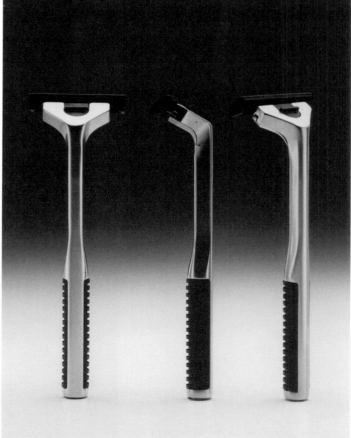

6 / 7 / 8 / 9. A selection of plastic models made by the team in Grange's workshop at Pentagram, exploring a range of concepts for ergonomic and attractive razor products.

Many did not progress to production, but the model in image 8 later evolved into the commercially successful women's Lady Protector razor.

5

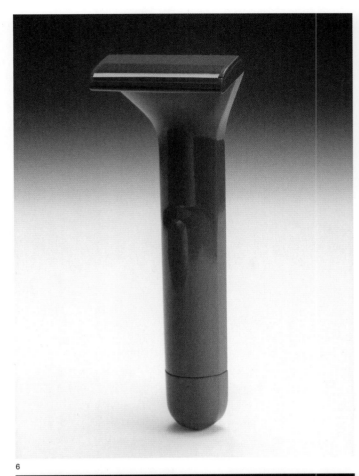

6

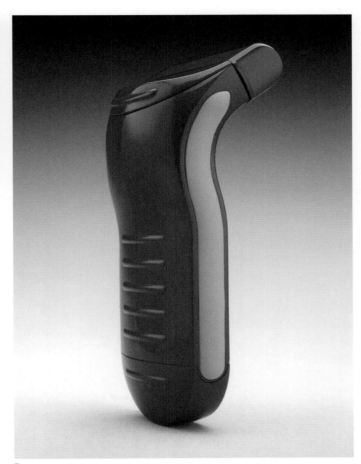

7

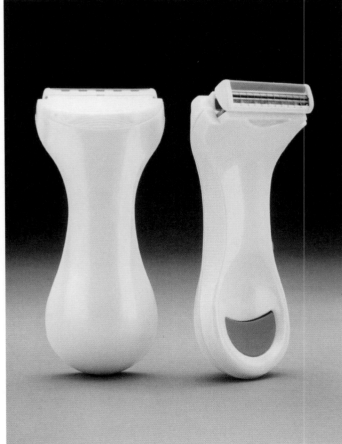

8

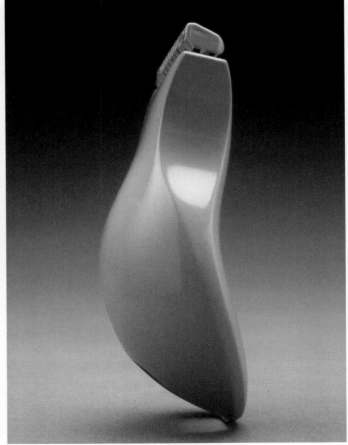

9

10. Grange's original Protector razor, recognizable for its distinctive sculptural handle, demonstrates Grange's dedication to understanding the behaviour of products held in the hand. It was this product that famously introduced the daring choice of red as a colour in the shaving market.

10

By the turn of the decade the market for easy-to-use wet shaving products was picking up speed with the birth of the single-edge razor, first introduced by Gillette. Wilkinson Sword had also been working on its own blade technology in this field, and in the early 1970s introduced its next innovation: the bonded razor blade. This involved precisely moulding a single blade into a plastic carrier, which enabled greater control of the angle of the blade when fitted to a razor, making it safer and reducing the risk of cuts. After the PTFE-coated blade this next key innovation was the tipping point for a huge shift in the market and would lead to the arrival of the dominating disposable razor we know today.

Grange was commissioned to design a razor to hold this new bonded razor blade, a product that was to be initially targeted at the sizeable US market. His design, with a sleek handle that evolved his previous design of the double-edge razor, featured a plastic handle and metal head with button to reject the used blade carrier for easy replacement. The design progressed to prototype stage, but was eventually shelved in favour of a concept developed by a US designer. Although disappointed, Grange later remarked philosophically that this was 'the proper choice' as consumer preferences were notably different in the USA when it came to the aesthetic of products, as he well understood from his work with both Kodak and Kenwood.

Grange's relationship with Wilkinson Sword continued, with him and his growing team, now at Pentagram, working on numerous conceptual handle and blade variations, none of which came to fruition. In 1977 things took another leap when he was commissioned to design a new premium product for the now booming single edge razor market; he was briefed specifically to ensure 'visible evidence of the company's commitment to making the best possible razors'. The design built on Grange's work from six years previously, and the company agreed to a specification of materials and construction 'of a level

far higher than had become standard in the market'. The resulting sophisticated product, fittingly called the Royale, featured a precision die-cast steel handle with satin chrome finish and a comfortable rubber grip. Launched in 1979, it became Wilkinson Sword's flagship product and a worldwide top seller, winning the coveted G Mark Award for foreign goods in Japan.

Numerous further designs for razors followed, along with studies for the accompanying structural plastic packaging, with substantial effort invested by Grange and his Pentagram team, as evidenced by the large volume of prototype models produced across the following two decades. Model making would always remain at the heart of Grange's studio process, and the volume of work completed for Wilkinson Sword is an exceptional demonstration of the sheer number of concepts it often took per each product that would get anywhere near to production.

The recession of the 1980s saw manufacturers vying ever more keenly for market share; designs focused on smart use of materials became a key differentiator to cut costs in the highly competitive disposable razor sector. During this period the competitor Schick purchased Wilkinson Sword, which had nearly been put out of business by the recent flooding of the market by the new Bic disposable razors; and as part of 'a proliferation of new appointments, coupled with strong investments to respond to the competition' as reported by *Marketing* magazine, Grange was appointed consultant design director to the company, a position he retained until his retirement from Pentagram in 1998. During his tenure he built strong relationships and worked alongside many engineers and marketing and sales people at the company, both in the UK and in Germany, recalling that Wilkinson had a strong reputation for 'hiring talent'. He struck up a cherished long-time friendship with sales director George Palmer and would also later reflect that although his work with Wilkinson Sword began with the UK team, his 'most significant designs' came out of his alliance

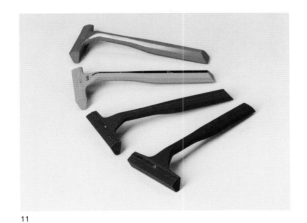

11

11 / 12. Wooden and plastic painted models, made by the team in Grange's workshop at Pentagram, showing colour variations for the Retractor disposable razor. A one-piece mould using a small amount of coloured plastic was proposed for the final product.

with the 'very impressive' German division of the business, the engineer in charge of which, Wolfgang Althaus, would also become a dear friend.

In this new working environment Grange's next highly successful product to come to market was the Retractor, which introduced the smart detail of a retractable blade, thus reducing costs as no separate protective cap was required. This was followed soon after by a fully disposable version of the Retractor, manufactured very cost-efficiently using a minimal volume of colourful plastic. The large volume of sales of this now ubiquitous model of disposable razor reinforced Grange's standing with the company, and led to him being able to propose ideas for product innovations rather than wait for briefs. One of these proposals, delivered to the new product development team, saw Grange conceive a travel razor that had the capacity to store a cartridge of replacement blades inside the handle, a pushback against the disposable mania, as he argued it would result in 'the use of less material overall'. The product, launched in the UK as the Compact and in Germany as the Kompakt, again saw positive sales figures as a distinctively different product, particularly in its later cast-steel form.

Grange's final razor design to be realized came in the early 1990s after a visit to the German site, where he was shown the engineering team's latest innovation: a razor blade wrapped in ultra-fine guard wire. Born of a desire to combine the safety of an electric shaver with the closeness of a wet shave, this wire technique ensured a very smooth shave while further preventing the user from being able to slice sideways and cut themselves. Grange recalled the engineering of the wire winding machine as being

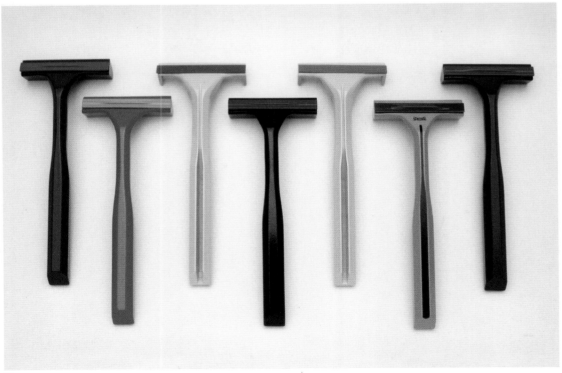

12

13. Exploratory sketches by Grange, from a presentation document for Wilkinson Sword, during the development process of the Compact razor; also showing glimpses of the form of the later Lady Protector razor (see p. 159, image 8).

14. The final Compact razor for men, which Grange devised to hold additional blade cartridges in the handle for convenient storage, especially when travelling.

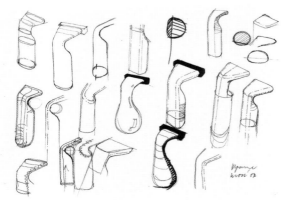

13

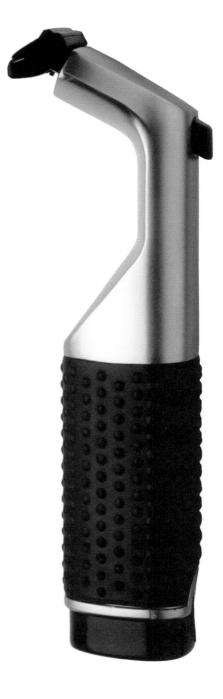

14

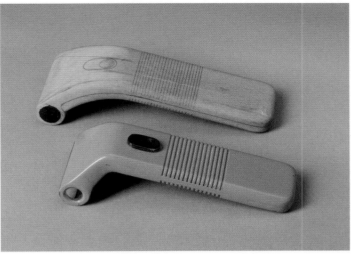

15

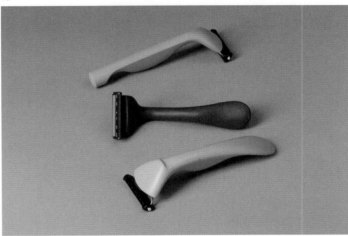

16

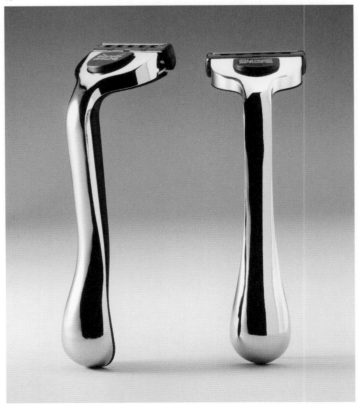

17

15. Painted wooden models of an early concept for a sturdy men's shaver handle, proposed to be used with another Wilkinson Sword innovation, the curved foil style of cutting surface.

16. Painted wooden development models, alongside a final plastic prototype (black), of the highly successful Protector razor.

17. The Protector razor was launched in striking red and also in a sophisticated chrome finish, seen here. The design would spawn many variations, and its influence is still clearly visible in the competitive shaving market today.

'little short of a work of genius', greatly praising the design engineers responsible, Max Lembke and Jochen Thoene, whom he much enjoyed meeting. Inspired by their invention, Grange conceived a similarly creative razor design, the shapely Protector, which launched as a men's product in 1992, followed by a women's version in 1994, and later spawned other variants. Wilkinson Sword staged its biggest-ever product launch for the product, backed by substantial marketing spend, with the press release claiming that the Protector promised 'the biggest revolution in shaving technology in 30 years'.

The sculpturally ergonomic handle of the Protector – born of the recognition that 'a user will change his grip on the handle many times during the shaving process' – demonstrates, perhaps more than any other in his archive, Grange's dedication to understanding the behaviour of products held in the hand to ensure the best possible user experience. And it was also this product that famously first introduced the daring choice of red as a colour in the shaving market, while also being produced in solid steel. In the press release Grange is quoted as saying: 'It is a remarkable razor, and I have made a wilful attempt to give it a strong personality and to make it as functional and cheerful as possible.'

By the time of his retirement from his consulting role, Grange had been instrumental in the evolution of an industry and helped turn an early utility into a safe, comfortable and style-conscious consumer product. Meanwhile, concurrently with his work for the shaving division, across the two decades he had also been variously commissioned by other divisions of Wilkinson Sword's constantly diversifying business. These projects included designs for kitchen knives, scissors, garden shears and snips, lighters, domestic electrical products and even a fencing foil, together making for one of the biggest and most fascinatingly diverse portfolios within Grange's archive.

Standard Telephones and Cables

1 (opposite). Painted wood and plastic model, made by Grange's team in the workshop at Pentagram, of a concept for an early folding telephone handset during his earlier work with the GPO and, by association, STC.

2. Grange's first direct commission from STC was for the casings of omnidirectional microphones; pictured is the STC 4113 Ribbon Cardioid, used for recording speech and music.

3. The STAR radiotelephone range of products, designed by Grange for the newly formed STC Mobile Radio Division, was intended predominantly for use by taxi companies.

2

Standard Telephones and Cables Ltd (STC), was a British manufacturer of telephone, radio and telecommunications equipment and a leading innovator in communications technologies through much of the twentieth century. Although the company had substantial engineering expertise it employed few in-house designers, so would regularly commission consultants to work on certain products when they required a particularly considered level of user experience design.

Grange first came to be commissioned by STC in 1967, after being connected through his work with the General Post Office (GPO; see pp. 72–77), which was a major commissioner and purchaser of STC products. Grange worked closely with STC's chief designer, Michael Gayford, and his first two early designs were for the casings of omnidirectional microphones. First was the 4113 Ribbon Cardioid, for which Gayford had obtained a patent for the technical design in 1963. Intended for professional

and amateur use in recording speech and music, the 4113 was a cube-shaped device fixed to a compact desktop stand. Reviews from the time describe its small size and good performance, and although it was presented as the cheapest of STC's product range it was renowned for an unusual and innovative design. This was soon followed by the 4114 Moving Coil microphone, this time housed in a more shapely, moulded case that could be placed directly on a desk or held in the hand. A threaded insert in the base also enabled it to fit onto a standard camera tripod.

When in 1968 the STC Mobile Radio Division was formed to focus on the fast-growing UK market for mobile telecommunications, Grange was brought in again as consultant designer for a brand new product range: the STAR system (Standard Telephones Advanced Radio). His brief was to use the 'most advanced techniques to produce equipment of minimum size and weight' that would also offer 'top-grade performance, reliability

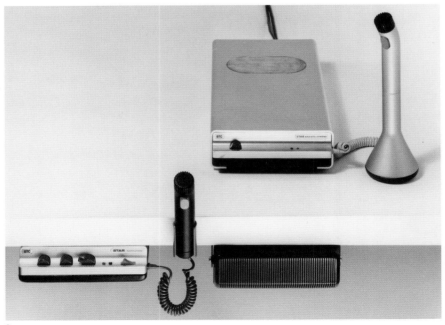

3

4

4 / 5. Prototype and working sketches for the Starphone, a nickel cadmium battery-powered pocket radio handset with internal aerial and early miniaturized printed circuits.

and convenience'. The project was led by the entrepreneurial director John Brinkley, whom Grange recalled as 'a larger than life character', who had recently joined STC after a previous role as chairman and managing director of Pye Telecommunications; he and Grange struck up a strong friendship.

Predominantly used by taxi companies, the first STAR products were an ultra-high-frequency (UHF) base-station control unit and desk microphone that served a remote vehicle radiotelephone unit, together known as the Star Mobile Radiotelephone system. The product development was rapid, taking just eighteen months from initial concept, and resulted in the first UHF products to gain industry type approval in the UK. Manufactured in compression-moulded melamine and injection-moulded ABS plastics, the housings of the units designed by Grange featured recessed buttons, avoided sharp corners and incorporated cushioning to protect the components from shock. The STAR range was soon extended with a portable UHF radio handset known as the Starphone, claimed in a press release to be 'the world's smallest UHF radiophone'; it operated from a rechargeable nickel cadmium battery and needed no external aerial, and the small size was achieved in part through advanced printed circuit designs. The whole range won Grange and STC a Council of Industrial Design (CoID) award in 1970. At this time STC was a member of the International Telephone and Telegraph group of companies, through which this range of radiotelephone equipment was exported across the world; as the CoID's magazine *Design* recorded, STC 'received orders from over thirty countries in the first year of manufacture alone'.

Grange's tenure with STC was short, but he went on to apply his experiences to the design of further telecommunications products for the GPO's division British Telecom and later also to electronics systems for Plessey (see pp. 226–231), alongside many other concepts across the fast-growing public telecommunications sector.

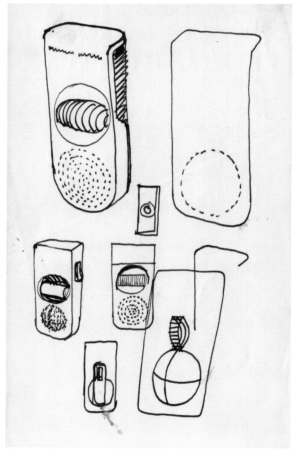

5

6 / 7. Working sketches and final prototype for a sleek desktop microphone, made in injection-moulded silver ABS plastic, which was attached to the base-station control unit of the STAR radiotelephone system.

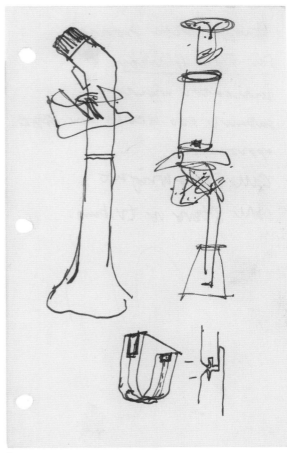

6

7

British Petroleum

In the UK the provision of private car filling station services can be dated back to 1919, but these were independent, attendant-operated sites; it would not be until the early 1960s that self-service stations first began to appear, ushering in a new era of modern convenience. The first of these self-service stations were still independently owned, but through the 1960s and into the 1970s the number of branded stations grew as oil companies looked to buy out sites, establish their own chains and consolidate the market. This resulted in the need for a more strategic approach to the retail of fuel and the associated competitive customer experience.

In the late 1960s the renowned design studio Crosby/Fletcher/Forbes (formerly Fletcher/Forbes/Gill), with which Grange had initially become acquainted through their shared client, Kodak, was commissioned by British Petroleum (BP) to conduct a review of the application of identity design across the business, ranging from typography to packaging and signage. This commission rapidly expanded to become a major study in self-service retailing, as BP looked to respond to the market opportunity and the growing competition. The project was not only to encompass graphic treatments but also to review the structure of the forecourts, the associated products and customer interfaces, and finally to deliver a full reappraisal of the function of the petrol pump. For this last part the trio recognized they would require the input of an experienced industrial designer to complement the architectural (Theo Crosby) and graphic design (Alan Fletcher and Colin Forbes) disciplines of their own studio, so they asked Grange to collaborate. The result was a substantial body of work – developed over two years and involving a large team of BP marketing staff and operations services alongside the capacity of the two small studio teams – which would provide the foundation for all BP's future service station developments.

The study began with a survey of existing self-service stations in northern Europe, where, according to an early Pentagram promotional book from 1972, their introduction 'had proceeded faster than in the UK' owing to acute labour shortages. The team made a systematic survey of practices, regulations and requirements across existing BP and competitor forecourts in the countries in question, together compiling reams of notes and sketches. This first chapter of work resulted in an initial summary concluding that 'the customer is used to the comfort of his vehicle and if he is to service himself he is entitled to equivalent protection and sophisticated equipment'. This led to a brief for the next stage of the project stating that 'each element of the station must therefore be reconsidered in terms of customer handling, cleanliness and convenience'.

In response to the report's conclusion, one of the most notable innovations recommended, and subsequently introduced, was the covered forecourt; it was advised that 'the way in which this is done will establish the quality and image of the station and the company'. This now commonplace feature was an almost non-existent element of service stations in the UK at that time, and Grange would later recall how challenging it was to persuade BP of the requirement; but the company would go on to set a precedent in the industry by implementing a 'modular, flexible, practical roof system' across its entire chain of forecourts.

Another major part of the study, the part for which Grange was predominantly engaged, was rethinking the function of the petrol pump, which had previously been designed for experienced garage staff but not for use by the general public. Grange's main design objective was to devise a mechanism that presented the self-service units to the customer in as simple a form as possible, with the report commenting that 'recent technological developments make it possible to separate dispenser from pump, relating push button selection to prices and gallonage' so that the interface presented to the customer could therefore be 'regarded as a selection and recording device'.

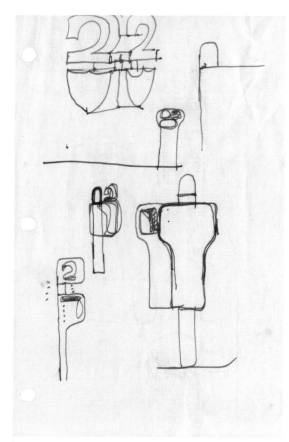

2

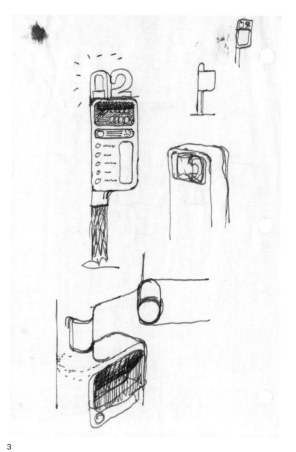

3

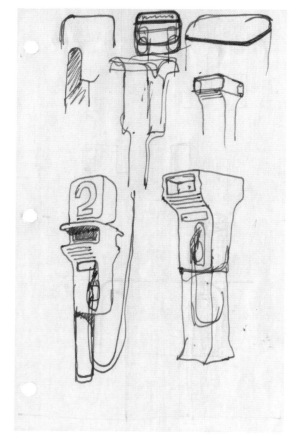

4

5

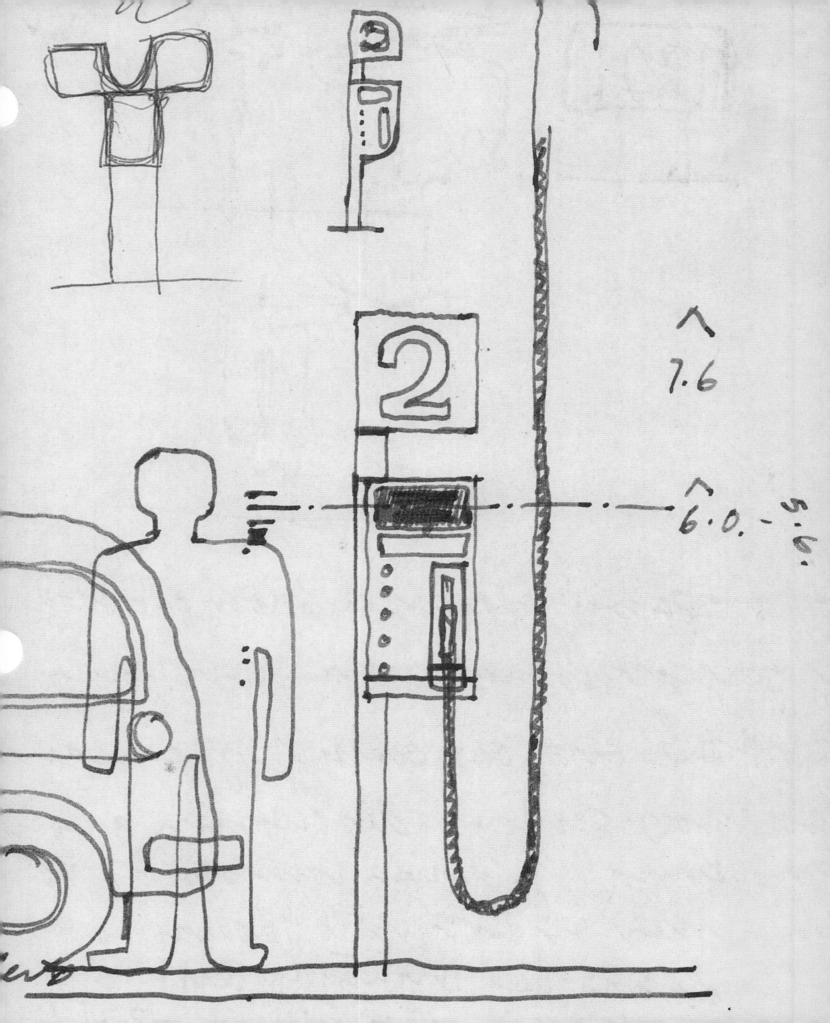

2

7.6

6.0. — 5.6.

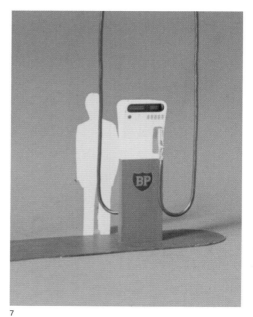

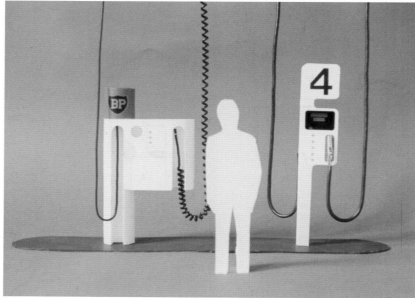

7

8

New technologies also made it possible for one electronic system to do all the work formerly carried out by individual mechanical computers at the pumps, providing one cashier with an overview of all pump positions.

From initial rough sketches, Grange and his team then progressed to making more detailed drawings of the concept units before converting these into early full-scale models to help the team visualize 'the real thing'. Made in the workshop at his Hampstead studio, these models would be presented by Grange when Crosby, Fletcher and Forbes came to visit,

greatly impressing them with his practical working processes. The initial models were constructed in wood and cardboard, to determine the ergonomics and allow for easy modification, while later versions were more advanced non-functioning prototypes using sheet metal forming, castings and fibreglass mouldings. Additional station services such as air and water dispensers, paper towels and a litter bin were later combined into a separate amenity unit for the forecourt. And once all the designs were finalized, a presentation set of general arrangement drawings was developed to complete the study.

This substantial piece of work – later recalled by Grange as 'a very enjoyable experience' – not only represented a milestone in the evolution of the consumer-facing segment of the petroleum industry in the UK, but also proved a major marker in Grange's career story. As mentioned previously, the Pentagram promotional book records that the BP project was recognized as 'outstanding among those in which Crosby/Fletcher/Forbes and Kenneth Grange discovered their mutual dependence', and the collaboration subsequently led to the formation of Pentagram in 1972, with Mervyn Kurlansky joining as the fifth partner.

7 / 8. Scale models of possible self-service fuel pump designs, made and photographed in the workshop at the Hampstead studio.

9. A later full-scale concept model for a pre-payment filling station pump solution for late-night customers.

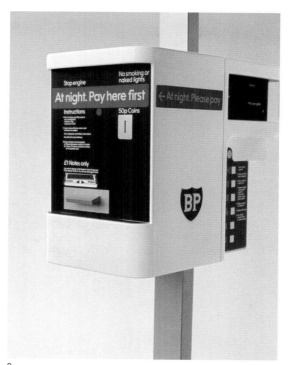

9

10

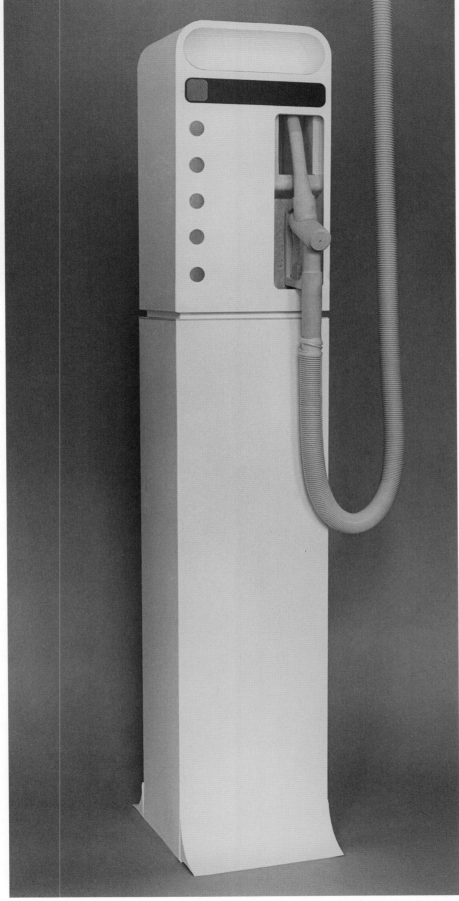

10 / 11. Further visual records of the full-scale models for double (above) and single (right) self-service fuel pump designs, built and photographed in the workshop at the Hampstead studio. Although this research project did lead to BP pioneering a new era of self-service filling stations, the models themselves are lost to time.

11

Harvey

1 (opposite). A promotional image, shot under spotlights in a photographic studio, for the launch of the Inter-space range of radically modern, modular office furniture.

2. *Business Systems and Equipment* magazine, November 1972. The cover caption (inside) reads: 'The man in the suit is Kenneth Grange. *BS&E* photographed him with some of the desks he has designed for G. A. Harvey, during launching ceremonies in Amsterdam. The desks are part of the Inter-space range which is being pushed with great ballyhoo into the £100 million-a-year European furniture market.'

Founded in the late nineteenth century, G. A. Harvey became a leading British manufacturer of all-metal storage units in the first half of the twentieth century, providing industrial, office and academic premises with a range of products from industrial storage tanks and vast shelving systems to filing cabinets and changing room lockers. By the late 1960s the enterprising company directors were refocused on gaining a larger share of the emerging modern office furniture sector in the UK, while also spotting a developing opportunity to increase exports to the booming, design-conscious office market in Europe, through Britain's upcoming joining of the EEC (European Economic Community).

To meet this vision, and also ensure a strong proposition to counter stylish European imports, it was felt that the company required a suitably 'futuristic new look' for their office furniture offering, which included desks, storage, trolleys, partitioning and filing systems. So, via an introduction from the Council of Industrial Design (CoID) through the Design Selection Service, the company directors turned to the person whom they considered – as reported in *Design* magazine – 'the best man for the job to predict future trends in office furniture'.

For Grange, this would be a rare foray into the world of furniture design, though during those same few years he was also working on the highly futuristic Confravision video conferencing studio concept for the GPO (see pp. 72–77), which also involved consideration of furnishings for an efficient and comfortable working environment.

Explaining the reasoning behind the brief, and describing a vision for 'the end of box-shaped metal desks in box-shaped, overcrowded rooms', a Harvey report forecast that 'work patterns are changing; the more boring clerical tasks are gradually being taken over by computers and calculators. Different projects require different office configurations to achieve rapid results.' The brief requested that Grange's design solution be 'compatible for volume sales' and deliver an 'untraditional twist' on the conventions of office furniture. But beyond that it was also a future-gazing brief: a consideration of trends in the future of the working environment. Since new commercial furniture designs could take from two to five years to come to market and further years to reach peak sales, and taking into account that these furniture pieces would be in use around the world for a substantial period, Grange was required to 'predict the preferences and requirements of office workers a decade into the future'.

Forecasting a move away from small, walled rooms towards more flexible open-plan office layouts, Grange chose 'space utilisation, flexibility and appeal' as the three most important attributes, explaining this in terms of the increasing expense of office space, the fact that workers 'wanted to better adapt their surroundings to suit their working preferences' and

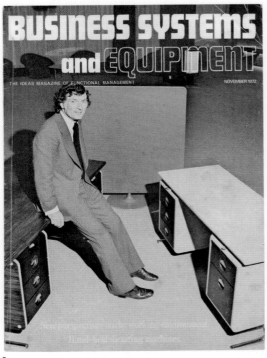

2

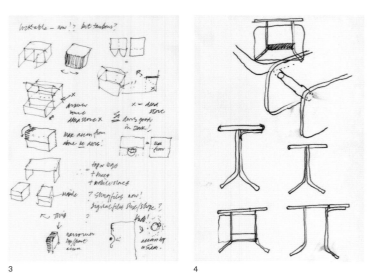

3

4

3 / 4. Exploratory sketches for the desk system functionality, including how two storage pedestals might suspend under a desk and how the bent tubular-steel desk legs might be shaped to avoid the risk of bruised knees.

5 / 7. Various storage units, featuring tambour shutters, that could be fitted into a modular desk and shelving layout as required.

6. A magazine advertisement for the Inter-space furniture range, featuring a suitably futuristic font.

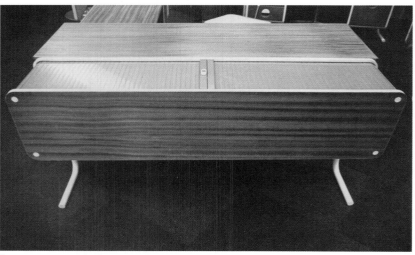

5

6

7

8. A pedestal filing system referencing the same bent tubular steelwork as the desk legs, in this context not to avoid bruised knees but to allow easier access to the storage tray below.

8

that they were 'becoming more concerned about the way their environment looks'.

His resulting design solution presented a modular system of units intended to 'fit any office environment, whether administrative, secretarial or top executive'. Hard edges and corners were replaced with smooth curves, bent steel was combined with a choice of hardwood or veneer surfaces, and light, cheerful colours were introduced. *Design* magazine noted that 'Grange's principal innovation lay in convincing the firm of the economic and structural advantages of using timber as a material', while the 'untraditional touches' requested in the brief were to be found 'in the splay-footed tubular-steel framework and the intelligent linear filing boxes' that featured slatted roller shutters (tambour shutters). Overall this new range was quite a departure and the media joyfully reported the additional benefit in the way in which the curved steel structures avoided the 'leg in every corner' and much reduced the risk of 'bruised knees and laddered tights'.

The range was priced competitively with existing modern furniture brands in Europe, and Harvey stated in the official press release that it would 'appeal to the lower/middle end of the market because of its pricing and to the higher end because of its aesthetics, versatility and flexibility'. The final range, named Inter-space, was first presented in London and Copenhagen before being officially launched in Amsterdam in late 1972, where the presentation was, according to media reports, unveiled to the futuristic theme music from the film *2001: A Space Odyssey*.

AJ Binns

1 (opposite). The award-winning Variset cloakroom system comprised a wall-mounted modular system of extruded-aluminium hooks, with slim-profile acrylic coat hangers later being added.

2. A page spread from Grange's sketchbooks capturing his evolving ideas around the shape of the wall hooks for the Variset system.

In 1964 a young product designer by the name of Julian Binns, recently graduated from London's renowned Central School of Arts and Crafts, came to work for Grange as an assistant designer at the Hampstead office. Three years later he would depart to take on the running of his father's ironmongery business, AJ Binns, in Leicester. However a year later, in 1968, he called the studio to ask if Grange might be interested in designing some new products for the company, an approach that sparked a new working relationship between the two that would endure for more than three decades.

AJ Binns had been established by John Binns in 1937 after he previously worked as a director of the Dryad Metal Works, a renowned British ironmongery manufacturer that Grange had known in the days when he worked for Jack Howe. When Grange first visited AJ Binns, in 1969, the business had recently been split into two specialist divisions:

one for industrial fencing and gates, and the other specializing in cloakroom ironmongery for the emerging sports and leisure industry. The latter would be the division with which Grange would work.

Grange's first commission was a new modular hat and coat hanging system, predominantly for cloakrooms; the brief asked for a versatile wall-mounted system based on 'good looks, high quality materials and the flexibility to suit a wide range of applications'. Grange took as his starting point the consideration that 'fixtures in hard-wearing environments can become quickly tarnished by re-painting or by the work of vandals' and the observation that hooks were 'all too often simply fixed by caretakers to haphazard wooden battens'. With both these points in mind he devised an aluminium internal spine for the row of hooks, which would permanently fix to the wall; over this a variety of colourful modular cover segments with double

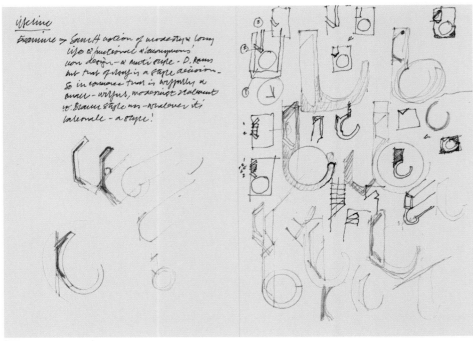

2

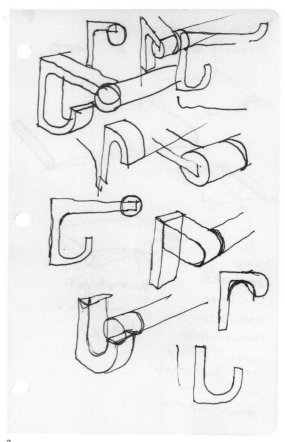

3

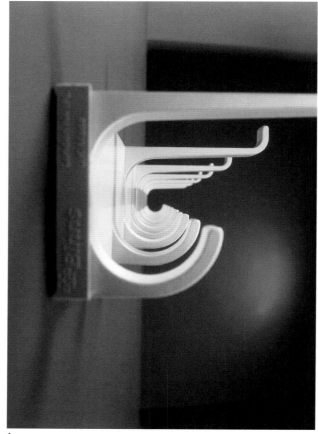

4

and single hook components could be slid with ease, and equally easily replaced. The hooks were fabricated from extruded aluminium, sliced in profile – a manufacturing method he knew from experience with Hope's (see pp. 90–93) and Taylor Instruments (see pp. 114–117), and chosen for its low capital cost during mass production – and then anodized or coated with epoxy resin. Managing to 'gracefully combine style with a robust high-functioning structure', Grange explained that when providing the framework to hang a lot of coats the weight consideration becomes 'really very formidable', stressing that the functional aspect of a component as simple as a coat hook in a public place 'is much more complex than it looks'.

The resulting range was named Variset – referencing the variable, modular nature of the system – and won a Council of Industrial Design (CoID) award in 1972; the awards issue of the CoID's *Design* magazine noted it as 'one of the first adjustable systems of integrated hat and coat hooks in aluminium'. The standard of AJ Binns' manufacture was renowned for its precision and material finish and the range was immediately highly successful; it is still in production today and, although additions and updated features have been introduced, the core design remains unchanged. Its success sparked

Grange to comment that the design was a good example of 'the value of raising the quality of the most seemingly mundane everyday product'. The AJ Binns catalogue proclaimed: 'Variset multiple hook units will save labour costs – simply screw backplate to wall, slide on hooks and spacers, screw in end pressure plates and finally snap in end caps. It's easy! No need for careful measuring to obtain even spacing and alignment – Variset ensures this.'

Over the following years Grange developed further coat hook systems for the company, including a high-density solution for use in commercial cloakrooms and the Reverse hook system for safety in schools, as well as a beautiful line of beech-slatted cantilever benches.

3 / 4. A further page of sketches of a more refined final form of the Variset hooks, from Grange's notebooks, with a side image of the final system with semicircular central profile.

5

6

7

5 / 6. The Variset cloakroom hook system features a sturdy wall bracket onto which hook and panel modules can be easily slid, making it simple to change the arrangement or replace damaged units.

7. An alternative hook system, the Reverse, offered increased safely in school cloakroom environments.

8

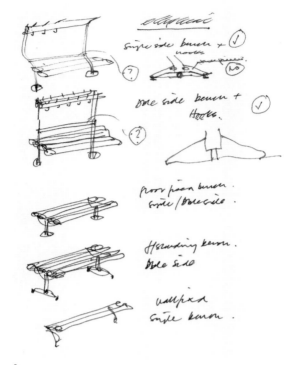

9

8. One of many certificates in Grange's archive, this one awarded to AJ Binns for the Variset range in the CoID Design Awards 1972.

9. A page from Grange's sketchbooks exploring ideas for a wooden slatted cloakroom bench system with variable widths, as part of the Variset system.

10. A three-slat bench option in the cloakroom bench system, here installed in a sports changing room setting.

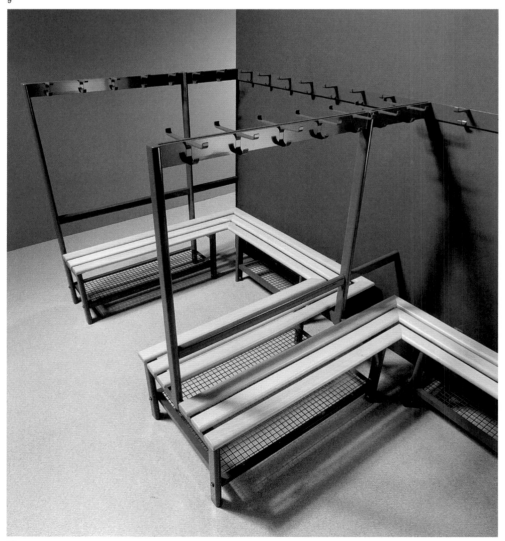

10

11. A page spread from Grange's sketchbooks exploring ideas for another bench system to expand the Variset offering, this time as a stand-alone solution for floor or wall fixing.

12. A detailed drawing of a cross-section through an extruded aluminium slat, which was a material option for the final bench specification.

13. The final bench design, named the Elliptical range, pictured here with hardwood slats. The bench units can be fabricated to be one, two or three slats wide.

11

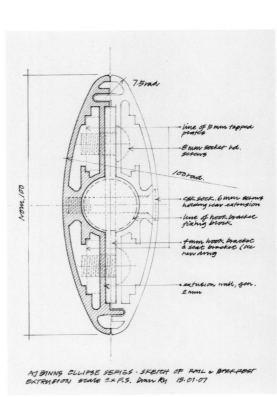

12

13

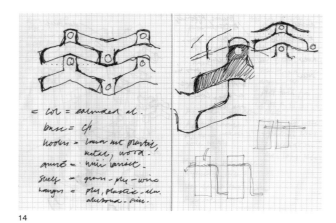

14

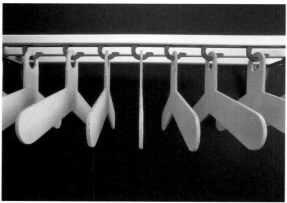

15

Grange recalled that he and the AJ Binns team 'really pushed the boat out' when conducting product development work trialling 'new techniques for prototyping' during this time. And this period of work would also lead to Grange conceiving another notable design icon for the company: a slim-profile coat hanger, which was produced for years after. The acrylic hanger was applied to a sliding captive system with nylon straps for hospitality applications, or offered as individual units hooked onto Variset pegs for changing rooms and personal wardrobes. This second application also involved a variation in the hanger design that featured an open corner: Grange described this as 'allowing trousers to slide off easily, removing a real irritation found in normal coat hangers'.

The AJ Binns chapter is a good example of the strong, long-time client relationship for which Grange became renowned. This relationship endured well beyond his retirement from Pentagram in 1997 and he continued to work on new product designs, including variations on the concept he had developed for a cloakroom bench, in the years following his return to practising as Kenneth Grange Design and until Julian Binns retired from the business in 2003.

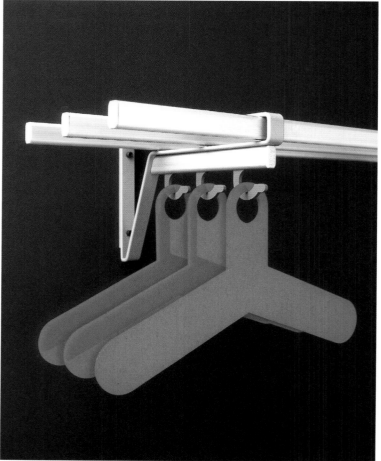

16

14. Notebook sketches of the flat hanger system devised by Grange to make manufacture as cost-efficient as possible through tessellating the hanger shape to make the most of the sheet of material from which they were cut.

15 / 16. The final Variset flat hangers, in plywood and acrylic, fit neatly onto a variety of pegs or hooks at different orientations, or can slide onto a fixed pole for an option where the hangers cannot be removed.

17. The 'moulded hanger' option for changing rooms, devised by Grange to make it easier to slide a pair of trousers on and off the hanger, a pet frustration of his.

17

Tribute to Johan Santer

1

In 2021 a long-time friend and valued design assistant to Grange and later designer at Kenwood, Johan Santer, died; he had been a healthy seventy-one-year-old and this was a shock to everyone who knew him. Another good friend, Paul Anthony, set about designing a tribute to Santer, whom he had known for many years when they had both worked at Pentagram. Anthony had worked for Alan Fletcher, one of the original partners with Grange, and he and Santer had worked together as part of a close-knit team on product and graphic designs for AJ Binns. After Santer died, spotting that the distinctive hook of the Variset range was shaped like a 'J' for Johan, Anthony transformed this icon into a beautifully boxed gift to be given to everyone at the funeral. Grange remarked that this ingenious creative gesture demonstrated the 'real affection' and pride the team had felt for one another and for their projects together at Pentagram.

'Perhaps the most rewarding aspect of working as a team was how interdependent we became, with consequent friendships lasting our entire lives. Such teams have key figures, and Johan was our key. He was stone-deaf to any entreaty when busy finding solutions to a design problem …'

Kenneth Grange

1. The boxed tribute gift set in memory of Johan Santer.

Clark Design

Recorded in Grange's archives is a concept for an early liquid crystal digital clock that never made it into production. The only physical record that exists is an immaculate working prototype in Grange's collection of models, made during the early years of Pentagram.

The project was commissioned in 1973 by young business entrepreneur Gerald Clark, of G. D. Clark Design Co. Ltd, a small consumer goods consultancy based in London and Perth, Scotland. Clark had persuaded financiers to back a new product during the early days of the highly competitive electronic clock boom; so, in a story told by Grange that has settled into legend, Clark visited the studio in Hampstead to propose a brief for the design. As *Design* magazine later reported, he brought with him a 'beautifully made Scandinavian peppermill' to illustrate the kind of quality he was after – elegant, solid and purposeful – while Grange was quoted as saying, 'there aren't too many clients who come to you and impress upon you that the look of their product must be as good as what's inside it', especially in mass production, where 'so many mass-produced items today look almost tired'.

On departing after the meeting, this 'greatly likeable character' left the team with a number of sample components and brimming with enthusiasm. Given the encouragement to explore something 'a little unusual', Grange and the team set to work and devised a prototype with 'a very conspicuous cantilever' that gave the product the appearance of defying gravity. The motherboard was housed in the stem, while the interface board and display panels were fixed at right angles. The body, proposed in a range of colours, was made in ABS plastic, sand-blasted and lightly oiled to prevent finger marks.

When they presented the prototype to Clark he was delighted with it, commissioning product photography and printed promotional materials in which the clock was named the Alto. However, following this flurry of activity, and despite the design attracting positive early attention and coverage in

Design magazine, with claims of confirmed orders from European distributors, the funding never materialized, the clock never went into production and the client was never seen again.

More recently Grange critiqued his design as not the most intelligent as far as problem-solving design for simple production was concerned, as it would 'wilfully fall over' were it not for the additional weight that had to be included in the base. But he acknowledged the great value to entrepreneurial clients of being able to cost-effectively test new product ideas through design studios such as his, as well as the fact that it gave him and his team a chance to 'indulge their design enthusiasms'. And he appreciated that the promotional materials for the clock anyway produced 'a lot of good PR mileage'.

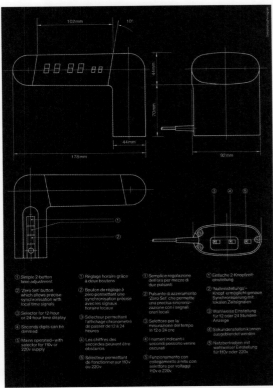

2

Reuters

1 (opposite). A later-edition NPK colour monitor and keyboard, displaying the 'much praised, much copied and never bettered' logotype designed by Alan Fletcher, a commission that later led to Grange's involvement in the design of the terminals themselves.

2. The clean and simple original keyboard, in pressed aluminium, was part of Grange's first design for the company: the industry-changing Reuter Monitor.

3. Following the initial success of the Reuter Monitor, Grange developed a smaller workstation solution for dealers, to be more economical on desk space.

Founded in London in 1851, the international news agency Reuters rapidly built up a formidable reputation both for the rigour of its early financial news reporting and for the speed at which it could deliver the latest reports to its subscribers. The organization had more staff and stringers across the globe than any of the competition and being based in London, the unrivalled centre of news reporting, it benefited greatly from British control of cable lines.

Innovation was always at the forefront of the Reuters service, with substantial investment made in employing the latest communication technologies. The organization's expansion into Asia and South America in the 1870s had been made possible by advances in overland telegraphs and undersea cables, while in 1883 Reuters became the first news agency to begin transmitting messages electrically to the London newspapers. By 1923 it had pioneered the use of radio to transmit news internationally, and in the early 1960s it became one of the first news agencies to transmit financial data globally via computer.

However, the decades since the Second World War also saw the business making substantial financial losses and slowly declining as competition increased and the market moved ever faster. When Gerald Long was appointed as new managing director in 1963 he set out to aggressively transform the fortunes of Reuters and reignite the organization's image as an innovative, cutting-edge player.

Spurred on by Long, Reuters initially approached the architect and designer Theo Crosby to design an interior scheme for the organization's new Fleet Street headquarters. Soon afterwards Crosby joined forces with the renowned graphic designers Alan Fletcher and Colin Forbes to form the highly acclaimed studio Crosby/Fletcher/Forbes, and through this alliance encouraged Reuters to commission Fletcher to design a new corporate identity. The resulting logotype, unveiled in 1965 and based on the pattern of punched holes in teleprinter tape, subsequently became one of the world's most recognized and enduring identities, in Grange's words 'much praised, much copied and never bettered'. This was followed by further typographic work in the form of a more legible alphabet for a proposed new range of Reuters electronic information terminals – the point at which Grange would be brought on board.

By the late 1960s, with Long's assurance to the board of Reuters that the investment was sound,

2

3

4

5

6

the Reuters Economic Services (RES) division was well down the path to developing an advanced computerized financial information system run from Fleet Street, to support finance houses and traders in the global financial markets. Long had recognized that, in the fast-moving world of trading, the speed of access to the latest financial news was critical to success; just as key was the ability for a user to quickly interrogate the data and retrieve only that which they personally required.

Managed by two bright talents, Michael Nelson and Glen Renfrew – the general managers of RES in the UK and the USA respectively – the underlying proprietary technology in this new information terminal was to become a game-changer both for Reuters and for the industry. However, to meet Long's vision of international brand recognition, the physical terminal needed to 'function impeccably and look the part too'. And so it was that Crosby/ Fletcher/Forbes, which had recently collaborated with Grange on the BP research study and were in the process of joining forces with him and Mervyn Kurlansky to form Pentagram, recommended that Grange join the project and work with the Reuters team on the design of the terminal. So, in the early 1970s, Grange embarked with the engineering team at RES – then headed by David Ure, whom Grange came to know well – on developing a distinctive form for the first generation of the revolutionary

4. Early sketches from Grange's notebooks, exploring options for a desktop stand for a monitor, to lift the screen to comfortable eye level.

5 / 6. The original Reuter Monitor, with separable keyboard, had a highly recognizable profile formed from pressed aluminium sheet, and became a distinctive symbol on desks across international trading floors.

7

7. Grange ensured the ventilation holes on the reverse of the monitor reflected the revered Reuters logotype, which references the punched holes in a teleprinter tape.

desk-based terminal that would become known as the Reuter Monitor.

The terminal was designed specifically for its particular function and environment, and with the visionary aim that it would become highly recognizable, respected and essential desk equipment across international trading floors: the first machine of its kind. With this in mind Grange conceived the design as a 'fitting physical representation' of Reuters' status – as a prestige piece of equipment of higher quality than the normal office standard. The design introduced an upright display with separable keyboard that could either tuck neatly under the overhang of the screen or be pulled closer to the user. The striking shape of the case was formed in heavy-gauge aluminium sheet, creating a sharply modern profile. Turning out to be to the stylistic benefit of the product, sheet metal had been specified instead of injection-moulded plastic in order to keep the tooling costs down for an initial small production run forecast to be just fifty units.

The Reuter Monitor Money Rates (RMMR) service was launched in 1973, presenting the international trading sector with a first generation terminal that Grange described as demonstrating 'a strong design thrust and a clear message to their customers that Reuters are a visibly progressive company'. The industry response was phenomenal and immediate, with thousands of RMMR service subscriptions placed and monitors rapidly appearing on desks across the world's trading floors. Within a decade of launch, and just as Long had envisioned, the RMMR service had rebooted both the image and the profitability of the company. The Reuters publicity reviewed the monitor as having enabled the company to 'continue to be in the thick of it, at the forefront of emerging industries', while *Design* magazine reported that 'the increasing miniaturisation of the hidden microelectronics offer the designer liberating opportunities for exploring the visual, tactile and other sensory aspects of the product'.

8. A large sheet of sketches exploring a later model of the Reuter terminal, with a more angular, futuristic feel to suit the confidence of the 1980s.

9 / 10. Building on the success of the original terminal, Grange proposed further iterations, here a solution that offered a tilting monitor screen for improved visibility.

8

9

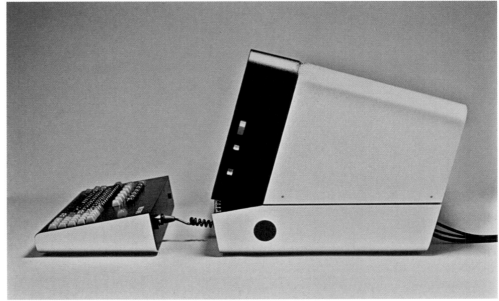

10

'You learn by disassembly. That's one of my great enthusiasms. You learn more by taking something apart than ever trying to invent it to start. In fact, all good engineering is about disassembly. I still practise it today.'

Kenneth Grange

11. One of a number of proposals for colour-coded keyboard layouts for the later NPK colour monitor.

Grange proceeded to design further variations of the keyboards and displays over the following years, including a mini monitor version, an iteration with adjustable anti-reflection screen, a colour monitor and even a complete trading desk unit with in-built terminal. He continued to work with Nelson and Renfrew well into the 1980s, the latter becoming the new managing director of Reuters after Long's retirement in 1981. The Reuters story as a whole is an excellent example of the Pentagram business model working as intended – as a multidisciplinary offering comprised of solo talents but collaborating variously on client projects.

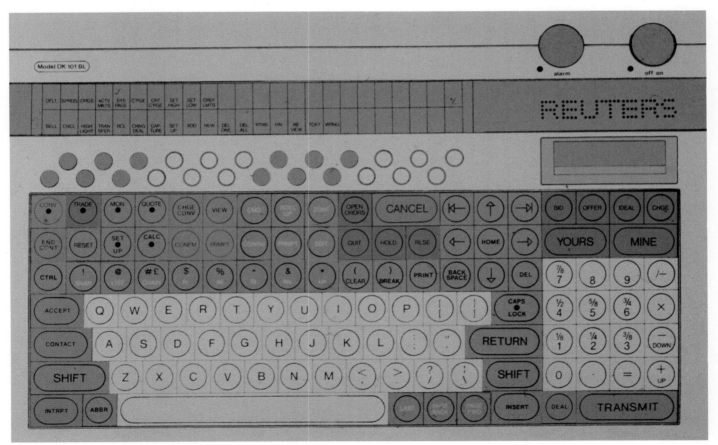

Glug Bottle

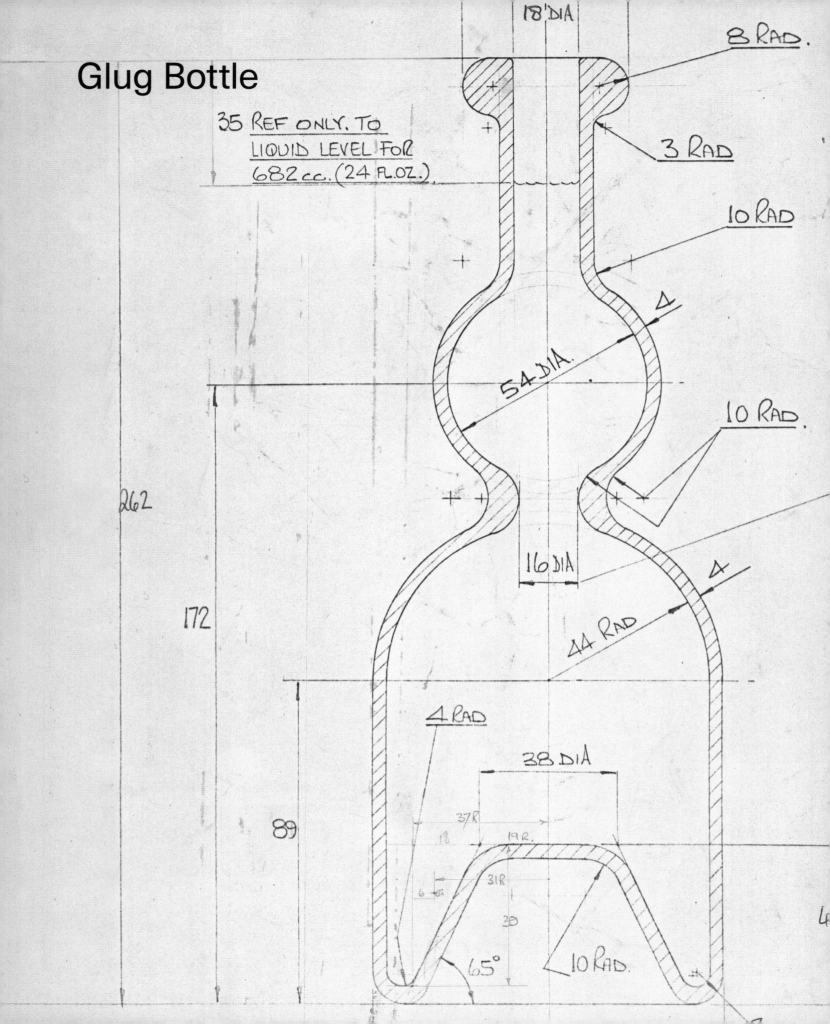

18'DIA

8 RAD.

3 RAD

10 RAD

35 REF ONLY. TO
LIQUID LEVEL FOR
682 cc. (24 FL.OZ.)

10 RAD.

54 DIA.

262

16 DIA

4

172

44 RAD

4 RAD

38 DIA

89

37R

18

19R.

31R

6

30

65°

10 RAD.

1 (opposite). Scale drawing of the final design of a sherry bottle proposed by Grange, with a carefully calculated bubble in the neck to cause a 'satisfying glugging sound' on pouring.

2. Three full-scale models showing the development of the proposed sherry bottle, from wooden version used to perfect the dimensions, through a polystyrene whole form, to the final glossy-painted presentation model for the client.

Grange has often commented that 'a pleasure much sought but not often associated with product design is wit', following this with the conjecture that 'if it is functional, beautiful and has some element of the unexpected, then surely this is the product we would most like to own and keep'. An example he has often referred to in this context – a project where he once attempted to 'bring some wit to a solemn situation' – is his bottle design for Cock, Russell & Spedding Ltd, a London wine merchant.

This was a loyal client of the celebrated graphic designer Alan Fletcher, who in the early 1970s was one of the five founding partners of Pentagram. Over the years Fletcher designed many striking labels for the bottles introduced by the merchant to the UK market from Europe. So when in 1974 it asked Fletcher to design a distinctive new graphic identity for its La Riva sherry, in the new-found Pentagram collaborative style he and Grange immediately discussed how they might deliver a response

'employing more than one creative discipline'. The pair shared the approach of always delivering 'more than was originally asked', so they settled on Grange devising a new bottle design to accompany Fletcher's graphic solution.

In devising the bottle, Grange drew inspiration from the 'cheerful noise made by a special shape of sake flask' that he had enjoyed during his recent business trips to Japan to visit Maruzen, so he set about creating a similarly pleasing effect for the sherry bottle, to 'enhance the moment of pouring'. After much testing, the design Grange settled on featured a 'perfectly balanced balloon' incorporated into the neck of the bottle, which, on tipping the bottle to pour the sherry, momentarily trapped a small amount of air; this captured air, once released by the force of the descending liquid, would cause 'a pleasing glug sound'.

Endless models were made by Grange's workshop team, and much time invested in sculpting and

2

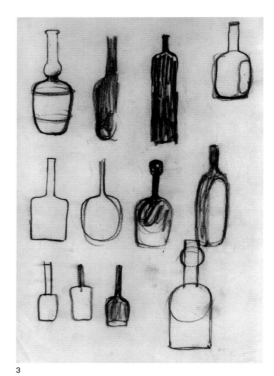

3

measuring the optimum volume and flow of liquid, before a preferred solution was reached. It was just this sort of project that highlighted the 'exceptional skills' that Grange often championed within his team, particularly those of his long-time friend and 'genius constructor' Bruce Watters, who had joined Grange in the Hampstead studio in 1968 and continued to run the workshop activities for three decades, right through Grange's years at Pentagram. Watters was a traditional model maker by trade, and Grange never ceased to marvel at his expansive ingenuity, problem-solving abilities and superlative talent for 'a spray and rub-down finish'. Grange acknowledged that it was Watters who had dedicated himself to making the numerous models for the evolving sherry bottle-with-balloon design, happily employing his latest 'workshop toy', a vacuum former, to great effect in the process.

By all accounts, although they had set out to commission simply a new graphic identity, the client did love the distinctive design and the 'surprise element of theatre' of the bottle concept; and Grange admitted that it 'gurgled beautifully'. However, as is so often the case when it comes to commercial production, the reality of the cost of manufacture for the relatively small number of bottle units required was deemed financially unviable. So the client progressed only with Fletcher's graphic elements. But the story of this much-enjoyed project, which far overstepped its original brief, was joyfully celebrated in Grange's exhibition 'Those That Got Away' staged at the Pentagram studios in 2003.

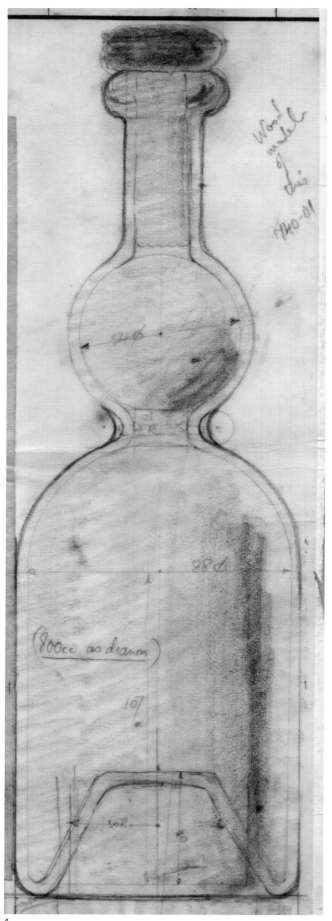

4

3. Early sketches of various bottle forms, finally arriving at the beginnings of an idea to introduce a bubble in the neck.

4. A drawing exploring thickness of glass walls, moulding of the base, and the resulting internal dimensions, given to Grange's head of workshop, Bruce Watters, to make a wooden model, as the note instructs.

5 (right). A glossy presentation model of Grange's final design, complete with gold branding. Unfortunately the client could not be persuaded to take it on, so the 'glug bottle' never made it to production.

ANT. DE LA RIVA
REZ DE LA FRONTERA
ESTABLISHED 1776

LA RIVA AMONTILLADO SHERRY

PRODUCE OF SPAIN
SHIPPED BY
COCK RUSSELL & SPENDER
FROM THEIR OWN
VINEYARDS
MIN. CONTENTS 26 FL. OZ

Parker

Since launching the revolutionary, bestselling Parker 51 in 1939, marketed as 'the world's most wanted pen', the Parker Pen Company had been synonymous with high-quality, innovative – if expensive – fountain pens. But by the 1960s, with the evolution of the rollerball pen offering cheaper and easier options for everyday use, and companies such as Bic flooding the market, fountain pens were on a downward trend. Parker especially had gained a staid image in Europe, so in 1971 a research report by the European marketing team recommended that as it was schools and younger users in particular that were transitioning to using the hassle-free rollerball, they should therefore be the target audience for a new range of pens by Parker. In response the company developed a carefully targeted brief for a 'student pen' that would be 'more affordable, fun and innovative' than anything Parker had previously released, aimed at the eighteen-to-thirty age group, a market in Europe calculated at a potential ten million users.

Having until this point always undertaken the design of new pens in-house in the USA, with only minor adjustments made for European manufacture, Parker decided this time to commission a European designer for the job. The team at Parker's US advertising agency, J. Walter Thompson, immediately recommended Grange, who was at that time just transitioning to work under the banner of Pentagram. He had originally come to their attention a few years previously when he designed a new typewriter for Litton Industries, the US owner of Imperial Typewriters, which also employed J. Walter Thompson as its advertising agency.

Grange would later credit how insightful the well-researched brief had been, as it 'stepped so boldly outside their traditional market'. The brief stated that the new pen design should focus on being 'cost-effective for mass production to enable it to retail affordably', and therefore should 'have as few parts as possible, be designed for automatic assembly,

apply minimum finishing processes and restrict the requirement for servicing'. The production of the pen would benefit from Parker's existing sophisticated manufacturing capabilities, including the ability to deep-draw pressed stainless steel, an 'impressively efficient' production process much admired by Grange that had first captured his imagination when inspecting how aluminium cigar tubes were made.

At the time of Grange's receiving the brief, in 1972, the NASA Apollo missions had not long concluded and the space-age theme had been sweeping across style and popular culture. Starting with an existing nib and ink cartridge unit, Grange opted to design a rocket-shaped profile for the casing of the new pen, featuring a stepped barrel that allowed the pen lid to slip over the end without overlap, giving a sleek outline when the pen was in use.

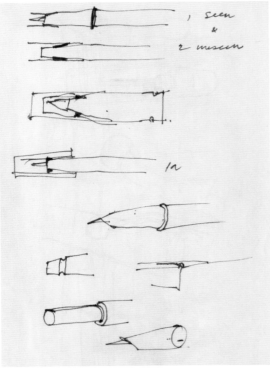

2

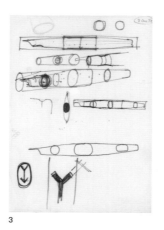

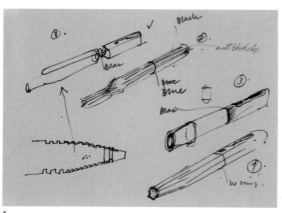

3

4

At the same time, a substantial share of the design and development period was dedicated to rethinking the classic symbol of the Parker pen – the arrow clip. The brief permitted this to be reworked, as it was judged it might otherwise inhibit a new style. In place of the original metal arrow, Grange devised a simple, efficient stainless steel strip with a small rounded plastic button to act as a buffer against the fabric of a pocket.

These various stylistic judgments and material specifications together resulted in a cost-efficient and visibly futuristic departure from traditional pens, and immediately attracted attention when the final production pen was presented by Parker at an annual sales conference in 1975. The first version launched to market was a stainless steel fountain pen, known as a flighter; and what had started life intended as a pen for students fast became a sophisticated modern status symbol for a style-conscious, upwardly mobile younger market: the Parker 25 was born.

The pen was a huge commercial success, with millions of units sold, and became the principal product in the international Parker range. In 1978 this European design was introduced into the US catalogues, which extolled its 'rugged, functional, space-age' design. Other variations, including a rollerball, felt tip and ballpoint version, would launch across the following years, in various colourways. And the Parker 25 series continued to be manufactured, design unchanged, until the mid-1990s – a lifetime of twenty years.

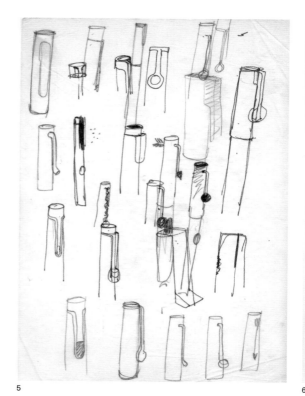

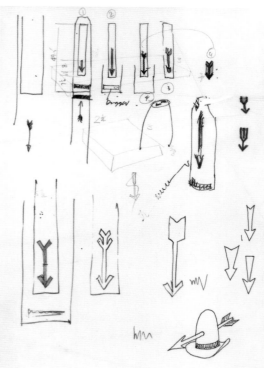

5

6

7. Side view of the Parker 25 fountain pen showing the stepped profile – inspired by the forms of rockets, following NASA's recent Apollo missions – which allowed the lid to fit neatly over the barrel.

8. Parker 25 rollerball, felt tip and ballpoint versions would launch in subsequent years, produced in smooth matt plastic and available in a range of colourways. The series was continued for twenty years.

7

8

Bowers & Wilkins

1 (opposite). Close-up detail of the front of a DM3000 loudspeaker, showing the attention to detail in the fixtures framing the iconic gold Kevlar-fibre speaker cone, an innovative feature unique to B&W.

2 / 3. Early explorations in response to the brief for a loudspeaker cabinet shaped to house a linear phase arrangement of the three driver units, stepped gradually backwards from bottom to top.

The premium British loudspeaker brand Bowers & Wilkins (B&W) began life in a small radio and electronics shop in the seaside town of Worthing, Sussex, after the Second World War where, alongside Roy Wilkins's turntable sales and TV rentals, John Bowers would assemble speaker systems for private customers. In 1966, after inheriting £10,000 from a satisfied customer, Bowers invested in setting up a separate loudspeaker manufacturing business.

The first B&W loudspeaker models developed by Bowers rapidly built a strong industry reputation for their technical performance and, although initially comprising a team of only five, the company punched well above its size, winning a Queen's Award to Industry in 1973. Around this time the visionary Bowers, recognizing the commercial potential of securing a designer to work alongside his world-class team of engineers, was recommended to meet with Grange by Antony Armstrong-Jones, Lord Snowdon, who knew Grange through the Design Council (previously the Council of Industrial Design). This introduction to Bowers would lead to one of Grange's most long-lasting and treasured client relationships: the two men forged a strong working rapport from the start through 'a shared passion for delivering excellence', and together established an enduring culture of design within the business. Grange was appointed the company's consultant designer in 1974 and would deliver on designs for a wide variety of loudspeaker cabinets across the following four decades.

Grange quickly gained respect throughout the business for his in-depth understanding of the engineering requirements as well as the design

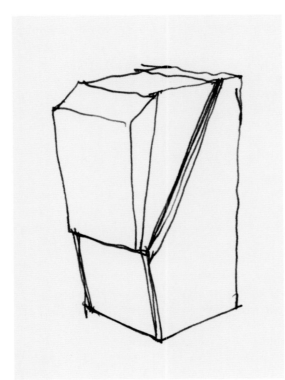

2

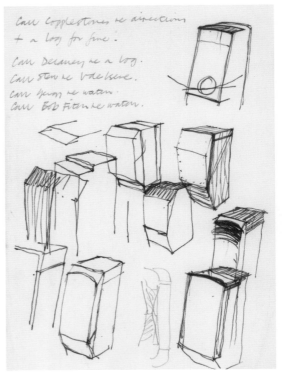

3

4. A further sketch as the final stepped design solution becomes gradually clearer and more refined.

5. Outline drawing of the final volume of Grange's first speaker cabinet design, which would become the DM6.

4

potential of the speaker cabinets, and would always engage at an early stage with the engineering team as each new acoustic prototype was established. He would later recall that the B&W team were 'a very active, inventive team of engineers, coming at it almost exclusively from the point of view of acoustic performance' – whereas he would always come at it 'from two points of view: performance, principally, but also style'.

Grange's first design, the DM6, launched in 1976, was Britain's first linear phase loudspeaker and quickly gained the affectionate nickname 'the pregnant penguin' for its distinctive black-and-white form. It was the first speaker to explore a 'phase-optimized' arrangement of the three driver units inside the cabinet, meaning that the bass, mid-range and tweeter were each stepped back from the façade, thus creating the unusual profile.

This design solution enabled B&W, for the first time in its evolution, to achieve 'the holy grail of linear phase sound', where sound waves from the different drivers, travelling at different frequencies, would all meet with clarity at the ear of the listener.

The DM6 was rapidly followed in 1977 by the DM7, which took the industry-leading step of 'liberating the tweeter' from the cabinet for the first time, bringing greater clarity to the delicate treble output. Grange's now famous tweeter-on-top solution – the speed of development and testing of this innovation significantly facilitated by investment from B&W in early computer-aided design (CAD) – received Design Council recognition, and was henceforth integrated across the majority of the company's products.

However, it was Grange's subsequent design that would be hailed as the model that truly introduced 'the modern era of hi-fi', bringing all existing research and engineering innovation together to revolutionize the listening experience. The iconic 801, launched in 1979, responded to Bowers's free-rein brief to create something that was 'clearly superior to anything that had come before', and which would be 'the best loudspeaker the world had ever heard'. Across an extraordinary four years of in-depth research, facilitated by B&W's further investment in state-of-the-art acoustic testing equipment, the combined team more than delivered.

Through the process Grange and his workshop team would build full-scale models of the volumetric parts of the design – such as the tweeter casing and the mid-range box – which the B&W engineering team would then use to analyse the acoustic performance, applying the novel process of numerical optimization, measuring and comparing the working model with a computer-simulated ideal. Grange would subsequently receive the test results, refining the forms and the structural detail accordingly; and thus, gradually, the design of the 801 was honed.

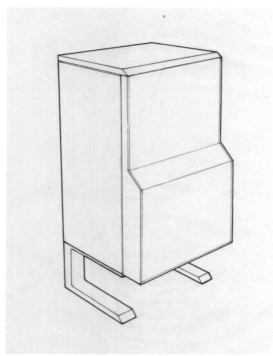

5

6. The DM6 was the first commercial loudspeaker in the UK to deliver a phase-optimized listening experience, and helped to secure B&W as a pioneer at the forefront of loudspeaker innovation.

7. The DM7 placed the tweeter clear of the main cabinet for the first time – another B&W innovation made visually eye-catching by Grange's design solution.

6

7

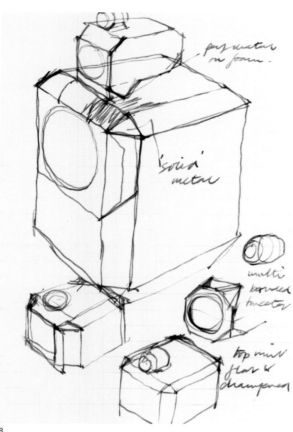

8

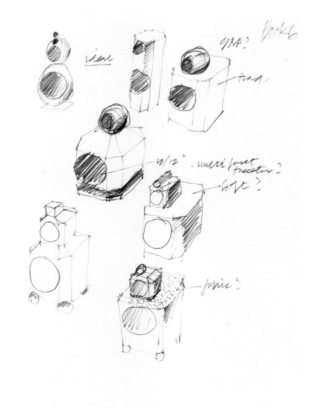

9

8. The late 1970s brought Grange his most widely celebrated brief from B&W, the cabinet design for the 801. Seen here are early sketches where Grange is separating out the tweeter, mid-range and bass drivers into separate casings.

9. For optimal acoustics Grange had wanted to house the mid-range driver in a spherical casing, perched on top of the bass, but the fabrication technologies of the time could not accommodate his vision. So he settled on an octagonal box.

10 (opposite). A later iteration of the hugely successful 801, introducing B&W's 'matrix' structural innovation and here finished in black lacquer.

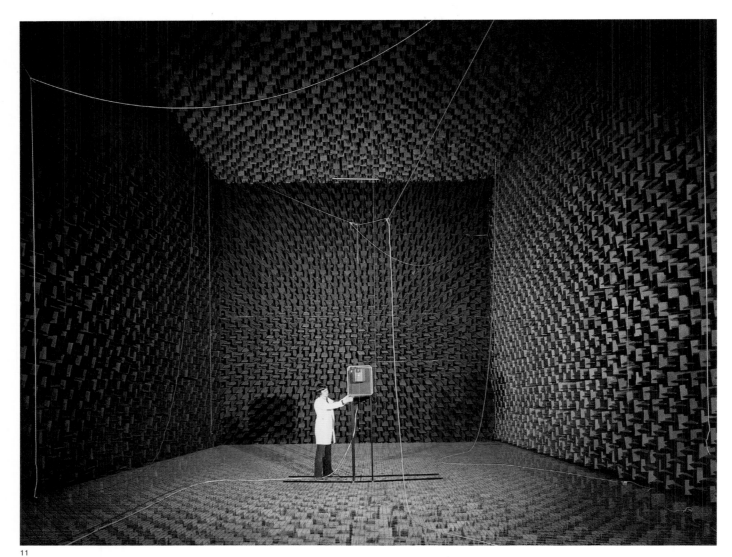

11

12

11. An immaculate full-scale prototype of the 801 cabinet, made by Grange and his team, being tested in the advanced acoustic chamber at the National Physical Laboratory in 1979.

12. A pair of the iconic 801 loudspeakers, pictured here on stands in Abbey Road Studios after being specified as the reference monitor of choice by EMI. The design defined a new era of quality for the listening experience, the culmination of years of B&W research and engineering innovation.

'I could call John Bowers any Sunday through the whole year, at the works, and he'd be there. He'd always be working, always experimenting with another speaker. So he made a marvellous client.'

Kenneth Grange

13. An immaculate, small-scale model of a later floor-standing cabinet design made when Grange was exploring the potential of a loudspeaker to also be a 'piece of beautiful furniture'. Here narrow doors and a fold-back tweeter panel could disguise the product's function when not in use.

13

Embodying the 'form follows function' approach, the 801 was the first loudspeaker to house the driver units in three separate – and visible – stacked volumes, allowing the sound emitted from each to flow without disruption. It was also an early demonstration of the company's quest for ever-improved performance through applying new material technologies, such as Fibrecrete (fibre-reinforced concrete) in the formation of the octagonal mid-range box. For this volume Grange had wanted to create a spherical form – 'a football' – to deliver the 'ultimate look and acoustic performance', but the financial investment required to manufacture such a challenging form proved too costly at the time, hence an octagonal volume was devised instead. It should be noted, however, that in recent years B&W has finally been able to realize Grange's spherical vision in models such as the 800 Series Diamond.

The 801 greatly amplified Grange's industry reputation and design celebrity, setting the bar for every loudspeaker that followed; its professional adoption culminated in the record label EMI installing the model as the reference monitor – the most exacting role demanded of any loudspeaker – in all the recording studios at its flagship Abbey Road Studios. Many other world-class studios around the globe followed their example, and continue to specify next-generation B&W monitors to this day. A second Queen's Award soon followed, sales doubled, international exports accelerated and B&W gained global press. *Design* magazine noted that 'although designed principally for studio monitoring applications, the 801 has been styled and finished so as to be equally at home in domestic surroundings' – a growing market for status audio equipment.

Always striving to excel, in the early 1980s Bowers founded the renowned Steyning Research Establishment (SRE), an R&D laboratory bringing scientists and engineers together with designers to push acoustic innovation to its limits. The constant iteration of new technical features and improvements flowing through these laboratories brought Grange

14

a steady stream of design briefs, and the opportunity to continually explore the role and form of the monitor cabinet.

Alongside delivering products for professional and domestic environments, the B&W business soon turned its sights on the accelerating market for automotive audio solutions. Grange's design for the compact LM1, the first of an in-car range initially introduced in 1982, featured a tough and heavy cast-zinc alloy outer enclosure to be inserted into a car's interior frame. Unexpectedly this chunky style and material specification also made the unit popular with the sailing community thanks to its resistance to the effects of salty air and humidity. And similarly, scaling down to target a new domestic market looking for 'a small yet premium speaker option', Grange's 1987 design for the CM1 boldly bucked the trend for large floor-standing cabinets by offering a compact monitor for table or shelf, featuring just a mid-range driver and tweeter. This model was rapidly followed by the CM2, integrating two backward-facing bass drivers in a pedestal. This design quickly established itself as the principal small hi-fi speaker, and opened up a significant market for B&W internationally.

One of the SRE's most important structural innovations of the 1980s, developed by chief electronics engineer Laurence Dickie, was the 'matrix', an internal bracing and damping structure of high-density particle board and acoustic foam that boosted driver performance by reducing vibration of the monitor cabinet. Grange would integrate this feature into multiple products from the latter half of the decade onwards, including a reworked 801 and a compact Matrix series and peaking with the totemic Matrix 800, a towering pair of angular cabinets unveiled in 1991. Fulfilling a brief to design monitor cabinets that ensured exceptional performance, the Matrix 800 also impactfully illustrates Grange's other remit: to consider how the requisite pair of

floor-standing speaker cabinets, which by now were a substantial presence in living spaces across the world, could be better presented as pieces of refined furniture or even sculpture. Grange was encouraged to explore materials and high-quality techniques of craftsmanship, which B&W keenly incorporated into its manufacturing processes, making the substantial investment in the tooling required to execute the production of every impeccably specified cabinet that left the Worthing factory.

Regarding B&W's investments in development, an earlier press release by the company had explained that 'B&W spend hugely more than some mighty rivals on research staff and equipment' in order to act on Bowers's ideas about 'the quality of musical appreciation'. Later a *Design* magazine review of the company remarked that 'one of the best acoustics laboratories in the world, computer-aided design methods, laser vibration-measuring techniques, and the long-term employment of one of Britain's leading industrial design consultants ... all these have helped B&W become one of the world's most successful manufacturers of quality loudspeakers'.

15

17 / 18. Exploratory sketches for a sculptural, floor-standing design of cabinet, which would really push the concept of 'the loudspeaker as a piece of furniture'.

19. A sketch of Grange's final design for his totemic Matrix 800 cabinet design (see also image opposite).

20 / 21. Two small models of other elongated forms considered for the Matrix 800, with folding panel to hide the iconic golden Kevlar drivers when not in use.

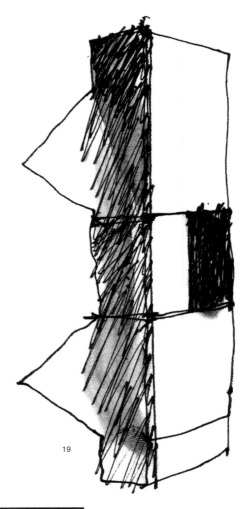

19

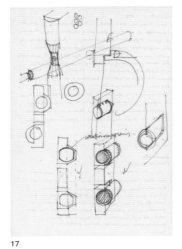

17

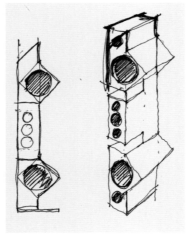

18

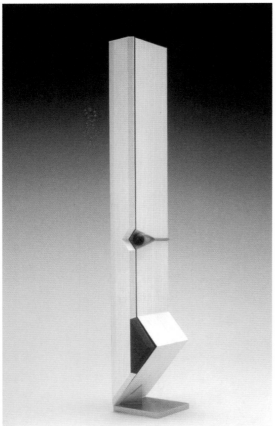

20

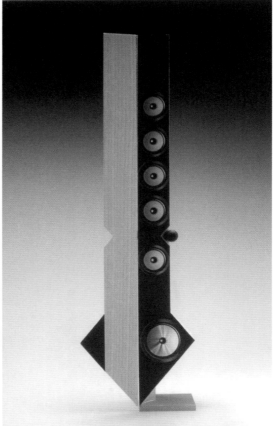

21

22 (opposite). A production pair of the Matrix 800, which stand 208 cm (82 in.) tall.

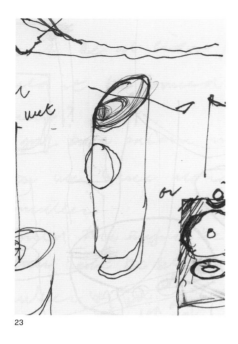

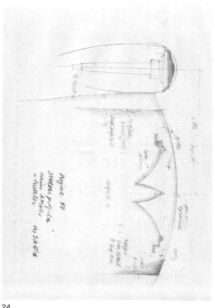

23. A small sketch picked out from a page in Grange's sketchbooks, capturing a moment in his thought process part-way through refining the design of his last product for B&W, the Signature Diamond.

24. A longways cross-sectional scale drawing through the tweeter and mid-range driver section of the evolving design for the Signature Diamond, as Grange neared a final design solution.

Grange continued to have input into designs from the B&W stable until the mid-2010s, long after he had left Pentagram and returned to practising independently as Kenneth Grange Design. The final special commission model to come to market from his hand, in collaboration with B&W's celebrated engineer Dr John Dibb, was the Signature Diamond, made for the company's fortieth anniversary in 2006, as one of the evocative Signature series, itself created in tribute to John Bowers, who had died in 1987. According to B&W, the Signature series was conceived to deliver 'no-holds-barred performance, distinctive beauty and special-edition exclusivity'. Grange's design for the Signature Diamond featured a tweeter-on-top with a diamond-dust diaphragm, a new innovation from B&W in audio quality, housed inside a solid, polished ovoid of marble – including a sample from Carrara personally selected by Grange. The sleek matrix-braced curved pedestal was formed of layer upon layer of expertly curved beech ply, lacquered to a high shine using an exquisite technique that had first inspired Grange when watching the hand-making of traditional lacquered wooden bowls and trays on his visits to Japan in the 1970s. In the creation of the Signature Diamond this technique was translated for high-end European craftsmanship, as a final flourish in his B&W portfolio.

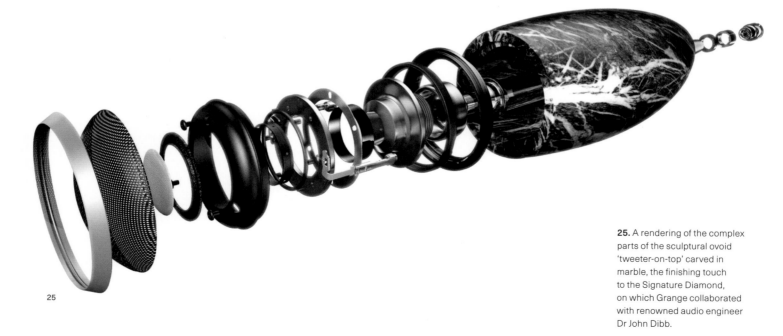

25. A rendering of the complex parts of the sculptural ovoid 'tweeter-on-top' carved in marble, the finishing touch to the Signature Diamond, on which Grange collaborated with renowned audio engineer Dr John Dibb.

26

26 / 27 (below). The final impeccable Signature Diamond, featuring a curved ply pedestal expertly finished in layers of traditional lacquer, a technique much admired by Grange on his work trips to Japan.

Through Grange's work with Maruzen from the late 1960s, and particularly the design celebrity brought about by his creation of the Cub sewing machine in the early 1970s, his reputation as 'the European innovator' grew rapidly across Japan's consumer industries, where the sensibilities of Western design were considered highly desirable to the Japanese customer. Concurrently, the profile of Pentagram was rising and attracting international attention, so it was not long before other Japanese companies started approaching the studio with a brief to bring a European design sensibility to their products. One of the most high-profile clients to arrive this way was Shiseido, the Tokyo-based brand giant and one of the oldest cosmetics companies in the world; and a company that had only ever once before commissioned design work from outside its own walls. Having set their sights on working with Grange, but not having managed to make contact with him at the Pentagram studio in London, they would determinedly track him down for an introductory meeting at his hotel in Osaka in 1976, while he was on one of his trips to Maruzen.

Grange proceeded to receive an 'impressively comprehensive' brief for a brand new cosmetics line aimed at the stylish, cosmopolitan Japanese man: ahead of the Western industry, the men's cosmetics market in Japan was already a notably large and valuable sector. Once the project commission was confirmed and Grange returned to London, a group of representatives from Shiseido was duly dispatched to take up residence at the Pentagram studio, following traditional Japanese practice and reporting back to Tokyo on the progress of this important project via daily telexes. A revolving team remained in the studio for nine weeks, with Grange confessing he and his team 'did not know what to do with them'. Shiseido's expectation, learned from the US style of working, was to receive a continuous stream of updates and visuals to demonstrate 'how much work was being done' each day, but as

Grange acknowledged, this 'simply did not align with Pentagram's more relaxed style of delivery'. Eventually the Shiseido team's patience paid off with Grange's final presentation of the proposed concept for the new men's line, including a cologne bottle, plus a graphic identity and outer packaging by Mervyn Kurlansky. The duo also conceived the brand name: Tactics. This they had settled on after reading the client's brand-positioning document for the new range, which described in detail the 'games and strategies for life', from physical sport to cerebral business thinking, that were projected to apply to the target customer. The accompanying graphic identity hinted at both the structure of a board game and the visual games played by an artist that distorted patterns on a canvas, in this case inspired by Op artist Victor Vasarely.

The presentation was very well received, save for one aspect that met with doubt: the proposed white opaque opal glass of the 'soft cube' cologne bottle. This 'cool and weighty' statement was devised by Grange after a visit to the V&A to study the collection of historical fragrance vessels, where he was inspired by Chinese porcelain bottles with 'stoppers shaped as inverted cups'. The glass-manufacturing specialist – who had been flown over from Shiseido for the presentation – responded that, regrettably, the white glass would be 'extremely difficult' to produce.

Somewhat deflated by his inability to sell this key part of the design to the client, but determined to ensure that the Shiseido team had a final good experience to round off their time in the UK, Grange and his team took their guests on a weekend trip to the city of Bath. Walking down a small street of boutiques, Grange happened to glimpse through the window of a chemist shop a display of classic fragrance bottles, including a Chanel bottle in white glass. He excitedly pointed this out to the client group, who duly rushed into the shop to purchase a large number of samples. Within days of the group returning to Tokyo they would inform Grange that

2

'a solution had been found' for the production of the white-glass bottles. Grange would later comment that 'every job needs its little bit of luck', this time occurring when 'one client responds to competition from another'.

The Tactics range went into production in 1978 – including bottles, jars, tubes and soaps – and rapidly became one of the most popular and recognized names in the Japanese market, further cementing Grange's celebrity in the country. The range is still retailed today, with the same identity and bottle, and is considered a modern Japanese classic.

Grange and Kurlansky were subsequently commissioned to develop the design of a vessel, packaging and identity for another men's cosmetics range, this time aimed at a younger, fashion-conscious customer; the product name, Trendy, had already been approved by the client. By the nature of its fashion-led positioning this range had a shorter shelf-life than Tactics, and did not remain in production for many years, although the product design won the prestigious ADC Tokyo Art Directors Club prize in 1988.

2. The complete range of Tactics cosmetics products for men, all presented in white glass vessels and pictured here with the packaging and identity designed by Pentagram partner Mervyn Kurlansky.

3 / 4. The Trendy men's cosmetics range targeted a younger, artier customer; the packaging, again designed in collaboration with Mervyn Kurlansky, won a prestigious art direction award in Japan.

3

4

Platignum

Founded in London after the First World War, the Mentmore Manufacturing Company quickly became known for innovative pen manufacturing. Its first product was a self-filling fountain pen, followed by a novel replacement stainless steel nib unit. The Platignum name was introduced by Mentmore in the 1920s to differentiate its range of pens from other stationery products being produced by the parent company, and soon afterwards it became the first brand to apply injection moulding to pen production. After the Second World War the company began manufacturing its own version of the recently commercialized ballpoint pen, followed by inventing the disposable ink cartridge, the felt tip and the retractable ballpoint pen through into the 1960s.

It was against this background of technological innovation that Grange later came to shape his designs for Platignum, when he was approached by the company in the early 1980s after they had noted the success of his design of the Parker 25 pen range (see pp. 198–201). The Platignum brand was

by then well known for its inexpensive, robust pens, but competition was increasing so the company needed a new, eye-catching offering. Grange's initial brief was less geared to an age range than the Parker brief had been, and more focused on designing a stylish pen with universal appeal that could be highly efficiently manufactured.

His first product for the company was an ultra-low-cost, all-plastic rollerball manufactured using the company's existing injection-moulding technology. As part of the cost-efficiency drive, Grange was careful to ensure that where possible the components could provide more than one function. So for example the plastic clip, which was still deemed a necessary feature in itself, also doubled as the button to retract the nib: therefore neither a separate button nor a separate protective lid was required, reducing the manufacturing cost. This colourful, robust pen was launched around the time of Grange's first solo exhibition at the V&A's Boilerhouse gallery – the predecessor of the Design

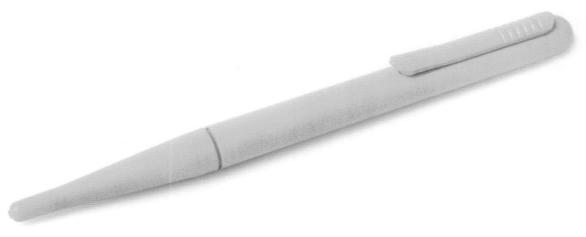

2

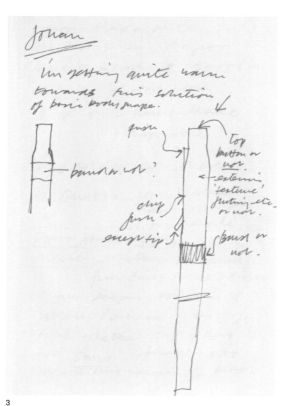

3

3. Sketches and note to Grange's design assistant, Johan Santer, regarding a preferred route for the body shape design of what would become the Accountant Pen.

4. The final Accountant Pen, a product aimed at professionals with a weighty stainless steel upgrade on his original all-plastic pen. Grange was proud of the design, but less proud of the product's role in encouraging waste in the manufacturing process.

Museum – in 1983, where a novel custom-printed version of the pen was presented to guests. Grange said at the time that the response to this design was 'very positive, and hopefully signals the start of a new rise in the company's fortunes'. And indeed it did.

Grange's next design, launched not long afterwards, was known as the Accountant Pen, targeting more directly the professional Parker market but still at a lower cost. It was a material upgrade on the all-plastic pen featuring, as Grange described, 'delicious pieces of engineering' in stainless steel for the nose cone and thin blade clip, with a separate button to retract the nib. When it came to choosing a production process for these steel details, Grange first proposed the same deep-draw technology as for Parker, but final analysis by the Platignum engineers deemed that advances in modern machining would make it 'faster and therefore more cost-effective' to start with a solid piece of steel rod and machine inside and out to turn away 95 per cent of the material; Grange would remark later with regret that this illustrated the attitude of an evolving modern era where 'speed of production trumped material waste'.

Following the market success of this second pen, Grange embarked on what would be his most celebrated design for Platignum: the Platpen. This robust, all-plastic pen sat at a price point between the two previous models and embodied the most contemporary style in its form. It sold in the millions, hitting the market during the booming fast-fashion

4

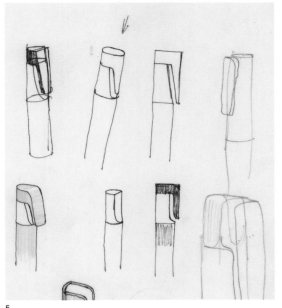

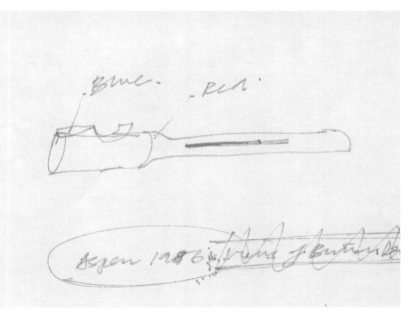

5

6

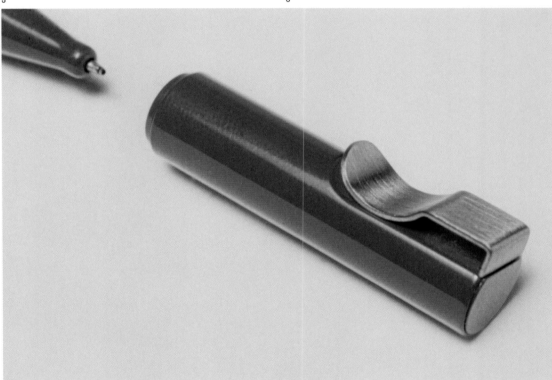

5 / 6. Exploratory sketches for the clip design and use of colour for the Platpen, the most recognizable and lasting of Grange's designs for Platignum.

7. Close-up of the final clip design for the Platpen, here in stainless steel, clearly showing the inspiration Grange took from traditional Terry clips used to hold tablecloths to tables and paper to drawing boards.

8. Profile of the Platpen, showing the careful consideration of the relationship of the clip to the pen lid, for good grip when clipped.

7

8

9 (below). A pile of Platpens: the clip colour and the disc in the base signify the colour of the ink.

era, to which it was well suited. The Platpen was available as a ballpoint or fibre tip. The key detail of its design was the chunky, colourful plastic clip; in defining the shape of this clip Grange had been inspired by the metal clips used to hold paper to drawing boards or to secure paper tablecloths in restaurants. He has always been very admiring of the ingenuity of this simple, ubiquitous device, known as the Terry clip, which was manufactured by Herbert Terry & Sons, leading British makers of metal springs. Grange, who had been aware of the firm since his childhood as his mother worked in a spring factory in London, came to be personally acquainted with

the Terry family two decades later, when he was appointed external design director for the company's Anglepoise lighting brand (see pp. 284–291).

When, in 2010, Grange designed a men's shirt in collaboration with Margaret Howell (see pp. 292–295), he integrated a breast pocket specifically intended to hold a pen with a clip, such as the Platpen. Nearly four decades on from the original Platpen design, and long after manufacture of it ceased, Grange was proud to have drawers of the pens still in use at home, proving Platignum's golden rule that, although they might be inexpensive to purchase, the brand's reputation for 'pens that work' must always hold true.

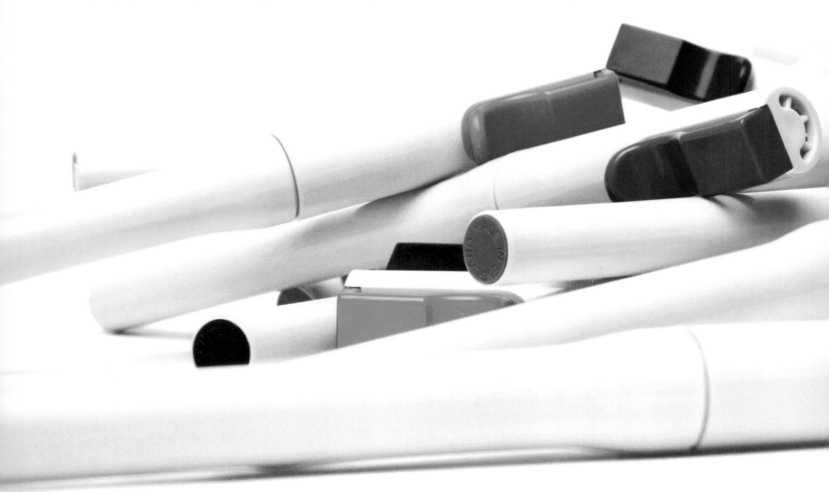

10. Three prototype pen lids, pictured in the pocket of Grange's shirt for Margaret Howell, showing Grange's explorations in creating a recognizable identity for the product using the clip.

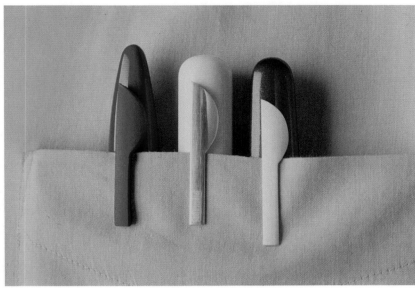

10

Plessey

1 (opposite). A later commission, from Plessey Displays, for a large floor-standing console for the Watchman air traffic control system, first used in defence operations and later in a commercial airport context.

2. The first commission Grange worked on, for Plessey Avionics and Communications, was the System 4000. The range of communications equipment, encased in lightweight, rugged die-cast aluminium alloy, needed to withstand extremely tough environments.

The Plessey Company was a major British manufacturer of electronics systems and equipment for telecommunications and defence, established in 1917, and is now part of GEC Siemens. Notable early contracts included manufacturing radios for Marconi, the first televisions for pioneer John Logie Baird, and telephones for the General Post Office, later British Telecom (for which Grange also later worked). The Korean War of the early 1950s brought Plessey critical work in developing modern defence communication systems, and henceforth Plessey Defence Systems became a significant part of the business, incorporating the development of electronic systems for land, air and marine operation.

It was from this division of Plessey that Grange first received an approach, the company having noted his reputation for intelligently simple, functional and enduring design, not least his award-winning 1970s work for the telecoms company STC, the avionics division of which Plessey had acquired. By the 1980s Plessey was looking to apply similar user-centric considerations to the design of the increasingly complex communications equipment used by military forces in the field. The brief to Grange would see him working on designs for a wide range of products for different divisions of Plessey across the following decade. For most of that time he worked day to day with Professor William Gosling, a leading electronics expert who had been headhunted by Plessey in 1980 to lead a world-renowned division of more than 1,500 scientists and engineers. Grange recalled Gosling as 'extremely intelligent and a thoroughly decent human being', and the pair maintained lifelong contact well after retirement.

3. The manpack was developed by Grange to hold the System 4000 range of modular communications equipment, for efficient portability in the field.

4. A monitor designed for Plessey Displays towards the end of Grange's consultancy period with the organization, demonstrating similar casing techniques to those developed for the Reuter Monitor (see pp. 188–193).

3

Grange's first commission, through the Plessey Avionics and Communications division, was the design of the System 4000 range of modular communications equipment components for portable manpack and vehicle installations. The range included a portable VHF transceiver with rechargeable power cell and manpack harness, and a vehicle-based intercommunication and radio control modular system. Working closely with the Plessey engineers, Grange devised a solution whereby the different components could be used individually or in a group configuration, depending on the specific assignment. The various units – protected in lightweight, rugged die-cast aluminium alloy cases – could be hooked together with heavy-duty quick-release catches, which also provided the electrical connections between components.

Grange would recall the consideration of 'human alliance' as being critical in the design development, as well as the requirement for a high level of 'simplified,

dependable functionality' owing to the extremely rigorous circumstances of use; for example the user might be wearing cumbersome gloves when handling the kit, often in severe environmental conditions involving water, heat and dust. Related to this, Grange was also required to thoroughly consider the maintenance of the products, and how this could most efficiently be conducted in challenging conditions and, ideally, minimized. When it came to the production process, Grange would later describe the 'fascinating glimpse' this project gave him into a different world of manufacture: unlike other factory formats and workshops he had been privy to during his work with a range of clients, the Plessey experience involved a 'highly sophisticated and protected working environment'.

While continuing to work on further iterations of personal and vehicle units for the Plessey Military Communications division, in the mid-1980s Grange also embarked on a separate commission for Plessey

4

5 / 6. Early sketches from a presentation document for Plessey, documenting part of Grange's thought process when developing an overall shape and efficient structure for the Watchman air traffic control console.

7. A more detailed presentation drawing of two Watchman consoles, demonstrating how the product design enabled a line-up of units providing a range of functionalities to be smartly positioned side by side.

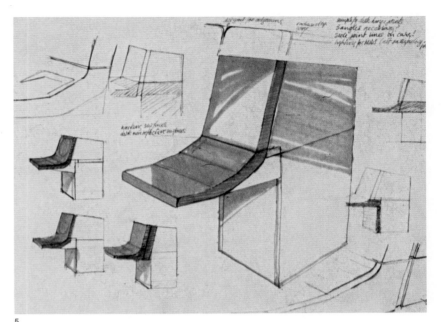

5

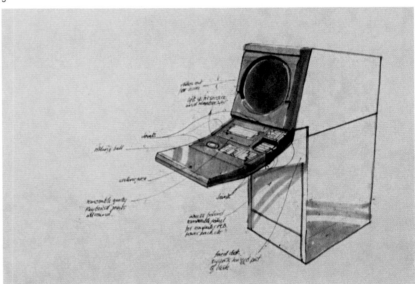

6

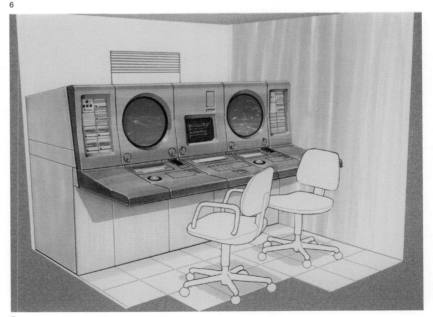

7

8 (opposite). A non-functioning prototype model in plastic of Grange's design for the PCN One personal phone, featuring a sliding cover over the keypad, an early contender in the nascent mobile phone industry of the late 1980s.

9. Working models of the evolution of the PCN One design, from first flat form to final curved profile with refined earpiece and rectangular keypad buttons.

Displays, this time the design of an intelligent console for the Plessey Watchman air traffic control system. This was initially developed by Plessey Radar in 1975 as a ground and air surveillance radar system for UK defence operational stations, while later versions were also widely integrated across commercial Air Traffic Services systems.

In 1989 came his last commission, this time through the Plessey UK telecoms division, for the design of the PCN One portable telephone concept. The product was developed by Plessey for a consortium including GEC and Philips, which were among many parties at that time looking to revolutionize telephone usage through nascent personal communication networks (PCN) operations. Grange described the phone as 'small enough to be truly a personal telephone, able to be taken anywhere'. Design features included a sliding cover over the keypad that incorporated the earpiece, to 'double the size of the unit' when in use and offer a 'satisfying everyday tool that is elegant and attractive'. The consortium's report at the time described the PCN system as 'a radio telephone network that will make this telephone as commonplace as a credit card'. This prediction did of course come to pass, with a proliferation of services gradually coming to market after numerous PCN licence applications were granted from the early 1990s. But the PCN One phone itself never came to fruition.

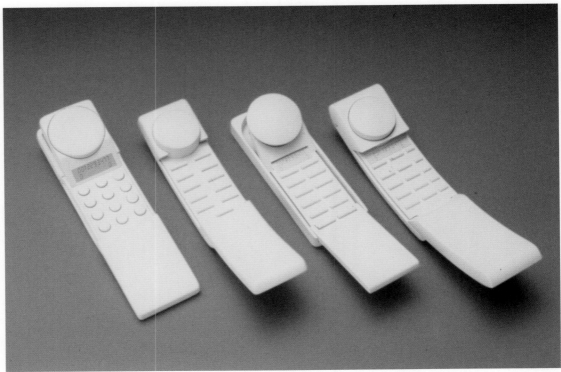

9

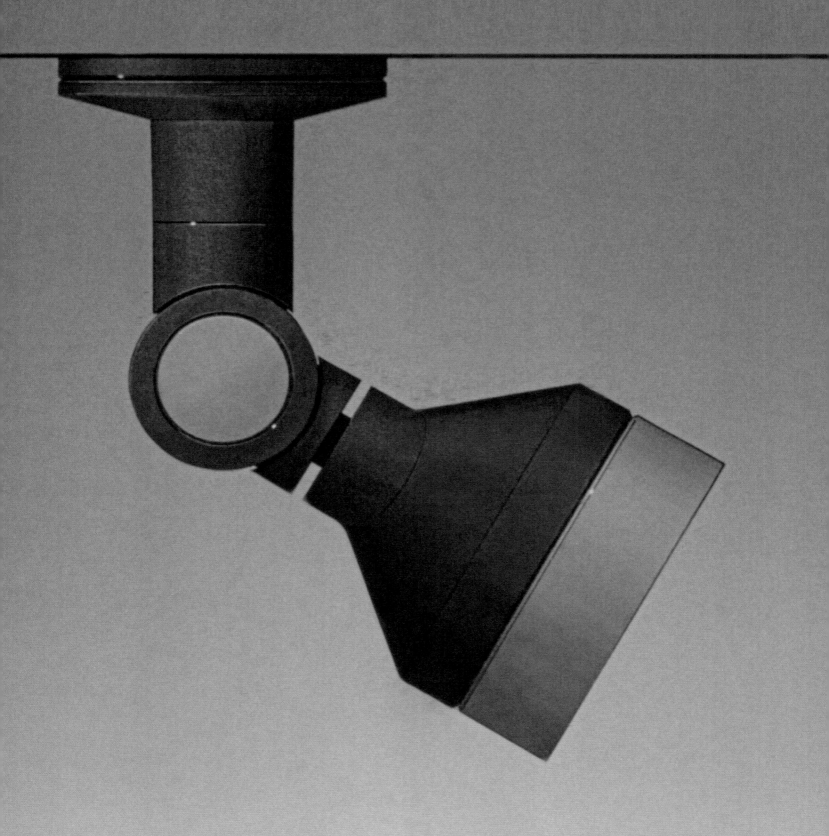

Thorn Lighting

1 (opposite). A precise side-profile photograph of a Lightstream 4 system spotlight, showing the circular joint solution capable of rotating and positioning the lamp at any angle.

2. A page of sketches exploring forms for ceiling-mounted spotlights, to be connected into tracks (detail bottom right).

Incorporated in the UK in 1928 as a dealer in electrical goods and radios, Thorn Electrical Industries first began manufacturing light bulbs in 1933. This division of the company grew rapidly, through investment in production facilities and a number of business acquisitions, to become Thorn Lighting, one of the world's largest producers of lighting components.

In 1945, as part of the company's expansion, Thorn Lighting signed a technical exchange agreement with Sylvania Electric Products, a US manufacturer of diverse electrical goods, to align on the development and manufacture of new lamp technologies. Notably in the late 1950s this included the development of the Flashcube, a disposable module of four expendable flashbulbs which fitted into a slot on the top of a camera. In collaboration with Kodak, this component was to become vastly successful as the amateur photography market took off, introduced to the new Instamatic camera range in the 1960s.

By then Grange had already been working with Kodak for a number of years (see pp. 78–89) and was in the process of working on the design of the European version of the Instamatic camera, which integrated the Flashcube, so he was aware of Thorn Lighting and they were aware of him. The company approached him separately soon after, connected via the Kodak team, though not initially to commission his industrial design input; as had also been the case in his early days with Kodak, his first job for Thorn Lighting was an exhibition stand design.

The stand was commissioned for the company's presence at a big London photography fair, promoting the Flashcube among other photographic lighting components. Commenting that Grange's 'sleek modern design style was all very well', the sales director for Thorn Lighting proceeded to dictate that what would work best would be for Grange to employ 'a team of pretty girls' to populate the stand as photographic models. Grange later recalled with good humour that he 'took the man at his word', setting about delivering a 'showstopper' of an exhibition stand. In the process he found himself not only designing the stand but also conducting auditions at which 'a sea of girls turned up', after his secretary put out a call to a number of London modelling agencies. By all accounts the resulting stand for Thorn Lighting was a 'terrific success' as amateur photographers flocked to try out the Flashcubes and snap the range of seasonally themed and vibrantly populated stage sets, which included a full beach scene complete with the requisite bikinis. In fact the response was so effusive that to Grange's lasting amusement police were required for crowd control, and he recalled the experience being for him 'a novel break from hardboard and glass'.

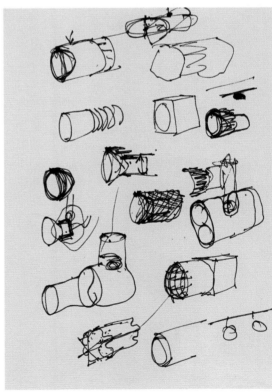

2

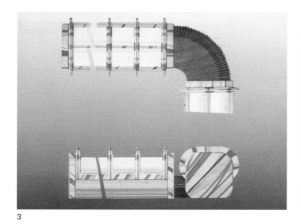

3

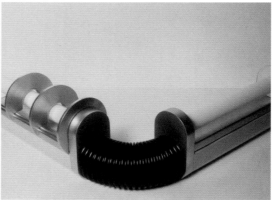

4

3 / 4. Presentation drawing and final production unit for the modular 2D lighting system using fluorescent batons, Grange's first product design for Thorn Lighting.

Separately, during the late 1950s, Grange had begun a significant long-term working relationship with the kitchen appliance manufacturer Kenwood (see pp. 94–107). When in 1968 it was bought by Thorn Electrical Industries, Grange was once again brought into contact with the Thorn business. While his output for Kenwood was copious throughout the decades, it was not until the early 1980s that he would again work with Thorn Lighting, this time in his capacity as an industrial designer. By this point the Thorn business had expanded further to become Thorn EMI and Grange was appointed consultant design director to the domestic appliance division. Alongside Kenwood, he subsequently worked across a number of projects for the group's brands, which also included Bendix and Tricity.

His first product for Thorn Lighting came after the company's advances in the manufacture of fluorescent batons, for which he initially designed a system of simple, refined modular steel fittings called 2D.

Then in 1985 the company introduced the Lightstream bulb, a 'radical' low-voltage version of its hugely successful tungsten halogen lamp technology,

for which Grange was briefed to conceive a sleek and functional ceiling spotlight system. This was described by the company as 'a product to show commitment to the interior commercial lighting market', which was at that time a lucrative sector still limited in options for quality lighting solutions. The track fittings and lamp holders Grange designed allowed greater flexibility in targeting the light beam and quickly proved popular for retail, office and gallery environments, opening up a new market for Thorn Lighting worldwide.

Two years later, in 1987, Thorn Lighting introduced another new product development, a single-ended metal halide lamp called Arcstream, which offered a brighter white light source. Grange applied these lamps to a sleek range of uplighters, called Legato, with floor-standing, wall-mounted and corner-fitting variants manufactured in grey powder-coated aluminium. After the opening of Thorn's lighting showroom in the Business Design Centre in London that same year – to which, as reported in *Lighting* magazine, the company estimated it would attract 'a quarter of a million visitors a year' – *Shop Equipment and Shopfitting News* described Thorn's 'startling

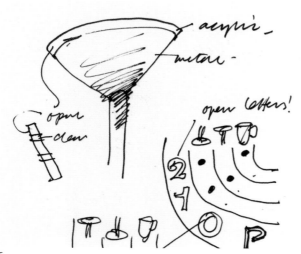

5

5. A quick sketch in Grange's notebooks (alongside notes for Kenwood on the same page), of the upward-facing shade of his Legato lighting solution.

6 (opposite). The final Legato range of uplighters, featuring Thorn's latest innovation in lamp technology, the single-ended metal halide Arcstream.

7 / 8. Presentation drawings of various options for adjustable, ceiling-mounted spotlights, proposed to Thorn for the Lightstream series.

9 / 10 / 11. The Aria collection of options for track-mounted spotlights and fittings, offered in the Lightstream lamp series, won Grange a prestigious product award at the annual Hannover Messe in 1989.

advances in display and commercial lighting', while *Lighting* quoted Grange as saying, 'It is encouraging to see Thorn ... known for its technical know-how and innovation ... becoming more alive to shifting trends and even more design-conscious.'

Following this success, Grange was briefed to devise a modular spotlight system using the Arcstream lamp, both for commercial interiors and also for the popular new market of exterior floodlighting, and his continuing work for the company in the following years involved further iterations of both the Lightstream and the Arcstream systems, as the lamp technology evolved, and also included a new fluorescent baton system called Modulight. His last design, a track-mounted spotlight system called the Aria, which used the latest Lightstream lamps, won Grange and Thorn Lighting a Die gute Industrieform award at the 1989 Hannover Messe, the huge, prestigious industry trade fair in Germany.

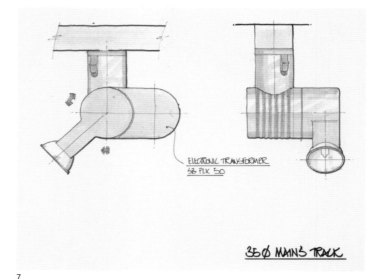

7

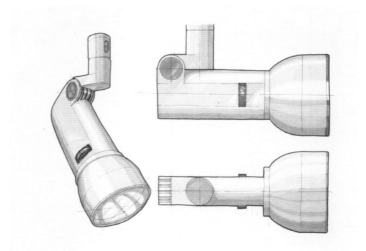

8

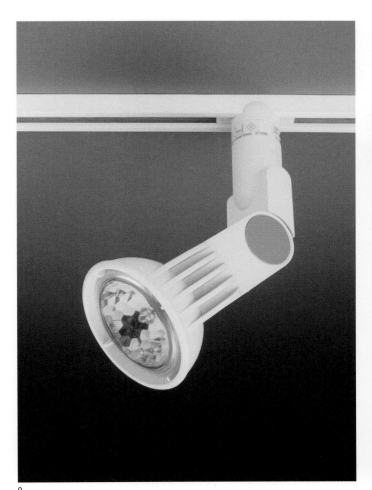

9

10

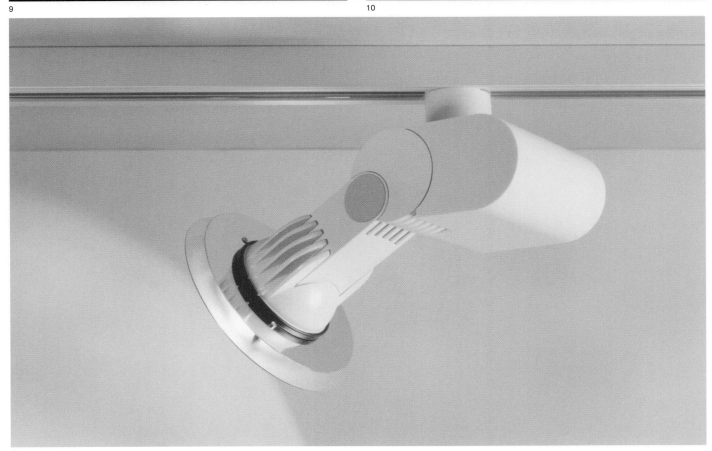

11

Thorpac

1 (opposite). Various designs for microwave-friendly containers developed as part of a research and development project undertaken by Grange for Thorpac.

2. Two lidded dishes and a jug from the final commercial range of microwave-friendly cookware that Grange designed for Thorpac through the Funded Consultancy Scheme initiated by the Design Council.

Thorpac Limited, later the Thorpac Group, was established in the UK in 1971 as a producer and distributor of packaging and accessories for the novel and fast-growing home freezer market: its product range included foil containers, plastic bags, labels and tools, and a range of injection-moulded plastic containers. Unlike other similar brands at that time, which retailed through catalogues or home visits, the Thorpac range retailed predominantly through the new freezer showrooms that were springing up around the country.

By the end of the decade a new domestic kitchen appliance was rapidly gaining in popularity: the microwave oven. And as the price of the appliances gradually became more affordable through the early 1980s, with Grange later recalling 'cooks on the TV demonstrating the tremendous speed advantages' of this latest innovation in cooking, Thorpac identified an opportunity to diversify and quickly started to expand into microwave-friendly cookware. Research commissioned by frozen food and electrical appliance retailer Bejam stated that 'in 1979 1% of homes had a microwave. But today 1 million homes have a microwave and this figure is expected to double in the next 3 years.'

Studying the science of microwaves passing through solid materials, the Thorpac team argued that both the design and the material of the cooking vessels could have a 'profound effect on the efficiency of the cooking process'. Alongside this they could see that there would be a niche for microwave-to-table cookware, enhancing the already time-saving promise of the microwave oven itself. Grange explained that the team's thinking was: 'If you could present the meal on the table in the same vessel it was cooked in, you bypassed the traditional step of using serving dishes and therefore avoided additional washing up!'

2

3

3. Side profile showing Grange's careful consideration of the handles of a lid and dish and how they curve upwards and downwards respectively, to make it easier to grip when carrying with oven gloves.

4. The complete range of microwave-friendly cookware and serving dishes, injection moulded in Udel polysulfone, a tough plastic through which microwave energy can easily pass.

Thorpac had identified the opportunity but, having no in-house design expertise, recognized the need to engage a consultant designer to give the company the best shot at developing a range of cookware that customers would be proud to present at their dinner tables. The team therefore applied to a newly launched initiative from the Design Council (formerly the Council of Industrial Design) called the Funded Consultancy Scheme, through which manufacturing companies could apply for fifteen days of funded design expertise from a recommended designer on the Design Council listings. Thorpac's application was accepted and the company was subsequently connected with Grange, whose credentials included his substantial body of existing work for Kenwood. Within the allocation of time, Grange and his team produced full concept drawings and block models suggesting styles, materials, capacities and colours. These proposals were very well received by the team at Thorpac and

from there the company extended their contract with Grange, during which time designs were developed and packaging was proposed. Within nine months the new microwave range launched and immediately began gaining widespread distribution in department stores and grocery, hardware and kitchen shops.

Describing the process of developing a product that needs to take into account the 'invisible science' of microwave cooking, Grange explained that his starting point for the design was realizing that 'a vessel with corners effectively multiplies the number of obstacles in the way of the microwaves' and that the truly optimum shape of a vessel for cooking in a microwave oven 'would be a balloon'. With this in mind he developed a range of dishes with well-rounded edges and lids, made in tough Udel polysulfone, a rigid, robust, heat-resistant plastic that is highly transparent to microwave energy and that will therefore stay cool to the touch. During the injection-moulding process the resulting dishes were

4

5

6

5 / 6. Grange's final project for Thorpac returned to the company's origins in freezer packaging and accessories with the design for a sturdy ice cream scoop, pictured here in Grange's favourite 'pleasing' solid cast-aluminium version and an ABS plastic version.

produced at a thinness that would further reduce obstacles to transmission. And an additional detail that Grange carefully considered was the design of the handles of the dishes and lids, to ensure the best grip when lifting them with oven gloves: the handles of the dishes tilted slightly downwards while the handles of the lids angled slightly upwards, ensuring a sturdy hold for the gloved hand.

Thorpac's press release at the time of launch in 1984 claimed that 'this is probably the first range of dishes to be designed scientifically rather than being based simply on traditional shapes. It will transform the company into a leader in this new field.' Sure enough, it opened new export markets, with twenty-five per cent of sales being overseas within the first two years of launch, and led to a further disposable range. Proud of the association with Grange, and seeing the commercial value in his design celebrity, during manufacture Thorpac introduced an embossed circular line of type to the base of many of the first collection of products, stating 'Made in UK. Design Kenneth Grange/Pentagram'.

Following this substantial project Grange was commissioned to design one other product, this time an ice cream scoop, referencing the origins of the company. The result was a pleasingly simple, streamlined form to be produced in either solid cast aluminium or injection-moulded coloured ABS plastic. The design solution, using just one piece of material, ensured that it was inexpensive to manufacture, and it would prove popular in the market. Grange explained that scooping out well-frozen ice cream can be 'quite an arduous task', so 'the force of your yield has to be very great': therefore the scoop needed to be both 'very comfortable and a real extension of the user's strength and dexterity', just as with any hand tool.

Alessi

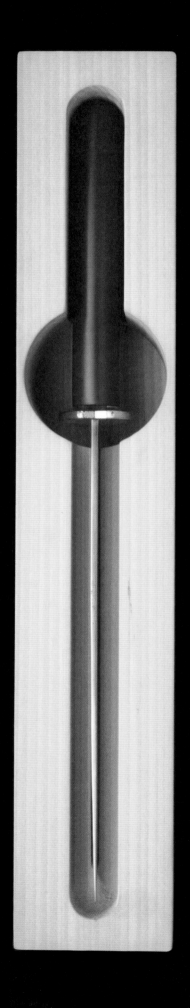

1 (opposite). The only prototype to exist of a proposed kitchen knife designed and made for a presentation to Alessi, for which Grange took inspiration from the Japanese knives he admired during his trips to the country. Pictured here presented in a wooden block.

2. The series of three different prototype kitchen knives conceived by Grange, the top one in particular clearly displaying design details inspired by Japanese samurai swords.

At a design industry party in the late 1980s Grange was introduced to Alberto Alessi, the third head of Alessi, the family-owned Italian homeware company known for its collaborations with a portfolio of names across the design world. Alessi happened to mention to Grange that he was considering a move into the crowded kitchen tools market, specifically premium chef's knives. So Grange, drawing on his past experience with Wilkinson Sword (see pp. 156–163), set about fashioning a proposal.

By that time Grange had been working for clients in Japan for more than two decades, during the course of which he had been greatly inspired by the country's approach to hand tools and the quality and dedication with which these items were crafted. He later described his admiration of the 'single-minded focus on the importance of performance and absence of style' he found in Japan, which had ensured many product additions to his own toolbox that he would 'revel in demonstrating' to visitors.

So it was that Grange set about honing a kitchen knife design that would reference 'the unsurpassable sharpness and distinctive style of Japanese knives'. The characteristic details of his concept were a swept-down handle, a hilt between handle and blade, and the upturned profile of the tip of the blade through which a continuous gentle curve meets a 'vicious point'. Grange explained that he hoped to show 'how a tool both common and celebrated across two cultures can amalgamate the special qualities of both'.

The Alessi team considered the concept for over six months but eventually declined to take it any further. So the immaculately modelled prototype knife remains today in its equally immaculately milled wooden block, stored in his archive. Grange did proudly display it as part of his exhibition 'Those That Got Away' at the Pentagram studio in 2003, as the closest he would ever come to designing a much-coveted samurai sword.

2

Helen Hamlyn Trust / Ideal Standard

1 (opposite). The production version of a domestic shower unit for the elderly, as featured in the Ideal Standard catalogue, initially designed by Grange for the exhibition 'New Design for Old' at the V&A.

2. A presentation diagram from 'New Design for Old' explaining the range of considered features of the shower unit, aimed at making the shower experience safer, easier and more comfortable for elderly users.

In 1986 the V&A staged the groundbreaking exhibition 'New Design for Old' in its Boilerhouse, a gallery conceived by Terence Conran and Stephen Bayley that was the predecessor to the Design Museum. The show presented proposals for new products designed to help older people stay independent at home, and was spearheaded by the British philanthropist Lady Helen Hamlyn, after she experienced substantial difficulty in finding suitable products to help her elderly mother remain independent. Witnessing at first hand how restricted and stigmatizing the market was, Hamlyn developed a vision to challenge perceptions through a public exhibition that asked fundamental questions about design and human dignity. The project was supported by her foundation, the Helen Hamlyn Trust, which works to change attitudes towards accessible design.

In curating the exhibition Hamlyn invited fourteen high-profile designers to take an everyday product – she matched and commissioned each from a list she had compiled of possible projects – and reimagine it in a way that would improve its experience for the older user. For the initiative she engaged an impressive line-up of eminent international names including Robin Day, Dinah Casson, David Mellor,

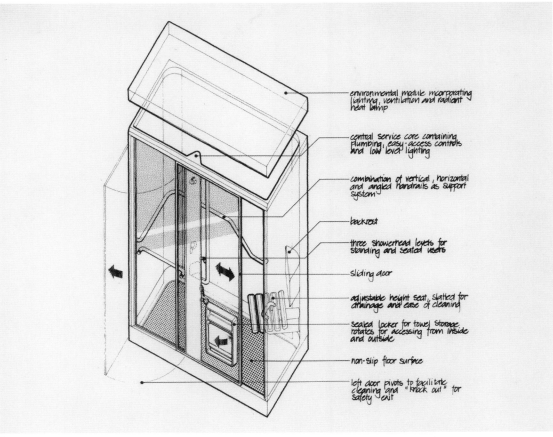

environmental module incorporating lighting, ventilation and radiant heat lamp

central service core containing plumbing, easy-access controls and low level lighting

combination of vertical, horizontal and angled handrails as support system

backrest

three showerhead levels for standing and seated users

sliding door

adjustable height seat, slatted for drainage and ease of cleaning

sealed locker for towel storage, rotates for accessing from inside and outside

non-slip floor surface

left door pivots to facilitate cleaning and "knock out" for safety exit

2

'There is a saying that nakedness is a great leveller, and so is age. Take washing your feet, for example. At age two sitting on your bottom to reach your feet is easy; by the age of twelve sitting on a seat would already be easier; and at age eighty-two you need to sit to reach your knees, let alone your feet. So the task of washing the whole body provides an acute focus on disability at all ages.'

Kenneth Grange

3. Cut-through axonometric presentation drawing of the shower unit, from the 'New Design for Old' exhibition, showing the in-shower features of the unit, including a warming cabinet for towels and overhead lighting.

Vignelli Associates, Hartmut Esslinger and Grange; the last, with characteristic enthusiasm, rapidly accepted the challenge set for him by Hamlyn to rethink the domestic shower unit. Grange later stated that he considered the commonplace shower-in-the-bath as 'the single biggest hazard' to the elderly, recalling that his mother never set foot in a bath in later life, instead using a basin on the floor.

Grange and his team at Pentagram consulted occupational therapists and then embarked on the project in conjunction with Ideal Standard, which had already been conducting research into future bathrooms for ageing populations in the USA and was therefore interested in rapidly putting a product into production. Grange's design response presented a self-contained shower unit that deliberately used the same footprint and plumbing source as a bathtub; so it could be easily installed in place of an existing unit without disrupting the rest of the bathroom. To further simplify installation it was proposed that the central column holding all the necessary piping would be pre-plumbed at the factory.

The shower unit offered plenty of safe and usable space around the flow of water, and also enabled the introduction of an adjustable fold-down seat with back rest and foot rest. Three shower heads were introduced at different heights, with controls to turn on the water before entering the unit; all water would be thermostatically controlled, and a digital panel would display the water temperature before entry. Plenty of sturdy vertical, horizontal and angled grab bars were integrated, alongside options for sliding or pivoting doors for access and cleaning. An overhead panel contained lighting, a radiant heat lamp and a steam extractor, while an additional thoughtful feature was a small in-built heated cupboard in the wall of the unit, accessible from outside and inside the unit, to store warm dry towels and clothing.

Following the exhibition, Grange's design was further developed based on visitor feedback, and Ideal Standard launched it to market in 1988

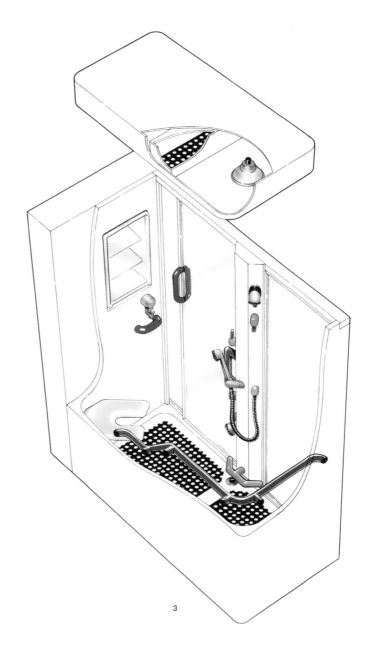

3

under the name ShowerAge. The brochure for the product described how the company had become increasingly aware of 'imaginative design being able to introduce more comfort, pleasure and safety to the lives of the elderly'. The concept was shortlisted as a finalist in the BBC Design Awards in 1990. But the product itself did not see a long life in the market, cost and perceived lack of ease of installation being barriers to adoption by the builders of the day.

The 'New Design for Old' exhibition, nonetheless, attracted widespread attention, sparked many conversations and proved an important catalyst for future pioneering initiatives in the field of age-conscious design. The Helen Hamlyn Trust proceeded to fund Design Age, a new research unit at the Royal College of Art, where Hamlyn had studied fashion in the 1950s. Since its founding in 1991 its remit has gradually evolved to promote 'design for our future selves' rather than simply focusing on ageing, as 'reduced mobility can happen to us all'. The research unit eventually became the Helen Hamlyn Centre for Design, a global leader in inclusive design that works with RCA graduates, businesses, government and the third sector (charities and social enterprises) – all of this originally sparked, in Hamlyn's words, by 'the enthusiasm and generosity' of fourteen designers, including Grange, 'in supporting the acorn which led to the oak tree'.

Oun / Dentsu

1 (opposite). A domestic gas heater designed by Grange for Osaka Gas, a leading Japanese company that he was introduced to by Oun.

2. Small, intricate painted models (approx. 15 cm / 6 in. tall) of some of Grange's gas heater designs for the Japanese market.

The success of Grange's initial design work for clients in Japan, particularly his sewing machines for Maruzen (see pp. 148–155) followed by the Tactics brand for Shiseido (see pp. 216–219), brought with it a significant degree of celebrity profile, arguably more so than he found in Europe. He became for two decades the name with whom Japanese companies wished to associate themselves, to benefit from the appeal to the Japanese customer of European design sensibilities.

One such company to align itself with Grange was Oun, a strategic agency offshoot of the giant and influential Japanese advertising agency Dentsu. As part of enhancing the consultancy service attentively delivered to its clients, the Oun team wished to be able to offer the promise of exclusive European design flair from highly respected designers. Both Grange and his Pentagram partner Alan Fletcher were approached with this proposal in the mid-1980s

by Ippei Inoh, a director of Dentsu and president of Oun, and over the following decade Grange would build up a dynamic relationship with the team at Oun, consulting on a wide variety of product concepts for the company's clients, and often describing Japan as a 'powerhouse for products'.

Notable among Grange's output for Oun's clients is his design work for Osaka Gas and its subsidiary, Harman Gas. Portable gas being the major fuel in Japanese homes, a proliferation of gas appliances was a critical part of domestic culture. Grange would often recall the 'boundless appetite' of the Japanese consumer for newer and 'seemingly better' products, including a constant demand for the latest designs of gas heaters, which played a very visible role in the home. So through the late 1980s Grange was often asked to devise new looks for these highly efficient heaters. He would attend regular presentation meetings at which, true to form, he always presented

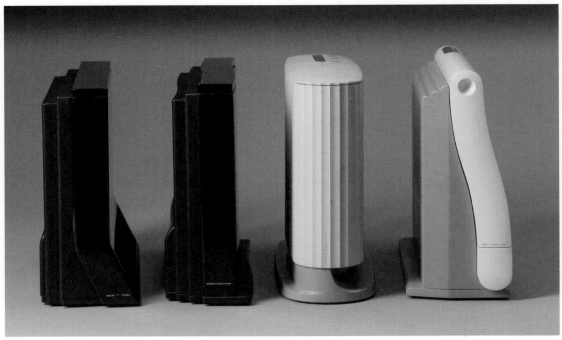

2

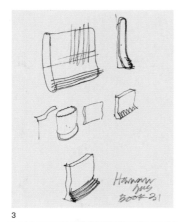

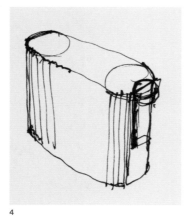

3

4

3 /4. Sketches for various formats of portable gas heater during the development process of products for both Osaka Gas and its subsidiary, Harman Gas.

5

6

impeccably produced models of his designs, all constructed and immaculately finished by his head of workshop, Bruce Watters. These models always met with much praise from the Japanese team, who greatly appreciated the effort and attention to detail that aligned so finely with their own cultural sensibilities.

Alongside gas heaters, Grange also tackled designs for gas water heaters and tabletop grills and cookers, the latter an area of domestic appliance design that fascinated him because of the 'sheer skill' with which the Japanese cook could create 'such superb meals using such a compact cooking device'. And he would subsequently win two prestigious G Mark awards, sponsored by the Japanese Ministry of International Trade and Industry, for a water geyser and a fan heater.

5. A sleek stainless steel tabletop gas cooker with integrated grill, for Osaka Gas. Compact gas cookers were another staple of Japanese homes, and Grange greatly admired their efficiency.

6. This refined design for a gas-powered hot-water geyser won Grange a prestigious G Mark product award from the Japanese Ministry of International Trade and Industry.

7 (opposite). This gently curving gas heater design (also seen in model form on p. 249) won Grange a second G Mark product award. Portable gas heaters were – and still are – the main solution for domestic heating in Japan.

8. An adhesive tape dispenser design, commissioned as a corporate gift by his client Dentsu, devised in the shape of a comma – the graphic icon of the agency.

9. A page – headed 'KG idea' – of sketches and notes from Grange's notebooks, outlining the concept for an electric pencil sharpener, responding to a brief from Dentsu for a desk-based product they could give as a gift.

10 (opposite). The final electric pencil sharpener, for which Grange designed special pencils with a flattened side, reflecting the shape of the sharpener, to stop them rolling across a desk.

Meanwhile for Dentsu, the parent agency, Grange designed two desk products for its traditional gift collection, a series of carefully considered items presented each year to its clients. The first, a 'solid and weighty' electric pencil sharpener with additional holes to display a collection of 'pleasingly aligned' pencils, was subsequently manufactured for Dentsu 'to a very high standard', with Grange much appreciating the 'impressive fastidiousness' of Japanese industry when it came to production. This attention to detail was also seen in the pencils, the shape of which exactly followed the sharpener and which had a flat edge that prevented them from rolling off the table and made space to print the product name. The following year he continued the theme with a similarly high-quality adhesive-tape dispenser; its curved cutter created the shape of a comma, which was at that time the graphic icon of Dentsu. However, much as the client appreciated Grange's signature wit in the design, unlike the sharpener, the tape dispenser never made it into production; Grange recalled that his proposal 'sadly coincided with the bursting bubble in Japan', and Dentsu reverted to more cost-effective gifting options. Grange would later display the tape dispenser in his 2003 exhibition 'Those That Got Away' at the Pentagram studio.

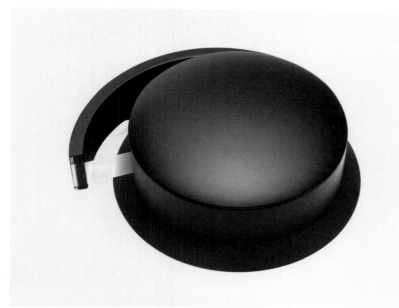

8

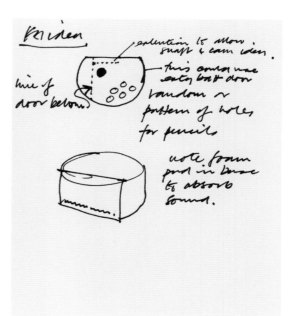

9

Polaroid
Eyewear

1 (opposite). Grange's sunglasses design for Polaroid featured a brow bar punctured with a meticulous formation of tiny holes, reminiscent of the cutter screen of his early design for the Milward Courier shaver (see pp. 108–112).

2. A quick sketch for the sunglasses design, from Grange's notebooks, showing his developing ideas around the relationship of the very thin profile lens frame and the brow bar.

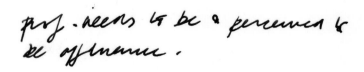

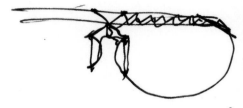

2

In 1929 Harvard academic Edwin H. Land patented his invention of a synthetic polarizing filter for commercial use; previous techniques had been attempted but it was not until Land's lightweight and inexpensive solution, based on a layer of polymer film, that a commercial market really opened up. This breakthrough innovation revolutionized the world of optics and remains the basis of all polarized eyewear, photography lenses and anti-glare screens to this day.

Calling his invention Polaroid – a combination of 'polarization' and 'celluloid' – Land established the Polaroid Corporation in 1937 and introduced the first sunglasses with polarized lenses. The Polaroid Eyewear division quickly took off, and became the most trusted name in eyewear in the world; if a pair of glasses had Polaroid lenses, the wearer knew their eyes were protected. Other applications of the polarized lens technology at that time included heavy-duty optics equipment for the military, eyewear for pilots and the first 3D eyewear for the cinema.

Fashion rapidly followed technological performance, and Polaroid's investment in frame designs alongside constant improvements in the lens technology saw the brand's sunglasses become the safe and stylish favourite of Hollywood icons, celebrities and sports stars throughout the 1950s and 1960s, while into the 1970s the ability to create a polarized gradient across the lens opened up new design possibilities.

By the 1980s the Polaroid Eyewear business was peaking, and international competition was tough. Polaroid met this challenge by securing collaborations with top designers to launch competitive new sunglasses models, including aviator styles with the novel proposition of interchangeable lenses. The brand's most high-profile collaboration was with Grange, who was not only the most renowned industrial designer in the UK at that time but was also seeing great success in Japan, a key market for Polaroid. He was approached by the company's UK representatives in 1986 to design a new model with

a European sensibility. It was to be called IMAGE, and had the aim of introducing a distinctive new take on the classic aviator style.

The fine frames of Grange's design were produced in drawn Monel (nickel, copper and other elements) alloy with a plated finish; the brow bar, in precision-cast copper-beryllium alloy, featured a pattern of tiny perforated holes for ventilation, inspired by the impeccable pattern of holes in the foil of the cutter screen of his award-winning design of the Milward Courier electric shaver back in 1963 (see pp. 108–112). When it came to the polarized gradient lenses, the company opted to manufacture them in exceptionally thin plastic rather than in glass. Whether this was for safety, financial or experimental reasons, Grange would never learn, but he later criticized this decision for 'making the product flimsy' when the lenses were clipped into the frame. And although the product still proved popular on launch in 1988, this situation would always frustrate Grange as he felt it 'let down the wearer's deserved experience' of a pair of supposedly premium sunglasses, and he has often referred to it as an example of the challenge faced by designers who are 'separated from manufacturing decisions involving their work'.

In the 1990s Grange developed some prototypes for the camera division of Polaroid; his concept work was amalgamated into the company's product development process although his specific designs were never produced. Later, in 2010, when Grange collaborated on the design of a men's shirt with Margaret Howell (see pp. 292–295), his favourite detail was a narrow double pocket on the chest of the shirt – perfectly sized to hold a pair of his IMAGE sunglasses and one of his Parker or Platignum pens.

Geeco

1 (opposite). The final design for the Jet watering can featured a forward-tilting style giving a sense of motion to the direction of pouring, while ribs on the body helped the user to judge the filling level.

2. A rough sketch of the watering can, hinting at Grange's idea for a detachable rose that fits into the opening on the top of the can for tidy storage.

3. The detachable rose, stored in the opening of the can, was just the kind of practical detail Grange found very pleasing.

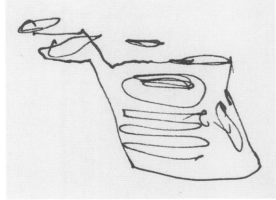

2

The British company G. & E. Engineering and Contracts, which traded as Geeco from the 1950s, was predominantly a manufacturer of domestic products in the hardware sector, notable for their enterprising prominence as manufacturers of early plastic-moulded items including washing-up bowls, kitchen utensils, coal buckets and pedal bins. As demand for plastic products rapidly increased, the company saw large growth through the 1960s, investing in further manufacturing facilities and extending production to include polypropylene chairs, petrol cans and gardenware. And by the mid-1970s Geeco was the biggest manufacturer of plastic watering cans in Europe.

By the 1980s the plastics manufacturing sector in the UK was feeling increasing competition from overseas so, looking to regain competitive advantage for their watering can division, the Geeco directors turned to the then much-promoted solution of 'investment in design'. Approaching Grange at Pentagram via an introduction through the Design Council, they commissioned him to design a modern range of colourful watering cans that 'reinvented the expected shape', aimed at a design-conscious younger generation of gardening enthusiasts.

In previous decades Geeco's plastic watering cans had mainly been modelled on the traditional circular galvanized can, with spout and handles manufactured as separate parts. However, Grange could see a solution that would be more cost-efficient for production and also improve the functionality of the can. Nicknamed by Grange 'the go-faster can', his first design for Geeco was officially called the Jet Can; both names derived from the dynamic forward-angled direction of the body that integrated both handle and spout within a single form. The body was heavily ribbed to 'improve rigidity and aid water level assessment', and the spout rose could be stored neatly in the filling hole when not needed – a tidy and thoughtful detail typical of Grange's designs.

From a user perspective the angled form offered a more comfortable position for the hand and wrist against the handle when positioning the can to pour. From a manufacturing perspective the single volume was extremely cost-effective to produce, applying, as Grange described, the 'primitive' blow-moulding technique and needing no final construction of parts. It simply required the rose to be added before the product was packaged for retail.

On launch in 1988, introduced by Geeco as 'a revolution in gardening product technology', the Jet Can initially proved highly popular. But its presence in the market, and Grange's association with the company, was short-lived; under increasing financial pressure the company subsequently went through a number of changes of ownership, and product lines across the business were reviewed. None of Grange's further designs were realized.

3

INAX

1 (opposite). Grange devised a complete, modular bathroom system called Xstage for Japanese tile manufacturer INAX, which looked at every detail from the geometry of the tiles to the fitted units and even an integrated speaker system.

2. A little sketch from one of Grange's notebooks, recording the dimensions of a traditional upright bathtub.

3. A view of the precise modular geometry of the Xstage bathroom; the 200 × 200 mm (7⅞ × 7⅞ in.) square tiles were intended for the traditional dimensions of a Japanese bathroom, to fit perfectly without any tiles needing to be cut.

By the mid-1980s Grange had been consulting for clients in the Japanese market for two decades, with highly acclaimed results, and his profile in the country was at its peak. It was around this time that he was first contacted by Motoo Nakanishi, founder of a brand strategy consultancy in Tokyo called PAOS, who was developing a new business image for a major Japanese manufacturer of decorative tiles. Called Ina Seito, the family-run business had an illustrious heritage as the makers of the tiles for the Imperial Hotel in Tokyo, designed by the celebrated US architect Frank Lloyd Wright in 1923. Substantial commercial success had followed but by the 1980s the company was facing tough competition from larger manufacturing corporations and needed to diversify. First introducing a new brand name, INAX, Nakanishi then persuaded the company to launch its fresh identity with a strategic expansion into new areas of manufacture, in particular the design and manufacture of complete bathroom systems, called XStage, rather than simply the tiles.

It was as part of this strategic process that Nakanishi first approached Grange, proposing he design a complete bathroom concept to launch

this new era for INAX. Named the KG Bathroom, to benefit from Grange's profile in the country at that time, the resulting project would see Grange oversee the design of every aspect of the bathroom proposition, including the bath, shower, basin, toilet, taps, lighting, storage solutions and, of course, the floor and wall tiles.

Much enamoured of the traditional bathing rituals in Japan and the cultural belief in the power of water for well-being, Grange was immediately keen to collaborate with INAX to bring a compact version of such rituals into the modern home. So over a period of eighteen months he proceeded to work with a large team of production engineers at INAX to steer his vision for a comprehensive bathroom system that could be planned and installed 'as logically as a modern fitted kitchen': he proposed the bathroom should be similarly treated, as the only other 'sophisticated work space' in the home.

He would later recall with great respect the way in which the company's working sessions were orchestrated during the development process, describing how the entire team of engineers, each responsible for a small piece of the complete system,

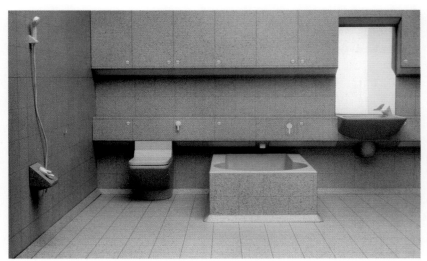

2

3

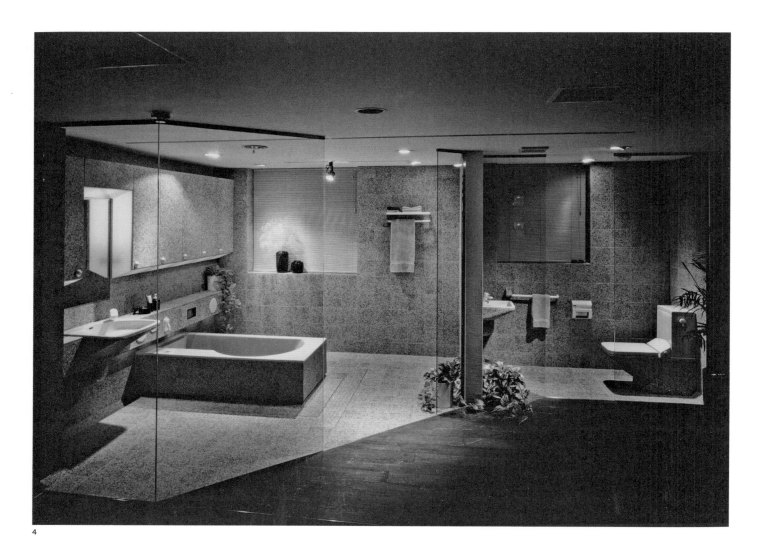

4

5

would sit in rows in the meeting room listening to the proceedings, waiting to be called forward to present their latest work to Grange and the directors for review. This 'carefully choreographed process' would continue across three or four days at a time and, as much as Grange acknowledged that to a Western eye it might appear 'a terrible waste of company resources and time', he thoroughly appreciated how valuable it was to the dedicated team 'for everyone to see how all the pieces fitted together'.

Three years from commissioning, in 1989, the final XStage KG Bathroom modular system went into production, showcasing the exceptional manufacturing quality of a company dedicated to 'the techniques and spirit of craftsmanship, and a relentless pursuit of quality'. The various elements, designed to 'seemingly grow out of a perfect grid floor', included: a deep upright bath with side seat for children, into which fresh hot water would constantly flow and refresh in the Japanese *onsen* (hot spring) style; a modular basin, toilet and storage units; wall-mounted shower fittings in a wet-room style with floor drainage, allowing for the tradition of showering before moving to the bath; and an ingenious series of floor and wall tiles produced with a range of angled borders designed to precisely fit any Japanese room layout on a meticulous 200 mm (7⅞ in.) grid without the need to cut a single tile. Never faulting on attention to detail, Grange even conceived the final finish of these tiles, in a 'soft granite texture, pleasing to the touch' and available in a range of colours.

The launch was met with high praise and helped INAX rapidly rise to become one of the most innovative and respected bathroom manufacturers in Japan, a position it still holds today. Its literature proudly explains its vision of 'beautiful bathrooms that make everyday life easier, healthier and more enjoyable, enabling everyone to live well', a sentiment of which Grange has always very much approved. And six

months after launch, as a gesture of gratitude to Grange, a complete modular bathroom in large boxes arrived at his home in Devon, where it was duly installed and is still in use to this day.

Following the success of this collaboration, Nakanishi introduced Grange to other clients of his over the next few years, resulting in further design briefs to round off a long and impactful chapter in Japan. Most notably, these final projects included three-generation family housing concepts and ranges of bathroom fittings for the innovative prefabricated urban housing developers Sekisui Heim.

6

1 (opposite). The curved roof and integrated curved metal bench of the flagship Sigma bus stop, the first of Grange's designs to launch as part of the Townplan 2000 scheme.

2. Detail of the changeable signage system, also designed by Grange, affixed to the roof of the Sigma bus stop.

3. Annotated presentation diagram showing the intricate construction of components at the point where the glazing meets the roof of the Insignia bus stop design.

2

Entrepreneur Rory More O'Ferrall founded the billboard advertising company More O'Ferrall in the UK in the 1930s following a visit to the USA, where he witnessed the dynamic outdoor advertising scene. Creating the first outdoor advertising network in cities across the UK, his billboard business would grow dramatically after the Second World War through the opportunity to build hoardings around the large number of bomb sites awaiting redevelopment.

In the 1960s word reached More O'Ferrall of the first bus shelters to carry advertising appearing on city streets in France, and he immediately recognized a further business opportunity – a new stage for eye-level advertising across the urban environment. He launched a new company division, setting up a factory to manufacture modern bus shelter structures designed to hold a standard four-sheet advertising poster. His managers then began approaching local authorities around the UK with a proposition: the company would cover the cost of manufacturing and installing these shelters, in exchange for being allowed to sell the advertising space integrated within them. This financial model proved widely attractive to local councils and from 1969 the new division quickly

took off. To differentiate it from the billboard business a new brand name was devised: Adshel, derived from 'advertisement' and 'shelter'. This proprietary word grew to be so ubiquitous that it would become the generic industry term for any poster situated within a bus shelter.

Over the following two decades Adshel, with London Transport Advertising as its partner in the capital, grew rapidly to encompass a lucrative network of nearly 20,000 managed bus shelters across 360 local authorities, reaching millions of pairs of eyes every day. But by the mid-1980s this sprawling portfolio was looking tired and in need of a strategic review, as the dynamic European competition became more dominant. The new managing director of More O'Ferrall-Adshel in the UK, Vincent Slevin, recognized the opportunity to create a more impactful and high-quality outdoor advertising medium. This action would then, he argued, enable the company to finance 'a radical visual upgrade of its significant urban infrastructure' across the nation.

Putting this strategy into practice, the first innovation introduced was Adshel Superlight, a back-illuminated poster system that rapidly attracted new advertisers

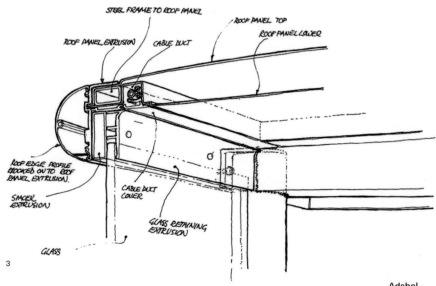

3

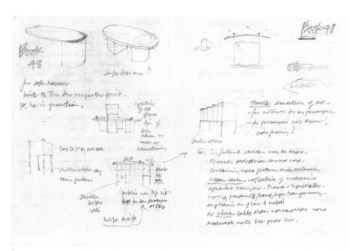

4

4. Early exploratory sketches by Grange, drawing on a number of references to various types of outdoor shelter, at the beginning of his period of work on designs for bus stops with integrated advertising space.

5 / 6. A later design for the Landmark, also known as the 'hi-tech shelter', when Adshel was looking for a new, cost-effective solution for nationwide rollout.

and revenues for the company. Thus began the upgrading of Adshel; the substantial Superlight income meant that it was now feasible to invest in a design overhaul of the network of shelters themselves. At this stage it was recognized that the time had come to bring in a consultant designer to help the company make the innovative leap that was necessary: this was the first time the company would strategically 'invest in design'. Enquiries were made within the industry, and Slevin would later recall that 'all roads led to Pentagram' and to Grange.

On being appointed to the job of reimagining the modern bus shelter, and able draw on his early experience working for Jack Howe on street furniture designs for the British Transport Commission, Grange quickly made an impression. Slevin described how Grange was commendably 'fastened to his principles of design excellence' but also had an 'unusually astute understanding' of the manufacturing cost implications of his design specifications, which proved 'immensely valuable' to the balance sheet of the company. And he credits Grange with being 'instrumental in greatly advancing the appearance of the nation's urban landscapes', at a critical time in the

shift towards recognizing the positive influence of good design in street furniture.

Work on the bus shelter designs was an evolutionary process; the company needed to manufacture shelters with enough flexibility to fit any urban situation and Grange responded to a brief for 'safe, vandal-proof, easily maintained structures of aesthetic appeal made in the best materials'. The overall system devised was called Townplan 2000, comprising a rigorous reappraisal of bus shelters and accompanying street furniture such as seats, signs and bins; this resulted in a range of designs launched across the following years.

The first design unveiled, Sigma, with its elegantly curved glass roof, became Adshel's game-changing flagship shelter, installed in premium city-centre locations from 1989. However, Adshel conceded that it would never be feasible to roll out this high-profile unit across the whole national network, so Grange also devised a more cost-effective alternative, the Landmark, to refresh the wider portfolio and ensure that a visible element of innovation was being introduced nationwide. Grange followed these with the Alpha and Insignia designs, each iteratively

5

6

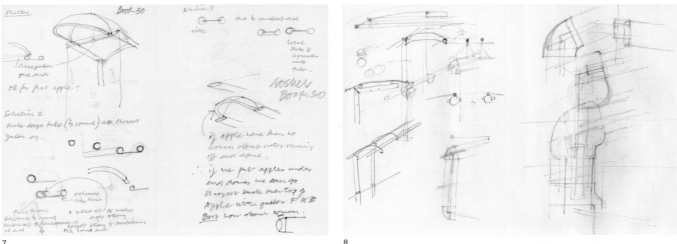

7

8

9

7 / 8. Various sketches form Grange's sketchbooks, as he evolved the designs for glazed roof shapes and fixtures.

9. The original flagship Sigma bus stop, in pride of place in London's Covent Garden, with the Westminster crest etched into the specialist toughened glass.

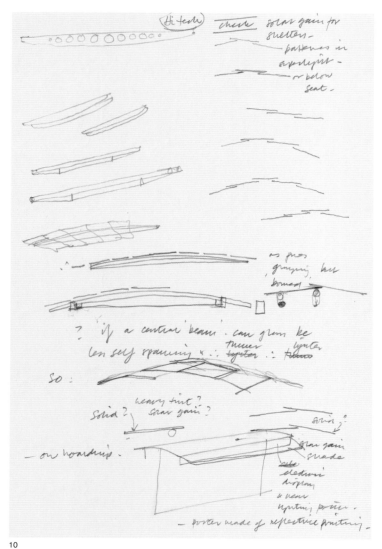

10

11

10. A sketchbook page showing Grange's thought process for later roof shapes using flat glazing panels; this exploration led to various iterations of the Landmark shelter (see p. 264).

11. A small model of a design proposal for the Westminster shelter, the brief for which required minimal visible structure for positioning on historically important streets.

12 / 13. A large model and a detail of an updated Insignia shelter, a cost-effective solution that was rolled out in towns and cities around the UK.

12

13

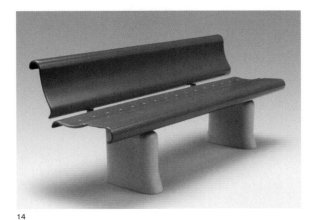

14

14 / 15. Small, impeccable models of stand-alone benches and bins, part of a range of street furniture also designed by Grange as part of the overarching Townplan 2000 scheme.

improving on visibility of advertising to passing traffic and pedestrians and delivering competitive solutions to fit every urban variation. The shelters were specified with a specialist toughened glass that does not fog when cleaned of graffiti, and a scratch-proof polyester-coated aluminium for the structure. A press release issued at the time stated that 'British bus shelters have never had it so good – the time, attention to detail and quality of materials bestowed on the shelter is second to none. This project will have major impact on upgrading the standards of Britain's streets.'

Townplan 2000 would also lead to further shelter designs by Grange into the mid-1990s, including to specifically suit the streets of London, with one variation introduced for Westminster borough that minimized the visible structural fabric of the shelter when installed along streets of national architectural importance. Another design contributed to the successful bid for the street furniture contract in the French city of Rennes, as Adshel expanded to become 'bus shelter builders to the world'.

Additionally, through his decades-long relationship with the company, which would continue for a few years after his retirement from Pentagram in 1998, Grange was also commissioned by the More O'Ferrall billboard division to devise designs for large-scale support structures for roundabouts and roadsides, alongside further street furniture designs such as benches and concept proposals for telephone boxes and display units for the company's clients in Europe.

15

Hippo

1 (opposite). Grange's production-ready prototype for the Hippo seat, an idea originally conceived by Tim Bentinck to make it easier and more comfortable to carry his toddler son.

2 / 3. Grange and his team worked on a number of prototypes in the workshop at Pentagram, before settling on this ergonomic, single-piece form in injection-moulded plastic with comfortable wrap-around straps.

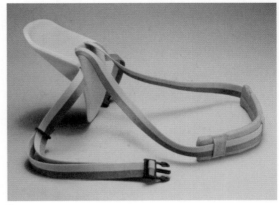

2

During the long duration of his consultancy for Wilkinson Sword (see pp. 156–163), Grange struck up a close friendship with his principal client there, the sales director George Palmer. In the late 1980s Palmer mentioned the ingenious invention made by another friend of his, the actor Tim Bentinck. Having reached the age of 'demanding to be carried everywhere', his young son was proving rather a weight, and Bentinck said that 'having little hip to carry the boy on' he felt he 'needed a shelf' to ease the strain. Having not been able to find what he needed in the shops, he set about inventing one: a small strap-on seat that fitted against a parent's hip. He made a few prototypes in wood, and proceeded to take out a patent.

On seeing his invention Palmer thought the device a 'brilliantly simple idea', so suggested that he introduce Bentinck to Grange, as he felt the seat could benefit from being 'properly designed', the thought being that it might have commercial potential

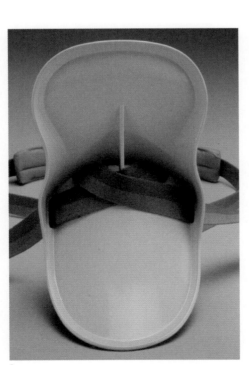

3

and find an outlet with a retailer. The two met and Grange happily engaged on the project with his team at Pentagram. He later described it as an example of the 'good fortune' of being connected through friends to 'someone with whom you might never otherwise have the joy of working'.

Grange and his team set about 'conducting many experiments' and developed a number of more advanced prototypes in the workshop to refine the ergonomics. One of Grange's secretaries, herself a young mother, gladly doubled as 'a perfect working model'. The team finally settled on a curving design in lightweight, injection-moulded plastic with a soft, supporting strap across the body and around the waist. Grange and Bentinck together also came up with the name Hippo, and Grange created a corresponding branding and packaging design.

By the mid-1990s, with the product ready to pitch to manufacturers, Bentinck, Palmer and Grange all set out to make enquiries and see if they might find a buyer among the high-street retailers. Grange and Palmer approached UK high-street chemist and retailer Boots, which initially expressed interest in purchasing the product if a manufacturer could be found. However, finding an interested manufacturer that could make the product cost-effectively in relatively low numbers proved a great challenge so, with the patent coming due for renewal, Bentinck made the decision that the project finances just would not balance any longer. The project was regretfully shelved.

Grange has forever wondered why the product could not find more support when the challenge it solved for parents is such a universal one. He later gladly gave it a spotlight when he included it in his exhibition 'Those That Got Away' at the Pentagram studio in 2003. And it is worth noting that a similar product came to market soon after the Hippo journey, and has proved popular with young parents, demonstrating that the trio were not so far away from finding success.

Boots

During Grange's tenure as consultant design director for Wilkinson Sword in the late 1970s (see pp. 156–163), one of his close colleagues in the sales division, Colin Weston, departed to work at Boots, the UK high-street chemist and retailer. Grange initially reconnected with him there when Weston was tasked with buying in a selection of Kenwood products, designed by Grange, to be retailed across the chain. Soon afterwards, Weston approached Grange and asked if he would be interested in designing a range of packaging for the retailer's own-brand products. Grange declined the commission, recognizing it would likely be more a graphic design job than an industrial design one. Instead he recommended a number of other design studios for Weston to consider, including the graphic division of Pentagram.

As a result Boots went on to commission the graphic designer and sixth Pentagram partner John McConnell, with hugely impactful results. After his initial packaging designs set a high-quality new tone for the Boots brand, McConnell was appointed external design director to the retailer in 1984. He became instrumental in the rise of Boots as a trailblazer on the high street for their effective design management and their investment in a big roster of design studios working across the company's many own-brand product lines.

In the early 1990s Grange was approached by a different division of the Boots business regarding the redesign of the ubiquitous shopping basket, a brief in line with the company's vision for 'offering better day-to-day design experiences'. Grange recalled the process of developing the prototype basket design as a 'very enjoyable experience', working alongside a specialist UK manufacturing firm to perfect a welded wire solution reminiscent of traditional wicker. He described this technique as requiring a 'very particular set of skills' and he greatly admired the firm, so he was dismayed when he later discovered that Boots had decided to engage a Chinese manufacturer to mass-produce the final product.

He would often later reference this manoeuvre as an example of the ruthless culture of modern commerce, which he saw as immoral. Recalling the positive attitude of his early clients at Kenwood and Bowers & Wilkins (see pp. 94–107 and pp. 202–215), who would 'reward' their loyal suppliers, Grange has always believed that a firm prospers through support from allies and in turn from supporting those allies, in this case loyal suppliers.

This aspect aside, Grange's distinctive design for the Boots basket, which launched in 1996, became a cheerful, thoughtful and recognizable high-street icon and is still in use today across the chain. The curved body of the basket, a comfortable moulded plastic grip for hand or arm – market research having shown that women in particular like to keep both hands free – and the moulded plastic clip-in tray for holding easily dropped smaller items, are all clear demonstrations of Grange's enduring consideration for the user experience and his belief that every interaction with a product in day-to-day life should 'encourage joy rather than frustration'.

2

Halfords

1 (opposite). The new shape of the bottle together with the pull-out spout made all the difference to the experience of pouring motor oil without spillage, and turned around the fortunes of this Halfords product line.

2. An early set of models made by Grange and his team, exploring different volumetric forms and clearly demonstrating the thoughtful introduction of a finger hold to the base to aid pouring.

Founded as a hardware store in 1892, Halfords has grown to become the UK's leading retailer of automotive parts and accessories and is recognized as a 'national business institution'. Its purchase by the Boots Company in 1989 further enhanced the company's growth, through which Halfords benefited from the parent company's highly effective management strategy of 'investing in design' to raise the profile of own-brand product lines to drive financial return.

One key own-brand product line in particular became a focus for Halfords in the early 1990s: motor oil. While it was widely understood that customers were happy to buy own-brand products rather than those from the premium-brand competition, studies showed that this was not the case with Halfords' motor oil range. The category was dominated by the big brands including BP, Shell and Exxon, and research reported that the majority of customers

were choosing to pay more for products from these brands rather than opt for the lower-priced Halfords alternatives, regardless of whether the product was in fact the same quality. But rather than scrap this underperforming line, the Halfords executives decided to commission a new packaging design and branding strategy in an attempt to turn it around.

A decade previously, through a connection via Grange, one of the graphic design partners at Pentagram, John McConnell, had been appointed external design director to the Boots Company (see pp. 270–271). So when Halfords set out to revive its motor oil range, it was to McConnell they first turned. Realizing that this project would require a significant level of structural design rather than graphic expertise, McConnell recommended the project onwards to Grange.

In order to respond fully to the brief, Grange and his team first conducted in-depth market research

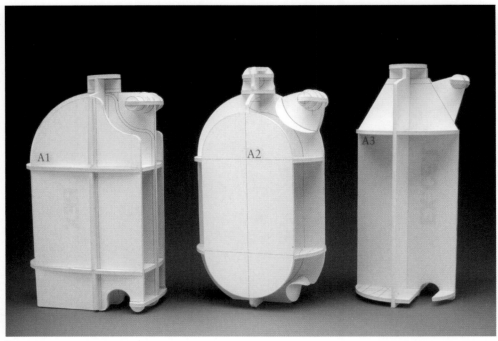

2

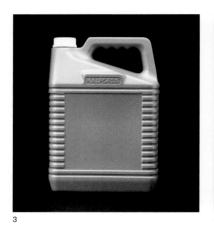

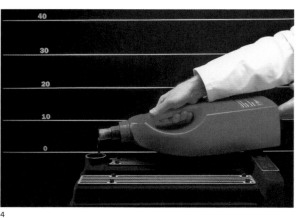

before embarking on the design process itself; and what they learnt proved hugely valuable. Setting up a focus group of 'DIY motoring enthusiasts' – the profile seen as the target customer for this product – the team was able to determine that these passionate car owners were happy to pay more for a product they 'perceived was higher quality and would give better performance'. Displayed on the shelf alongside the premium brands, the existing packaging for the Halfords product line was perceived to be 'cheap'; Grange critiqued the 'mundane, dreary polythene' rectangular cans as having a strong influence on customers' belief that 'even the Halfords top-grade engine oils were inferior', regardless of the reality of their competitive quality.

In response to these results, the overall design requirement was identified to be 'simply the creation of new containers with a classy shape, that more than matched the big premium brands'. However, Grange and his team at Pentagram, namely two of his lead

designers, Gavin Thomson and Peter Foskett, went a step further in identifying the specific mechanics.

Grange had always been a hands-on car owner and shared many of the frustrations felt by the market research group, especially, in the context of motor oils, the inability to accurately control aim and flow when pouring from a tall container, leading to unnecessary spillage. The team's resulting design would therefore be 'particularly pleasing' in that the shape 'made the pouring angle lower, therefore reducing waste'. Grange would reflect later that, in experiencing just that one detail, 'the customer thinks well of the brand'.

After a great many models had been made by Grange's team, overseen by head of workshop Bruce Watters – combining studies of volume and structural form – and after in-depth testing had been conducted on the pouring ability of the different vessels, the final design solution was revealed. It featured a flattened profile of container with a bulbous underside that,

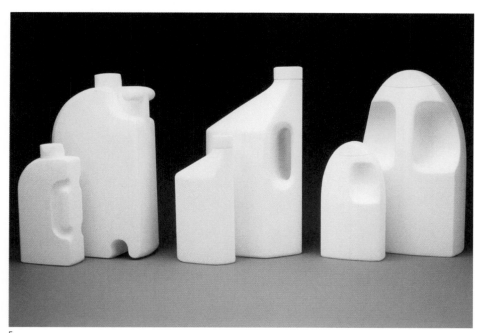

6. The line-up of final products in the range, introducing a new colour scheme and featuring new typography by collaborating design studio Lippa Pearce.

when tilted to the pouring position, held more liquid back before it reached the overflow point, thus allowing the mouth of the container to be positioned closer to the target before the pouring started. This was enhanced by a handle that was 'in-line with the mouth to accurately control the aim', and with a pull-up pouring spout and a simple supporting finger groove in the base. The traditional screw-on cap was replaced with a push-on top, which reduced manufacturing costs, while a transparent vertical strip was integrated up the centre of the flat wall of the container to solve the problem of measuring the liquid level.

In terms of labelling the customer's choice of options, the initial research report had also revealed that it was not always immediately obvious which product was which. Grange's solution clarified this communication by introducing impactful colours for the plastic containers to denote each grade. This was paired with clear and minimal typography, devised by design studio Lippa Pearce.

On launch in 1996 the design met with huge acclaim and product sales immediately took off; Grange later recalled that 'suddenly people thought that Halfords oil was classy'. And he would describe the project as a 'very clear example of how design equals commercial success' when not only did sales and profits increase substantially (showing a forty-five per cent uptick six weeks after launch) but, after a time, Halfords was able to increase the retail price. The project won a Retail Week Award, a DBA Design Effectiveness Award and a D&AD award in 1996, and is still much studied in business management today as an ideal case study of how a retailer's affordable own-brand lines can compete effectively on the shelf against the biggest brands in the market.

6

London Taxis
International

For Grange, the redesign of the London black cab in the mid-1990s represented 'the biggest responsibility of my career'; he described the enduring FX4 vehicle of the preceding decades as 'surely as iconic as a product can get' and his role in the redesign as a case of 'standing on the shoulders of giants'.

The first version of the official London black cab, the FX3, styled by Austin's chief designer Jim Stanfield, arrived on city streets in 1948. This was followed a decade later by a revised model, commissioned by Mann & Overton, which at that time was the largest taxi dealership in the UK. This version, the FX4, was styled by Austin's Eric Bailey and Jake Donaldson of coachbuilder Carbodies, with inspiration for the tail-light fins drawn from classic American cars of the era.

The intervening years were complicated: first Carbodies bought the production rights to the FX4 from Austin's owner, British Leyland, and twice attempted to produce a new cab design of its own. Then Manganese Bronze Holdings, which owned Carbodies, purchased the Mann & Overton dealership and formed London Taxis International (LTI). But through all the manoeuvres the FX4 endured; the internationally recognized icon was retained across various iterations for four decades, the last model being the Fairway.

After the economic troubles of the 1970s and 1980s had eased, agreement was finally reached between all parties to invest in developing a new black cab design; so in the early 1990s the internal design department at Carbodies set to work.

Around the same period Grange was sitting on the advisory board of the Design Council, where a fellow adviser mentioned the redesign project and asked if he might connect Grange with his friend Jamie Borwick, chief executive of Manganese Bronze Holdings. This contact explained that Borwick would appreciate it if Grange would take a look at the current concepts in development and give his opinion on their design direction. So Grange headed to Birmingham for a meeting with Borwick and, after putting forward his view that the 'icon should stay' and that 'no one would want a London cab to look like an ordinary modern car', gained the management's approval and was subsequently appointed consultant designer to the firm.

When Grange arrived to meet the design team at Carbodies, they were already far advanced with a new design and 'well on their way to radically altering the traditional style'. He recalled a scene where 'all these keen young car designers were enjoying getting their teeth into something fresh' after years of waiting for approval to redesign the black cab from scratch, rather than making incremental modifications. But into this environment Grange was launched, 'telling them to hold back', which at first 'did not make me

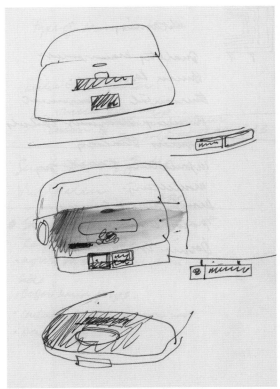

2

3

4

very popular at all'. But he was adamant in his view that the future of the firm and of the London black cab would rely on both cabbies and passengers being 'reassured that the icon was still there on the street', rather than 'blend[ing] in with the current trends in automotive styles'.

So Grange steered the team in a new direction, overseeing a design solution that balanced the remarkable visual cues of the FX4 with modern improvements to increase driver comfort, create more accessible passenger space and refine the engineering. Despite feeling the huge sense of responsibility, he also recalled the process as an 'exhilarating challenge' because 'if you get it right, here is something that will truly last'. And once the final design was completed it was presented to cab drivers for their approval, winning their acceptance as it 'sufficiently maintained the spirit of the London cab'.

The resulting TX1, launched in 1997, retained much of the original style and character of the FX4 while being 'equipped for modern use'; in the words

of the LTI project director, Jevon Thorpe, it also needed to be 'soft and friendly and have a sense of humour'. Notable elements of the new design included a windscreen that was substantially wider, giving the driver a much-improved view; doors that opened to a full ninety degrees, enabling easy access for wheelchairs and prams; and seatbelts for passengers, along with a built-in child's booster seat. On one further design detail, the distinctive rooftop 'for hire' sign, Grange worked hard to find an improved technical solution but with only partial success: the visibility of the orange light in sunlight has notoriously always been a weakness since the days of the FX4.

Remarking on the design's clear references to the past, Grange said that 'the job of the designer is not always to make something that looks dramatically new' and that sometimes the designer 'can and should bow to tradition'. The FX4 had represented such a reassuring, steady presence on the London streets that he questioned how it could ever have been possible to contemplate losing this huge asset, especially when one recalled the 'immense gratitude felt when a lit orange light miraculously appeared out of a dark wet London night'.

The TX1 remained in production with various modifications until 2017, leading Grange to remark that there is 'something very special in designing a product that lasts and still looks pretty convincing years later'. LTI has since been bought by Chinese automaker Geely and renamed the London Electric Vehicle Company (LEVC). The firm has replaced previous versions with the TX-E, an electric cab that yet retains many of those same distinctive design cues. Grange's only regret is that he never snapped up a first-edition TX1 for his personal archive.

3 / 4. A scale model crafted by Grange's team in his workshop at Pentagram, highlighting the streamlined bodywork. Grange spent endless hours working on a new solution for the for-hire sign that could be seen more easily in sunlight.

5. The cover of a brochure produced specifically for black-cab drivers. Grange gained huge support for his design from the taxi driver community for his thoughtful consideration of their needs as well as those of passengers.

The new TX1.
The taxi you told us you wanted.

TAXI

5

6. The TX1 model continued to be produced for two decades, and remains an icon of London's streets.

Royal Mail

Grange worked for a number of divisions of the General Post Office (GPO) across his career; beginning with designs for exhibition stands to introduce new GPO services to the public and later involving briefs for telephone handsets and future video conferencing services for the telecommunications division (see pp. 72–77); the organization eventually split to form the Post Office and British Telecom. Much later, in the 1990s, it would be Royal Mail – originally part of the Post Office – that came to Grange with one of his last iconic project commissions to land before he retired from Pentagram in 1997 and returned to working independently as Kenneth Grange Design.

Royal Mail, with origins dating back to the sixteenth century, provides mail collection and delivery services throughout the UK; it also owns and maintains the nation's network of distinctive red roadside postboxes. Introduced from the 1850s, the famous top class of cylindrical red pillar boxes was the first to be installed, mainly in highly populated areas. These were expensive to manufacture, so a smaller and more cost-effective class of box was soon developed for areas where the volume of mail was less, especially in rural areas. This class became known as 'lamp boxes' – literally postboxes that could be attached to lamp posts but were often also mounted on their own poles or embedded in walls.

Grange's commission to redesign this class of rural postbox came after almost a century of use for the original box designs, during which only incremental design modifications had been made.

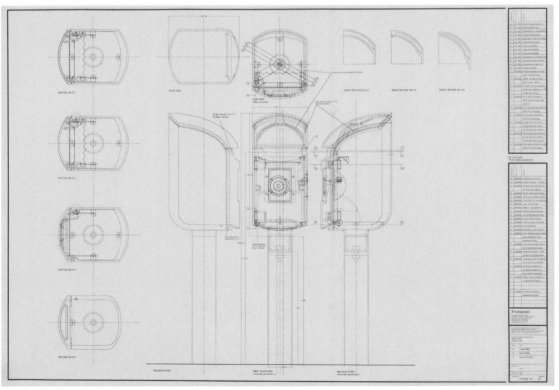

2

3

4

5

6

3 / 4 / 5 / 6. Despite the move to CAD and digital production of designs, Grange still insisted on making models of his design concepts as the 'best and only way I knew to really get a design across to a client'.

7

7. The shiny rural postbox, seen in situ on a leafy lane, was named the Bantam for its resemblance to the fuel tank of the classic red GPO Bantam motorcycle.

In contrast Grange's design was often described as 'ultra-modern', though he was openly mindful to retain the essence of the original. He later described that he 'kept it red and very shiny' but rounded off the shape to make it 'friendlier and more tactile'; and he also introduced a larger slot to accept the A4 size of envelope that was becoming more popular. When it came to the manufacturing specification, Grange insisted Royal Mail continue to invest in 'traditional cast iron, like the Victorian ones', so the boxes would 'last forever', once remarking they might 'perhaps last even longer than the client themselves', a comment referring to the privatization of the company at that time. The launch of Grange's design also came a couple of years after the retail and letters divisions of the Post Office had split, which necessitated the change of the embossed castings on all the postboxes, now to read 'Royal Mail' rather than 'Post Office'. So Grange's design was the first new box to carry this change, with 'Royal Mail' embossed across the lower belly of the box.

First unveiled in 1998, just after Grange left Pentagram, the new rural postbox was christened the Bantam. The name was chosen through a competition among Royal Mail employees, who suggested that the rounded shape of the box bore a resemblance to the fuel tank of the classic red GPO Bantam motorcycle, used by telegram boys in the early twentieth century. The Bantam was the final new design of postbox to be manufactured by Machan Engineering Scotland, the last foundry in the UK to make traditional cast-iron postboxes, which closed in 2015.

Anglepoise

1 (opposite). The beautifully refined base of the Type 3 desk lamp (see also p. 59), Grange's first design for Anglepoise after being appointed design director.

2 / 3. Sketches from Grange's notebooks capturing the articulation of a sprung Anglepoise lamp arm, and the detail of the central spring at the base.

In 1932, while exploring solutions for a vehicle suspension system, the British automotive engineer George Carwardine developed an elegant, flexible mechanism of pivoting arms and springs – the heart of the whole invention – that could be 'positioned and held at any angle with the lightest touch', as described by Anglepoise today. Recognizing that it would also work well as the support structure for a lamp, he took the concept to the biggest British springmakers, Herbert Terry & Sons. Immediately seeing a new commercial opportunity for making complete products alongside their mass production of individual components, the company licensed the design from Carwardine and soon afterwards began manufacture of the archetypal three-spring Model 1227 lamp. The impact and presence of this extraordinary product spread far and wide – from office desks, creative studios and workshop benches to libraries, living rooms and aircraft navigation tables – and the following decades would see Anglepoise Lighting produce a range of design variations on the original. However, by the turn of the twenty-first century the business was being undermined by many imitations and cheaper options flooding the market, and the brand was losing visibility.

It was at this point in the family company's story that Simon Terry, whose great-grandfather had worked with Carwardine, assumed the role of managing director of Anglepoise. Shortly afterwards he found himself seated next to Grange at a design industry dinner, where they got to talking about springs; Grange had recognized the Terry name from his childhood, through his mother's job at a spring factory in London and his own stint working there at weekends. Terry, in turn, was familiar with Grange's portfolio and had already noted comments made by him a few years previously when, as chairman of the judging panel for the BBC Design Awards in 1996, Grange had described the original Anglepoise lamp by Carwardine as 'a minor miracle of balance'.

Their immediate connection led to further conversations and a visit for Grange to the Anglepoise factory to meet with Terry and his father, John. Following this meeting, in 2003, Grange was

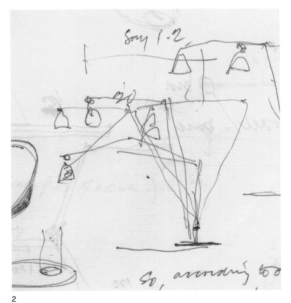

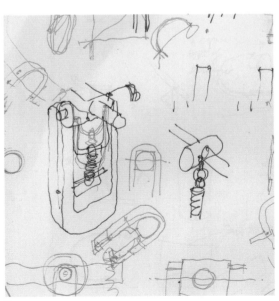

2

3

4. A view of the rear profile of the shade of the Type 3 lamp. One of Grange's key – but subtle – evolutions from George Carwardine's original design was to introduce a double layer and vent holes to the shade to prevent the outer surface from becoming blazingly hot to the touch.

5. A promotional photograph of the later Type 75 Mini, a table lamp aimed at a design-conscious home owner, which removed the spring mechanism in favour of a cost-effective static arm with a simple, robust hinge to tilt the shade.

4

5

appointed the company's consultant design director, with a remit to 'use design to pitch Anglepoise into modern life'. As Grange recalled, this rethink of the business and his arrival on the scene 'happened at just the right moment', transforming the business and placing it back in play at the centre of a new consumer era attuned to the values of impeccable, functional design.

Grange's first offering was the Type 3, brought to market quickly during his first year in the role. In a respectful refinement of the much-revered 1227, Grange's main revisions involved introducing a circular base and a double shade that 'formed a chimney, allowing the hot air to be ducted out between the two layers', greatly reducing the heat of the original surface. The initial Type 3 prototype was presented by Simon Terry at the Milan Furniture Fair that same year, 2003, where it met with high praise and was subsequently put into production.

Anglepoise was now back in demand, and the following year Grange focused on revising the original Model 75, relaunched as the Type 75, which has been a bestseller ever since. It was also the subject of limited-edition creative collaborations with fashion designers Margaret Howell and Paul Smith, and found quiet fame on many film sets. Grange noted that the spring mechanism in his reworked 75 remained virtually identical to the original, save for slight manufacturing refinements to make it more cost-effective to produce, which helped open up a new market by making the product more affordable. This design route was later followed up in the form of the Type 75 Mini, a smaller, cheerfully coloured and accessibly priced version targeting a younger audience, with a simple ergonomic switch in the base and limited adjustment of the shade.

6. The Type 75, a reworking by Grange of the original Model 75, is an enduring bestseller for the company, becoming a design icon in its own right.

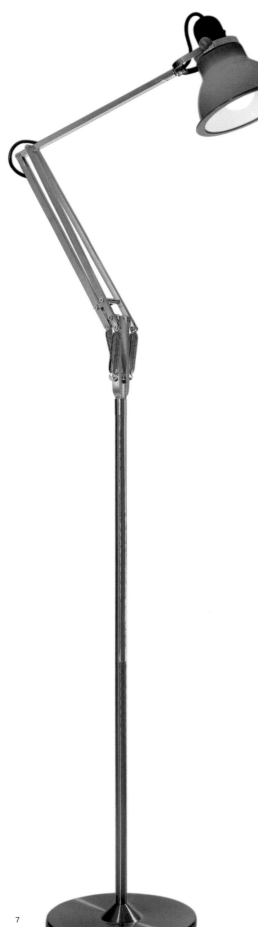

7 (left). Experimenting with colour and material, Grange devised the new 1228 range to introduce pops of glowing colour through moulded polycarbonate shades.

8 (opposite). A rear profile view of the glowing shade of the 1228, in a green reminiscent of traditional glass desk lamps.

Grange was further encouraged to experiment with new materials and the effects of colour in his brand new 1228 range, launched in 2008, which featured colour-popping translucent polycarbonate shades. The sleek lamp section could be fully rotated to act as an uplighter as well as a desk lamp, and the product was also offered as a floor-standing model. The design proved effective and highly popular but, to Grange's regret, has been shelved from production in recent years in favour of reducing the evident use of plastic materials and focusing on metal or even, most recently, glass shades.

A major challenge that had been undermining the business when he first came on board – the cost of sourcing components in an increasingly competitive marketplace – led Grange to make an introduction between the Anglepoise directors and Michael Lapham, an acquaintance and former client of Grange's as technical director and later group operations director of Kenwood. Of this successful connection Grange would later comment it was 'the happy consequence of working with a variety of businesses and their people'. Lapham subsequently drew on his exceptional knowledge of manufacturing in China to help steer Anglepoise through the bureaucracy and develop a route to making quality products with more manageable production costs. Grange considers this connection during his tenure to have been 'a most important thing' to have contributed towards the flourishing of the modern Anglepoise business.

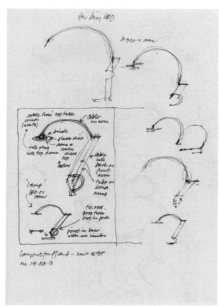
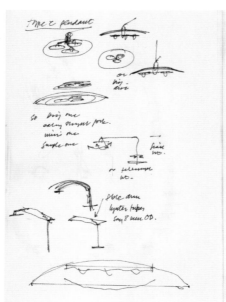
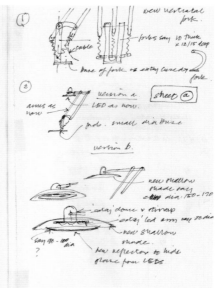

9

10

11

9 / 10. Exploratory sketches for a new product, responding to the early days of LED technology, introduced as the Type C.

11. Grange considered the high-tech design of the Type C to be one of his best, but it was too ahead of its time to succeed commercially.

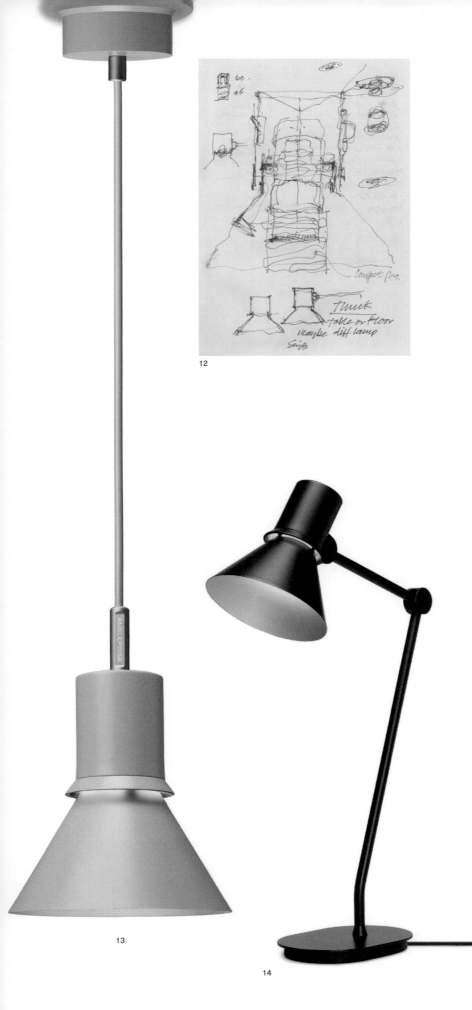

12

By the late 2000s the business was once again buoyant and the team could begin to explore new design ideas and innovations; it was now the dawn of the LED revolution, and lighting companies were quickly integrating this new technology. Anglepoise was no exception, and rapidly launched Grange's first offering of the new era, the Type C, in 2011, featuring three LED bulbs and a structure designed to fit over a computer screen. Grange considers it 'one of the best designs' he ever produced, but he also admits it was too far ahead of the pace of 'a lighting industry in flux' and, although it sold well initially, the manufacturing was ultimately let down by the weakness of the electronic components.

Nearly a decade later, however, LED technology was firmly established and made a trusted return in Grange's design of the Type 80, launched in 2019 to mark his ninetieth year. The design, also available as a pendant and a wall light, was deliberately less technically overt, concealing the classic springs inside the knuckles of the arm, in recognition that 'an industrial aesthetic is not always suitable' as part of interior placement, particularly in domestic schemes. Additionally, the shade design features a delicate 'halo' around the neck resulting in a soft glow over the outer surface of the cone – and a distinctive visual presence in low light – from just one small LED source.

At the time of writing, Grange continues to work closely with Anglepoise on the next generation of designs, himself as enduring as the products on which he works.

13

14

Margaret Howell

British designer Margaret Howell initially built up a strong reputation for exceptionally well-made shirts, setting up an independent business from her London flat in 1972. This staple wardrobe item for men and women, and for which she has become world renowned, remains central to her clothing label today; a trusted team of skilled machinists at her warehouse and small factory in the UK still oversees the making of every impeccably finished garment from start to finish. Five decades on from its foundation, her established business is now global and the label presents a wider collection of pieces beyond shirts, but her overall approach of 'focusing on making one thing, and doing it well' endures – and is highly respected and admired by Grange.

In 2007 Howell was awarded the coveted Royal Designer for Industry (RDI) distinction, regarded as the highest honour in Britain to recognize a wide range of design disciplines. Grange was awarded the same distinction back in 1969, and through this network the two have come to know each other well. Sharing Grange's ethos, Howell has described being often inspired by 'methods of making', believing 'good design has to work', and the pair are champions of British manufacture and of the appreciation of authenticity and 'design that is made to last'.

This meeting of minds, sparked when they initially met at an RDI summer school event at Dartington College in 2008 and underpinned by their mutual respect for each other's professions, led to Howell inviting Grange to collaborate on the design of a shirt for her collection. This would become the first of a number of collaborations for Howell, a series called Margaret Howell Plus, through which she looked to collaborate with designers from other fields whose work she particularly admired.

Howell explained of her invitation to Grange that 'good design, like good film music, often goes unnoticed ... we take it for granted, until we take the trouble to look, touch or listen'. So she questioned what might happen 'when a designer who excels in one area is asked to work in another'. Grange would describe 'my heart lifting' when Howell suggested the collaboration, as, 'ignoring the suit I made myself at art school, this would be my first venture into Howell's world'. He added that the project resulted in the discovery that their worlds were surprisingly alike, stating that 'it is in the details, as Mies van der Rohe said, that God lives'.

Grange opted to design a work shirt inspired by the collarless garments he had admired being worn in workshops during his time consulting for clients in Japan, as well as acknowledging his appreciation of the designs of Issey Miyake, from whose label he owns a few classic pieces. Howell began by selecting one of her existing pattern blocks for a relaxed shirt profile, from which she and Grange could gradually work out his preferences for the shaping and details. Grange wore the prototype shirt during his visits to Howell's studio so that she could make amendments directly onto his form as they discussed, and he could immediately visualize the results.

The final shirt was realized in a fine slate-grey Egyptian cotton (end-on-end two-fold 140 shirting), with a paler grey for the inner lining of the soft collar band and cuffs – a pleasingly subtle detail to be appreciated only by the wearer. Howell chose a soft construction for these details so the shirt 'would not feel too stiff and formal'. Of the collarless style Grange described his desire to 'remove any fuss', to ensure the comfort of the wearer while working. Howell introduced a wide pleat down the centre of the back, to allow for expansion and ease of movement when the wearer might be stretching over a work table, along with deep vents on each side of the hem so the shirt can be worn loose or tucked in. In trademark Howell style, the shirt features run and fell seams (a type of strong, flat seam) with immaculate, fine stitching that gives a lasting, smooth profile, while a wide, soft fly front hides the buttons. A narrow double-layered pocket on the left chest, specified by Grange, is perfectly sized to fit a pair of sunglasses

2

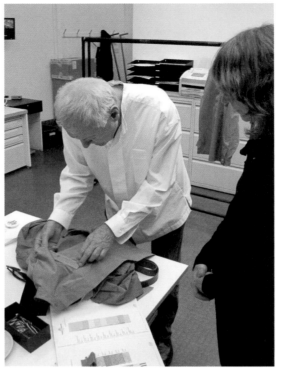

3

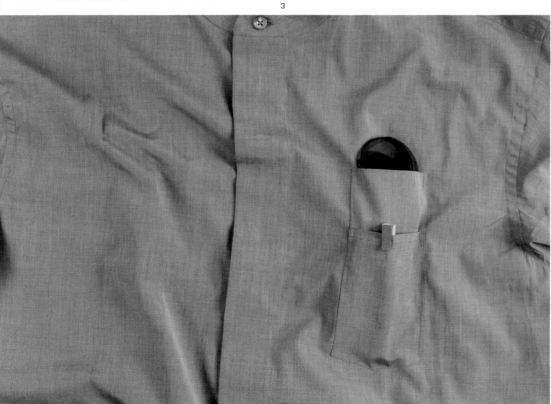

4

2 / 3. Grange and Howell at work in Howell's studio in central London, choosing fabric colour swatches and carefully measuring for a breast pocket.

4. The double-layered breast pocket was meticulously measured to neatly fit one of Grange's pen designs, here a Platinum Platpen in the outer pouch, alongside a pair of his sunglasses for Polaroid.

5. The window display in Howell's flagship store on Wigmore Street, on launch of the shirt design collaboration with Grange. The shirt hangs on the back wall, while in front is a small collection of his iconic designs from across the years (all of which feature as full stories in this book).

and a pen – naturally perhaps his sunglasses for Polaroid (see pp. 254–255), and one of his Parker 25 or Platignum pen designs (see pp. 198–201 and pp. 220–225).

The shirt was revealed in early 2010 and met with much admiration. Howell hosted the launch in her flagship London shop and studio, a beautiful space where she curates a thoughtful selection of mid-century-inspired furniture, books, accessories and homewares to complement and give context to her clothing collections. For the launch she introduced display cases holding a curated selection of Grange's classic designs, from Kodak cameras and the Milward Courier shaver to the Kenwood Chef and models of the InterCity 125 train.

Since then the pair have remained close friends, and Howell hosted Grange's ninetieth birthday celebration in the same space in 2019. They have also continued to cross paths professionally, as Howell later collaborated with Anglepoise (see p. 286), for which she applied her instinctive feel for timeless, nature-inspired colour palettes to a number of limited-edition Type 75 lamps – one of the most successful designs conceived by Grange.

5

Hitch Mylius

1 (opposite). In recent years Grange has appreciated the opportunity to design products that respond to his own requirements as an older customer: he is pictured here sitting in his 'chair for the elderly' designed for possible use by the NHS and care homes.

2 / 3. Sketches documenting the development of Grange's thought processes for a supportive chair for an elderly user – nearing a final design top right.

Hitch Mylius is an award-winning manufacturer of contemporary upholstered furniture made in the UK, established by designers Tristram and Hazel Mylius in 1971. At a time when 'the most exciting furniture designs in the UK were imports from Italy and Scandinavia', and frustrated by the lack of modern design visible in British-made furniture, the duo set out with a specific aim to offer simple, well-crafted furniture for both the domestic and contract markets. The company has gone from strength to strength over the decades, winning multiple awards, collaborating with many top names in design, and supplying prestigious clients worldwide.

Recalling how Grange came to work with the firm in recent years, Tristram Mylius described how he first encountered Grange when he was a

student at Hornsey College of Art in the late 1960s, where Grange – whose first design office was based nearby – would regularly visit and deliver talks to the students. Greatly inspired, on graduating Mylius would go on to work in the studio of Grange's later Pentagram partner, Theo Crosby, before coming to work for Grange in his Hampstead office for a short while, prior to establishing Hitch Mylius.

Much later, into the mid-2000s, once his business was well established, Mylius would have a chance conversation with a friend in the NHS who had experience in the mass-purchasing of chairs for healthcare environments; in this context Mylius was advised there was a substantial requirement for a chair designed specifically for the elderly. Following this discussion, and spotting a market opportunity,

2

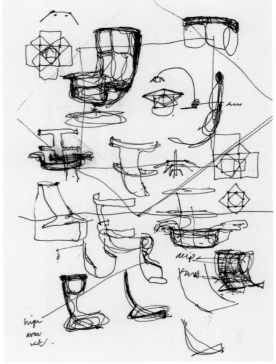

3

4   5

4 / 5. Further sketches for a low-backed version of what would become the Edith chair, exploring a comfortable and durable arm rest that could support the user in lowering and raising themselves.

6. A detailed diagram of the internal wooden skeleton of the final volume, showing intricate consideration of the ergonomics and supportive nature of the chair.

Mylius reconnected with Grange – who was by now a decade into his retirement from Pentagram and had returned to practising as Kenneth Grange Design – to ask him to consider tackling this particular design challenge.

The commission would represent a 'rare foray' for Grange into the industry of furniture design. The brief he answered was for an upholstered chair for the elderly user, to predominantly provide more support while sitting for extended periods of time. It was intended for use within a healthcare context across waiting and consulting rooms in hospitals, clinics and surgeries as well as in residential care and respite environments.

On accepting the challenge, Grange shared his view that the modern furniture design trend 'tends towards unobtrusive, low-slung furniture to make the volume of interior spaces appear more generous', but that this style 'does nothing to help the older sitter'. His design response would ensure that 'seat height was a key factor', because it 'impacted so much the ability to easily lower and raise the body' from a seated position. Grange and a small team, including his former senior designer Gavin Thomson from Pentagram, who had since departed to work freelance, set about constructing models in his home workshop, while Thomson also compiled the necessary CAD drawings. Grange then employed the advanced workshop team at the Royal College of Art, where he was engaged as a visiting professor, to manufacture the foam forms for the advanced prototypes, and to apply ergonomic rigs to 'tease out a good balance'.

The resulting hm82, or Edith, armchair collection launched in 2011, comprising high-backed and low-backed chair options, with or without arms and with steel or wooden legs. The seats were moulded in supportive high-density polyurethane foam over a steel frame, and upholstered in hard-wearing,

thickly woven British fabrics. The Hitch Mylius brochure describes the design as 'an exciting departure from the traditional and dated furniture currently available for this growing and increasingly sophisticated market'.

Grange has since expressed his admiration for the way in which Tristram Mylius insists on exceptional quality in the upholstering fabrics he uses and how he 'likens upholstery to tailoring', adding that he is 'very loyal to good suppliers, rather than being led by the most cost-effective options'. However, this quality gives the product a high price point, so although the Edith has been a much-praised design, gaining a lot of publicity and sparking much-needed discussion around 'design for an ageing population', it does not sell in big numbers and was not taken up by the NHS. It has however found a place in private settings, including in Grange's own home in Devon, where it is a favoured seat for watching television.

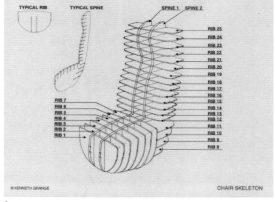

6

7 /8. The final hm82, or Edith, chair is made to order and is offered in a range of colours and with two leg style options to suit different environments and preferences.

9 (right). The chair is expertly and impeccably upholstered in the highest-quality, robust textiles specified by Hitch Mylius, as the detail of the chair arm here demonstrates.

7

8

Modus

1 (opposite). A stack of March
Lite chairs, developed by
Grange in collaboration with
star young designer Jack
Smith, of SmithMatthias.

2 / 3. Early sketches for
a soft seating solution
for commercial furniture
company Modus.

Following the positive reception for Grange's 'rare foray' into furniture design with the Edith chair for Hitch Mylius (see pp. 296–299), he was approached by Modus, another premium British furniture business. Founded in 2000 by Jon Powell and Ed Richardson with the idea of linking international designers with British manufacturing resources, the company predominantly focuses on the contract market, fitting out offices and academic buildings.

When he was approached by Powell and Richardson in 2013 with the proposal to work on a seating concept for them, Grange was pleased to accept the commission but suggested he would in turn employ Jack Smith, of young design studio SmithMatthias, to collaborate on the project. Smith was a rising-star graduate of the prestigious Design Products course at the Royal College of Art, where

Grange had for the previous eight years been a visiting professor, so Grange was keen to see if they might work on a commercial project together.

In a partnership branded Grange SmithMatthias, the duo embarked on their first project in 2014: the April soft seating collection, comprising slender two-seat and three-seat sofas and a compact armchair. The range, a formal lounge solution aimed at public and reception spaces, was designed, as Modus put it, to 'ensure good posture, with sculptural elegance and distinction', and launched to industry acclaim.

This collection was followed a year later by the April System, which transformed the elegance and flow of the original design into a modular system that offered complete flexibility, from 'simple straights to sinuous, flowing curves', to creatively divide up large spaces.

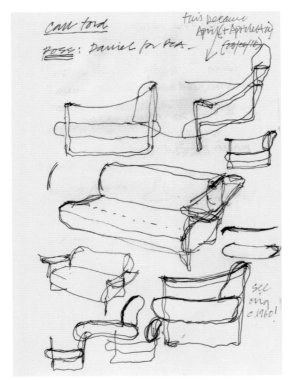

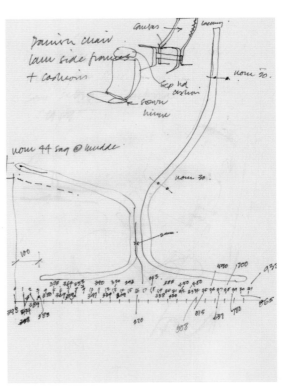

2

3

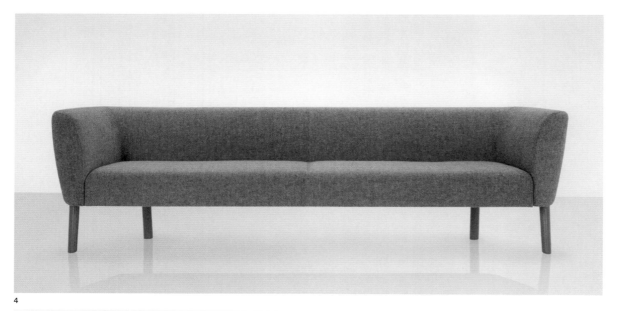

4

5

6

4 / 5 / 6. The first seating range resulting from Grange's commission by Modus and his subsequent collaboration with Jack Smith was the April sofa range.

7

7. The duo followed the success of the April sofa design soon afterwards with the April System, which offered a sleek, modular soft seating solution for larger open-plan environments.

8. A sketch for the March chair design, in which Grange is refining the subtle curves of the back and seat panels to make them 'unexpectedly comfortable'.

9. Alongside the launch of the March Lite, Grange and Smith collaborated on the Spring range of occasional tables, demonstrating similar honed consideration in the detail of the point at which the leg meets the tabletop.

10 (opposite). The March Lite chair design, in natural and blue water-based lacquer finishes, proved to be popular and sold well after Grange's revisions to the initial March design made the product more cost-effective to manufacture.

8

In the same year, 2015, Grange SmithMatthias also set about another commission, this time for a stackable wooden chair: the March. It was described by SmithMatthias as 'an all timber construction with an unexpected level of comfort' arising from the chair's meticulously sculpted back, which also 'contributes to its timeless aesthetic'.

The resulting chair, though praised in the design press, was costly to produce in any volume and consequently did not see good initial sales. So Grange took it upon himself to look at refining and 'shaving it down', to make it more cost-effective. The updated product then 'took off' in the form of the March Lite, launched in 2020. It is finished in a water-based lacquer, and Grange has described it as being more efficient in production and using 'fewer materials, boasting a more elegant aesthetic as a result'.

Concurrently with launching the March Lite, the duo also collaborated on a further commission, launched in 2021: a collection of occasional tables called Spring. The series comprises a coffee table and a side table, both of which were conceived in a variety of profile shapes – from circular to soft-cornered triangles – and in multiple sizes, making them suitable for 'interesting nesting combinations'. The distinctive leg-top detail is shared with the March Lite chair that Grange had refined the year before. The pieces are manufactured in veneered MDF with robust metal brackets deliberately visible, presenting, as Grange says, an honest product that delivers 'extremely economical use of materials'.

9

Lifelong Bookcase

The idea of designing his own 'really useful bookcase' seeded itself in Grange's mind soon after his mother died, in 2006, when one of the responsibilities that fell to him during the funeral arrangements was to choose her coffin. Sitting in the funeral parlour, leafing through 'page after page of the illustrated catalogue', he described the feeling of being 'acutely aware of the expectation' placed on him to make the right choice; to select 'the correct set of signals' through the style and cost of the coffin that would express a fitting homage to his mother in the eyes of family and friends. Yet, looking through the options, and recalling his mother's 'wonderful sense of humour', nothing seemed to do her justice. He would later criticize the designs in the catalogue

as seemingly 'locked in law, never to be altered, and for no good reason other than tradition'. In the event he chose a coffin that 'was not the most ornate but was also not the most modest', and everyone thought it appropriate. Except Grange.

So later, on retirement from Pentagram, and with time available to dedicate to crafting his own projects in his workshop, Grange set about designing a coffin of his own. He explained he was conscious that, when the time came, he did not want his family to feel the same strain of responsibility that he had, and wanted to ensure that even when he was not himself present 'at the final party', he would still be able to 'contribute to making the congregation laugh'. Additionally he has often stated that, without

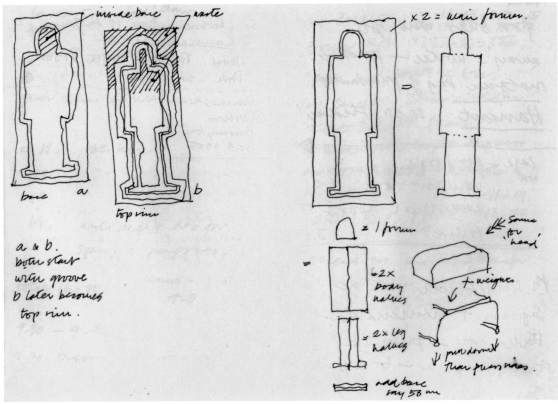

2

'There it is, my bookcase. A design developed because it might raise a smile at the end, just as at the beginning, and have a useful life in between.'

Kenneth Grange

3. Detailed construction drawing for the bookcase, front and side profiles, showing the sturdy sandwiched layers of milled plywood.

exception, all designers are 'ensnared by the notion of a device that has a hidden use' as well as some element of wit; and, to his mind, if it is 'of a blackish humour so much the better'.

The final design for the 'Lifelong Bookcase', crafted in his workshop in London and then transported to his home in Devon 'as a trial run', in Grange's words looks 'rather like a modernist Egyptian mummy case', although this reference had not actually been in his mind when he conceived the design. Having become interested in the 'age-old magic of laminating wood', he decided that for lightness and strength the body should be formed of laminated ply with the lid and back panel cut from ply sheet. As he explained, the great merit of forming the body in ply is that it is possible to 'simulate an appropriate outline of the occupant'. And most importantly, when stood up, 'it will not be crudely obvious that it is a coffin'.

Describing the proposition to be 'really very straightforward', Grange has often since explained to captivated audiences that 'the coffin can stand upright with its lid tucked away behind, and with temporary shelves inserted for books. And although I believe in my own immortality, conceivably one day I may die; in which case the books will need a new home and I will take their place. Then, lid on, it seems to me that my bookcase will produce a smile on the day – and what a nice way to go up to the great workshop in the sky.'

Then he admits with a grin, relishing the astounded expressions of his audience, that there was potentially 'one slight issue': that he has 'a terrible feeling the shoulders of the bookcase will be too wide for the doors of the crematorium ...'

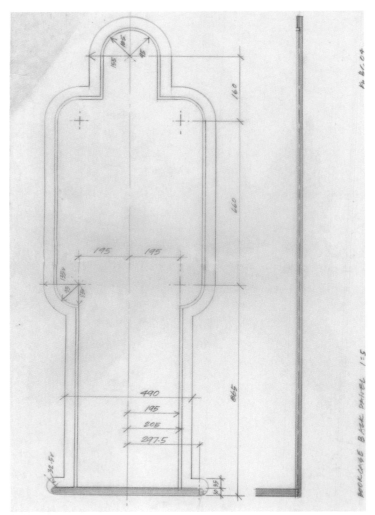

3

4 (right). The bookcase transforms into a coffin on the removal of the shelves, and the dimensions are sized for Grange himself.

Awards and Honours

Honours and Appointments

1955 Member, Society of Industrial Artists (SIA) (later Society of Industrial Artists and Designers (SIAD) then Chartered Society of Designers (CSD))

1959 Fellow, Society of Industrial Artists (SIA)

1961 Consultant Design Director, Kenwood

1969 Member of Faculty of the Royal Designers for Industry (RDI)

1978 Design Council adviser

1982 Consultant Design Director, Thorn EMI

1984 CBE in New Year Honours

1985 Consultant Design Director, Wilkinson Sword

1985 Honorary Doctorate, Royal College of Art (RCA)

1986 Chair of Judges, Design Council Awards

1985–87 Master of the Faculty of Royal Designers for Industry

1985–87 Member, RSA Council

1987 Honorary Professorship, Heriot-Watt University

1987 Co-chairman, International Design Conference, Aspen, Colorado

1987–89 President, Chartered Society of Designers (CSD)

1989 Chairman, Interior Design International (IDI) Awards

1990 Finalist, Prince Philip Prize for the Designer of the Year (Design Council)

1991 Design Business Association (DBA) council of management

1992 International Member, Industrial Designers Society of America (IDSA)

1993–95 Chairman of the Design Business Association (DBA)

1996 Minerva Gold Award, Chartered Society of Designers

1996 Co-chairman, Anice Alexander Award, Chartered Society of Designers

1998 Honorary Doctorate, Staffordshire University

1998 Honorary Doctorate, De Montfort University

2001 Prince Philip Designers Prize (Design Council) for lifetime achievement

2003 Honorary Doctorate, Open University

2003 Design Director, Anglepoise

2005–10 Visiting Professor, Royal College of Art (RCA)

2013 Honorary Doctorate, University of Plymouth

2013 Knighthood in New Year Honours for services to design

Product Awards

1960 Design Centre Award, Council of Industrial Design (CoID), for the Brownie 44A camera for Kodak

1961 Design Centre Award, for the Kodaslide 40 projector for Kodak

1963 Design Centre Award, for the Milward Courier shaver for Needle Industries

1963 Duke of Edinburgh's Prize for Elegant Design (CoID), for the Milward Courier shaver for Needle Industries

1964 Switzer Supreme Award for Good Design, for the Milward Courier shaver for Needle Industries

1964 Design Centre Award, for the Vecta camera for Kodak

1967 Daily Mail Ideal Home Blue Riband award, for the Rio hairdryer for Ronson

1970 CoID Design Award, for the Star radiotelephones range for STC

1971 CoID Design Award, for the Mariner range for Taylor Instruments

1972 CoID Design Award, for the Variset range for AJ Binns

1975 Design Council Award, for medical equipment for G & E Bradley Ltd

1981 Design Council Award, for refreshment vending service for VGL Industries Ltd

1989 Die Gute Industrieform Award, Hannover Messe, Germany, for the Aria range for Thorn Lighting

1989 Tokyo Art Directors Club (ADC) Award, for the Trendy range for Shiseido

1990 Finalist, BBC Design Awards, for ShowerAge unit for Ideal Standard

1991 Ideal Home Exhibition Blue Ribbon, for the Electronic Hi-Rise toaster for Kenwood

1991 Pifco Group/Electrical and Radio Trading Design Award, for the Electronic Hi-Rise toaster for Kenwood

1991 G Mark awards (Japanese Ministry for International Trade and Industry), for a water geyser and fan heater for Harman Gas

1995 Finalist, DBA Design Effectiveness Awards, for range of toasters for Kenwood

1996 DBA Design Effectiveness Award, for motor oil packaging range for Halfords (with Lippa Pearce)

1996 Finalist, DBA Design Effectiveness Awards, for 600 series loudspeakers for B&W

2001 Architectural Review Prize for Design Excellence, for ironmongery range for izé

Principal Clients, 1955 to Now

Addo

ADG Campingaz

Adshel

AJ Binns

Alessi

AMF

Anglepoise

Arm

Artemide

Association for the Blind

Aura

Avery Berkel

Avon Rubber

Bakelite

Barclays

Bendix

Biocompatibles

BMW

Bob Brooks

BOC

Boots

Bowers & Wilkins (B&W)

Breville Europe

British Aerospace

British Airways

British Oxygen

British Petroleum (BP)

British Rail

British Telecom (BT)

Brush Electrical Machines

Calrec

Caradon Friedland

Clark Design Company

Clarks Ltd

Coca-Cola

Commercial Bank of Kuwait

Crane Fluid Systems

Crosfield Electronics

Danfoss

Danish State Railways

Davall Gear Co.

Dent & Hellyer

Dysona

Eden Group

Edwin Mills

Ekco

Eurocellular

G. A. Harvey

G. & E. Bradley

GEC

Geeco

General Foods

General Instruments

Guinness

Halfords

Harman Gas

Heatrae

Henry Hope & Sons

Herman Miller

Hippo

Hitch Mylius

Holophane EU

Ideal Standard

Imperial Tobacco

Imperial Typewriter Company

INAX

izé

Junghans

Kenwood

Kodak

London Taxis International

Luciwear

Margaret Howell

Mars Foods

Maruzen Sewing Machine Company

Masoneilan

Micrologic

Modus

Mont Blanc

More O'Ferrall

Morphy Richards

Motorola

Musical Fidelity

National Westminster Bank

Needle Industries

Newhome Gas Appliances

Nichinan Corporation

Omega

Osaka Gas

Otis

Oun / Dentsu

Papworth Industries

Parker Pen Company

Parkinson Cowan

Peetee

Platignum

Plessey

Polaroid Eyewear

Post Office

Psion

Ransomes

Rediphon

Reuters

Rinnai

Ronson

Rotork

Royal Mail

Samsung Electronics

Sekisui Heim

Sheffield Brick Group

Shipton Automation

Shiseido

Sinclair

Sipple

Speak & Jackson

Stag Furniture

Stanley Garden Tools

STC

Sunbeam

Sutcliffe & Clarkson

Swatch

Takata Corp

Taylor Instruments

Transport for London

Thermos

Thorn EMI

Thorn Lighting

Thorpac

Thwaite & Reed

Toyota

Tricity

Tudor

Typhoon International

UK Atomic Energy Authority (UKAEA)

Unicorn Darts

Unilever

Valor

Venlease

Venner

Wilkinson Sword

W. M. Still & Sons

Wood & Wood

Woods

Select Bibliography

A selective list of material used in researching this book, along with some resources that readers might like to explore if they want to take their interest further.

Audio / Video
British Library Sounds – National Life Stories, 2003 (audio: 25 tapes). Kenneth Grange interviewed by Linda Sandino

https://www.bbc.co.uk/iplayer/episode/b084flz2/artsnight-series-4-7-the-brits-who-designed-the-modern-world
(BBC *Artnight* profile of Kenneth Grange, broadcast 25 November 2016)

UK Archive Collections
Kenneth Grange Archive, Victoria and Albert Museum, London

Kenneth Grange Archive, National Railway Museum Archive, York

British Rail Archives, The National Archives, Kew, London

Festival of Britain Archives, The National Archives, Kew, London

Kodak Archives, British Library, London

Jack Howe Archives, RIBA, London

Design Council Archives, University of Brighton Design Archives, Brighton

Design Council Slide Collection, Manchester Metropolitan University, Manchester

Library of Birmingham Archives and Collections, Birmingham

Websites
www.125group.org.uk

www.anglepoise.com/history

https://blogs.brighton.ac.uk/royaldesigners

www.bowerswilkins.com/en-gb/our-story

www.designcouncil.org.uk/who-we-are/our-history

https://gracesguide.co.uk
(Guide to British industrial history)

www.kenwoodworld.com/en-gb/history-of-kenwood

www.modip.ac.uk
(Museum of Design in Plastics)

www.railwaymuseum.org.uk/whats-on/intercity-125-sir-kenneth-grange

https://collection.sciencemuseumgroup.org.uk/objects/co8912366/kenneth-grange-interviewed-by-ellen-tait-oral-history-recording

https://sounds.bl.uk
(Wide-ranging recorded interviews archive, notably including Gordon Bowyer, previous employer of Grange)

www.thebaron.info/archives/technology/reuter-monitor-terminal-a-brief-history-of-its-development

https://vads.ac.uk
(Visual Arts Data Service)

Books and Publications
125 Group, *125: The Enduring Icon*, Stroud, 2018

B&W, *Bowers & Wilkins: Celebrating 50 Years of Audio Excellence*, UK, 2016

Boilerhouse Project, *Kenneth Grange at the Boilerhouse: An Exhibition of British Product Design*, exhib. cat., London, 1983

Boilerhouse Project, Helen Hamlyn Foundation, *New Design for Old*, exhib. cat., London, 1986

Breward, Christopher, and Ghislaine Wood, *British Design from 1948: Innovation in the Modern Age*, London, 2012

Council of Industrial Design / Design Council, *Design* magazine, complete set, 1949–1999

Crowther, Lily, *Award Winning British Design 1957–1988*, London, 2012

Design Council, *59–09: 50 Years of Innovation in Design*, limited edition booklet, London, 2009

Glancey, Jonathan, *Spring Light: The Anglepoise Story*, London, 2021

Harris, Jennifer, Sarah Hyde and Greg Smith, *1966 and All That: Design and the Consumer in Britain 1960–1969*, London, 1986

Haworth, J. E., 'Confravision', *Post Office Electrical Engineers' Journal*, January 1972, p. 220

Herring, Eleanor, *Street Furniture Design: Contesting Modernism in Post-War Britain*, London, 2016

Heskett, John, *Industrial Design*, London, 1980

Jackson, Tanya, *British Rail: The Nation's Railway*, Stroud, 2014

Lawrence, David, *British Rail Designed 1948–1997*, Hersham, Surrey, 2016

Lorenz, Christopher, *The Design Dimension: Product Strategy and the Challenge of Global Marketing*, Oxford, 1986

MacCarthy, Fiona, and Patrick Nuttgens, *Eye for Industry: Royal Designers for Industry 1936–1986*, London, 1986

MacCarthy, Fiona, Gemma Curtin and Deyan Sudjic, *Kenneth Grange: Making Britain Modern*, London, 2011

Martin, Nancy, *Post Office: From Carrier Pigeon to Confravision*, London, 1969

Nock, O. S., *Two Miles a Minute*, Cambridge, 1980

O'Carroll, Diana, *Kenwood: The Ultimate Guide to Kitchen Tech*, UK, 2022

Pentagram Design Partnership, *Pentagram: The Work of Five Designers*, London, 1972

Pentagram Design Partnership, *Pentagram: Living by Design*, London, 1979

Solanke, Tolu, *Avocet: In Pursuit of Style*, London, 2014

Sparke, Penny, *Did Britain Make It? British Design in Context 1946–86*, London, 1986

Stewart, Richard, *Modern Design in Metal*, London, 1979

Acknowledgments

The author would particularly like to thank Helena Johnston and Nick Johnston for their generous time and expert help with archive documentation and technical consultancy, respectively. She also wishes to thank Apryl Grange for her kind hospitality on multiple visits to Hampstead and Devon.

Kenneth Grange would like to give a special acknowledgment to Paul and Linda Anthony for their invaluable input and support throughout the project.

Wide-ranging appreciation and thanks are extended by Kenneth Grange and the author to the following people for their time, support and various involvement in the process and background of compiling this book:

Ian Buchanan, Elizabeth Burney-Jones, Debbie and Peter Foskett Hylton, Ron Major, Johan Santer, Gavin Thompson and Bruce Watters (KGD and Pentagram)
Angus Hyland, Mervyn Kurlansky, John Rushworth and Deborah Taffler (Pentagram)
Dido Crosby (daughter of Theo Crosby)
Carol Williams (daughter of Bronek Katz)
Susan Wright (daughter of Jack Howe)
Mary Archer, Baroness Archer of Weston-super-Mare (Science Museum Group)
Rosamind Julius and Mary Alexander (IDC Aspen)
Christopher Marsden (Victoria and Albert Museum, London)
Chris Wise (RDI)
Christopher Lucas (RSA)
Michael Lapham (Kenwood)
Andrew McLean (National Railway Museum, York)
John Zabernik (125 Group)
Bruce Holcombe and Sam Sugiyama (KG Japan team)
Christine and George Palmer, Wolfgang Althaus, Kurt Gruber (Wilkinson Sword)
Julian Binns (AJ Binns)
Danny Haikin and Evert Huizing (B&W)
Lady Helen Hamlyn (Helen Hamlyn Trust)
Vincent Slevin (Adshel)
Tim Bentinck (Hippo)
James Blyth, Baron Blyth of Rowington (Boots)
Simon Terry and Adam Wade (Anglepoise)
Margaret Howell and Kate Greenway (Margaret Howell)
Tristram Mylius (Hitch Mylius)
Jon Powell (Modus)
Dr Lesley Whitworth (University of Brighton Design Archives)
Jeremy Parrett (Special Collections Museum, MMU)
Fiona Orsini (RIBA)
Andrew Tweedie (Grace's Guide)
Trevor Burrows (photographer)
Julian Honer, Julie Hrischeva, Peter Dawson, Kirsty Seymour-Ure and Jane Cutter (Thames & Hudson)

Picture Credits

All images © Kenneth Grange archive. Courtesy of Kenneth Grange, Pentagram and the Victoria and Albert Museum, London, unless stated otherwise below.

11.1 © Kenneth Grange archive. Courtesy of Kenneth Grange, Pentagram and the Victoria and Albert Museum, London / British Railways Photographic Dept / NRM York
29.11 RIBA Collections
30.1 GB-1837-DES-DCA-30-1-POR-H-80-1. Design Council Archive, University of Brighton Design Archives.
37.9 Photo: Maurice Tuffin
42.2 © Kenneth Grange archive. Courtesy of Kenneth Grange, Pentagram and the Victoria and Albert Museum, London / Mel Calman
47.7 The National Archives
59.5 © Kenneth Grange archive. Courtesy of Kenneth Grange, Pentagram and the Victoria and Albert Museum, London / Anglepoise
62.13 Photo: Trevor Burrows
63.14 © Danny Howes
65 David Burton / Alamy Stock Photo
75.6 *Design* magazine, Issue 274, October 1971. Design Council Archive, University of Brighton Design Archives
79.2 incamerastock / Alamy Stock Photo
80.4 *Design* magazine, Issue 144, December 1960. Design Council Archive, University of Brighton Design Archives
82.8 *Design* magazine, Issue 186, June 1964. Design Council Archive, University of Brighton Design Archives
86.15–86.19 Photo: Trevor Burrows
89.25–89.26 Photo: Trevor Burrows
92.4 Hope's advertisement; various issues of *Design* magazine. Design Council Archive, University of Brighton Design Archives
107.36 Photo: Trevor Burrows
109.3 *Design* magazine, Issue 174, June 1963. Design Council Archive, University of Brighton Design Archives
111.6 © Kenneth Grange archive. Courtesy of Kenneth Grange, Pentagram and the Victoria and Albert Museum, London / Paul Anthony
112.7 *Design* magazine, Issue 174, June 1963. Design Council Archive, University of Brighton Design Archives
129.3 © Kenneth Grange archive. Courtesy of Kenneth Grange, Pentagram and the Victoria and Albert Museum, London / Illustration: Alan Fletcher
132.1 © Kenneth Grange archive. Courtesy of Kenneth Grange, Pentagram and the Victoria and Albert Museum, London / NRM York
133.2 © Kenneth Grange archive. Courtesy of Kenneth Grange, Pentagram and the Victoria and Albert Museum, London / British Railways Photographic Dept / NRM York
138.11 © Kenneth Grange archive. Courtesy of Kenneth Grange, Pentagram and the Victoria and Albert Museum, London / NRM York
138.12–138.14 © Kenneth Grange archive. Courtesy of Kenneth Grange, Pentagram and the Victoria and Albert Museum, London / NRM York
139.15–139.16 © Kenneth Grange archive. Courtesy of Kenneth Grange, Pentagram and the Victoria and Albert Museum, London / NRM York
141.18–141.19 © Kenneth Grange archive. Courtesy of Kenneth Grange, Pentagram and the Victoria and Albert Museum, London / NRM York
141.20–141.22 © Kenneth Grange archive. Courtesy of Kenneth Grange, Pentagram and the Victoria and Albert Museum, London / NRM York
142.23–141.26 © Kenneth Grange archive. Courtesy of

Kenneth Grange, Pentagram and the Victoria and Albert Museum, London / British Railways Photographic Dept / NRM York
143.27–143.29 © Kenneth Grange archive. Courtesy of Kenneth Grange, Pentagram and the Victoria and Albert Museum, London / NRM York
144.30–144.31 © Kenneth Grange archive. Courtesy of Kenneth Grange, Pentagram and the Victoria and Albert Museum, London / British Railways Photographic Dept / NRM York
145.32 © Kenneth Grange archive. Courtesy of Kenneth Grange, Pentagram and the Victoria and Albert Museum, London / NRM York
146.33 *Design* magazine, Issue 298, October 1973. Design Council Archive, University of Brighton Design Archives
146.34–146.35 © Kenneth Grange archive. Courtesy of Kenneth Grange, Pentagram and the Victoria and Albert Museum, London / NRM York
147.36 © Kenneth Grange archive. Courtesy of Kenneth Grange, Pentagram and the Victoria and Albert Museum, London / NRM York / Illustration: Per Arnoldi
157.2 Photo: Trevor Burrows
161.11 Photo: Trevor Burrows
163.15–163.16 Photo: Trevor Burrows
175.2 *Business Systems and Equipment* magazine, November 1972 / Kenneth Grange press cuttings archive
176.6 G. A. Harvey advertisement featured in various issues of *Design* magazine. Design Council Archive, University of Brighton Design Archives
178.1 © Paul Anthony / Photo: Heini Schneebeli / AJ Binns
180.4 © Paul Anthony / Photo: Heini Schneebeli / AJ Binns
181.6 © Paul Anthony / Illustration: Arboret Ltd / AJ Binns
181.7 © Paul Anthony / Photo: Heini Schneebeli / AJ Binns
182.10 © Paul Anthony / Photo: Heini Schneebeli / AJ Binns
183.13 © Paul Anthony / Photo: Heini Schneebeli / AJ Binns
184.15–184.16 © Paul Anthony / Photo: Heini Schneebeli / AJ Binns
184.17 © Paul Anthony / Illustration: Arboret Ltd / AJ Binns
185.1 © Paul Anthony / Photo: Peter Matthews
195.2 Photo: Trevor Burrows
208.11–208.12 © Kenneth Grange archive. Courtesy of Kenneth Grange, Pentagram and the Victoria and Albert Museum, London / Bowers & Wilkins
214.25 © Kenneth Grange archive. Courtesy of Kenneth Grange, Pentagram and the Victoria and Albert Museum, London / Black Dog Press / Bowers & Wilkins
215.26–215.27 © Kenneth Grange archive. Courtesy of Kenneth Grange, Pentagram and the Victoria and Albert Museum, London / Black Dog Press / Bowers & Wilkins
221.2 © Kenneth Grange archive. Courtesy of Kenneth Grange, Pentagram and the Victoria and Albert Museum, London / Black Dog Press
223.8 © Kenneth Grange archive. Courtesy of Kenneth Grange, Pentagram and the Victoria and Albert Museum, London / Black Dog Press
224–225.9 © Kenneth Grange archive. Courtesy of Kenneth Grange, Pentagram and the Victoria and Albert Museum, London / Black Dog Press
249.2 Photo: Trevor Burrows
262.1 © Kenneth Grange archive. Courtesy of Kenneth Grange, Pentagram and the Victoria and Albert Museum, London / Adshel
263.2 © Kenneth Grange archive. Courtesy of Kenneth Grange, Pentagram and the Victoria and Albert Museum, London / Adshel

264.6 © Kenneth Grange archive. Courtesy of Kenneth Grange, Pentagram and the Victoria and Albert Museum, London / Adshel
265.9 © Kenneth Grange archive. Courtesy of Kenneth Grange, Pentagram and the Victoria and Albert Museum, London / Adshel
266.13 © Kenneth Grange archive. Courtesy of Kenneth Grange, Pentagram and the Victoria and Albert Museum, London / Adshel
278.3–278.4 © Kenneth Grange archive. Courtesy of Kenneth Grange, Pentagram and the Victoria and Albert Museum, London / Black Dog Press
279.6 Oleksandr Ivanchenko / Alamy Stock Photo
283.7 © Kenneth Grange archive. Courtesy of Kenneth Grange, Pentagram and the Victoria and Albert Museum, London / Black Dog Press
284.1 Courtesy of Anglepoise / Photo: David Hitner, A Common Purpose
286.4 Courtesy of Anglepoise / Photo: David Hitner, A Common Purpose
286.5 Courtesy of Anglepoise / Photo: Tim Young
287.6 Courtesy of Anglepoise / Photo: Anglepoise
288.7 Courtesy of Anglepoise / Photo: David Hitner, A Common Purpose
289.8 Courtesy of Anglepoise / Photo: David Hitner, A Common Purpose
290.11 Courtesy of Anglepoise / Photo: David Hitner, A Common Purpose
291.13–291.14 Courtesy of Anglepoise / Photo: Anglepoise
292.1 © Kenneth Grange archive. Courtesy of Kenneth Grange, Pentagram and the Victoria and Albert Museum, London / Black Dog Press
294.2–294.3 Courtesy of Margaret Howell
295.5 Courtesy of Margaret Howell
296.1 © Kenneth Grange archive. Courtesy of Kenneth Grange, Pentagram and the Victoria and Albert Museum, London / Black Dog Press / Hitch Mylius
297.3 © Kenneth Grange archive. Courtesy of Kenneth Grange, Pentagram and the Victoria and Albert Museum, London / Hitch Mylius
299.7–299.9 © Kenneth Grange archive. Courtesy of Kenneth Grange, Pentagram and the Victoria and Albert Museum, London / Hitch Mylius
300.1 © Kenneth Grange archive. Courtesy of Kenneth Grange, Pentagram and the Victoria and Albert Museum, London / Modus / Photo: Angela Moore
303.7 © Kenneth Grange archive. Courtesy of Kenneth Grange, Pentagram and the Victoria and Albert Museum, London / Modus / Photo: Angela Moore
304.8 © Kenneth Grange archive. Courtesy of Kenneth Grange, Pentagram and the Victoria and Albert Museum, London / Modus / Photo: Jake Curtis
304.9 © Kenneth Grange archive. Courtesy of Kenneth Grange, Pentagram and the Victoria and Albert Museum, London / Modus
305.10 © Kenneth Grange archive. Courtesy of Kenneth Grange, Pentagram and the Victoria and Albert Museum, London / Modus / Photo: Angela Moore

Index

Cover. All cover images © Kenneth Grange archive. Courtesy of Kenneth Grange, Pentagram and the Victoria and Albert Museum, London, unless stated otherwise below. Additional front cover picture credits, left to right: Anglepoise Type 75: courtesy of Anglepoise / Photo: Anglepoise; Kodak Instamatic 33: Richard Brown / Alamy Stock Photo; Modus March chair: courtesy of Modus / Photo: Modus; InterCity 125: © Kenneth Grange archive. Additional back cover picture credits: Kenneth Grange in his Hitch Mylius hm82 Edith chair: courtesy of Black Dog Press and Hitch Mylius.

Frontispiece. A Kenwood promotional photograph of Kenneth Grange with his Cuisine food processor, 1970s. Grange's most radical design, the nose of the InterCity train, appears as the backdrop. © Kenneth Grange archive. Courtesy of Kenneth Grange, Pentagram and the Victoria and Albert Museum, London.

Page 7. Sir Jonathan Ive. Photo: Alasdair McLellan, 2022.

Lucy Johnston is a curator, commentator and advisor on design, technology and science innovation. She develops international exhibitions, hosts events and podcasts, and is the founder of a national task force championing innovation and talent across UK industry. She is the author of *Digital Handmade* and *The Creative Shopkeeper*, both published by Thames & Hudson.

Sir Jonathan (Jony) Ive KBE HonFREng RDI is a designer and currently Chancellor of the Royal College of Art, London. He joined Apple in 1992 and led the company's design of the iMac, iPod, iPhone, iPad and Apple Watch, and of Apple Park, the corporate headquarters of Apple Inc., in Cupertino, California. In 2019 Sir Jony co-founded the creative collective LoveFrom, based in San Francisco.

First published in the United Kingdom in 2024 by Thames & Hudson Ltd, 181A High Holborn, London WC1V 7QX

First published in the United States of America in 2024 by Thames & Hudson Inc., 500 Fifth Avenue, New York, New York 10110

Kenneth Grange: Designing the Modern World © 2024 Thames & Hudson Ltd, London

Text © 2024 Lucy Johnston
Foreword © 2024 Sir Jonathan Ive
Images © 2024 Kenneth Grange archive. Courtesy of Kenneth Grange, Pentagram and the Victoria and Albert Museum, London, unless stated otherwise on page 314

Copy-edited by Kirsty Seymour-Ure
Designed by Peter Dawson, with Ronja Ronning, www.gradedesign.com

British Library Cataloguing-in-Publication Data
A catalogue record for this book is available from the British Library

Library of Congress Control Number 2023945481

ISBN 978-0-500-02486-7

Printed and bound in China by C&C Offset Printing Co. Ltd

Be the first to know about our new releases, exclusive content and author events by visiting
thamesandhudson.com
thamesandhudsonusa.com
thamesandhudson.com.au